AF335623

Leaves

MANY MEN HAVE DIE
BRITISH
SANDS
RS OF
O DIED
DURING
WAR

Tales of Development

LEAVES

Miles Wortman

DE STAEL

ALSO BY MILES WORTMAN
Zoo Story
*The Road to Help: The Revolution in Charity, Philanthropy
    and International Development*
Latin America
*Notable Family Networks in Latin America
    (with Diana Balmori & Stuart Voss)*
Government and Society in Central America, 1680-1840

CONSULTATIONS
Argentina, Bolivia, Brazil, Chile, the Dominican Republic,
Mexico, Uruguay, Spain, Albania, Bulgaria, Romania, Russia,
Slovakia, Angola, Burkina Faso, Cape Verde, Egypt, Ethiopia,
Ghana, Ivory Coast, Mozambique, Nigeria, South Africa,
Togo, Tunisia, Uganda, Zambia, Zimbabwe, Cambodia,
India, Japan, Mongolia, Singapore, Thailand, Vietnam, and
the Marshall Islands.

Designed by *The Frontispiece*
Typeset by *Kevin Barrett Kane* in 10/14 ITC Galliard

Thanks to Fred Stouder, my pen pal for half a century, who
preserved and protected my scribbles upon which much of
this work is based, to all those who rippled my stream of
life and to my editor-in-chief of all things,
Myrna Chase Wortman:

> *Behind the screens of leaves, still shining through*
> *As good as gold, as beautiful as you.*
>
> —Clive James

Cheers to Kevin Barrett Kane and Emma Christine Hall
of *The Frontispiece* who designed this book, shaping my
words so artfully.

CONTENTS

FOREWORD

Trippers and askers surround me,
People I meet, the effect upon me of my early life or the ward
and city I live in, or the nation,
The latest dates, discoveries, inventions, societies, authors old and
new,

My dinner, dress, associates, looks, compliments, dues,
The real or fancied indifference of some man or woman I love,
The sickness of one of my folks or of myself, or ill-doing or loss or
lack of money, or depressions or exaltations,
Battles, the horrors of fratricidal war, the fever of doubtful news,
the fitful events;
These come to me days and nights and go from me again,
But they are not the Me myself.

Apart from the pulling and hauling stands what I am,
Stands amused, complacent, compassionating, idle, unitary,
Looks down, is erect, or bends an arm on an impalpable certain
rest,
Looking with side-curved head curious what will come next,
Both in and out of the game and watching and wondering at it.

Backward I see in my own days where I sweated through fog with
*   linguists and contenders,*
I have no mockings or arguments, I witness and wait.

———

These are really the thoughts of all men in all ages and lands, they are not original
*   with me,*

If they are not yours as much as mine they are nothing, or next to nothing,
If they are not the riddle and the untying of the riddle they are
*   nothing,*
If they are not just as close as they are distant they are nothing.

This is the grass that grows wherever the land is and the water is,
This the common air that bathes the globe.

———

The spotted hawk swoops by and accuses me, he complains of my
*   gab and my loitering.*
I too am not a bit tamed, I too am untranslatable,
I sound my barbaric yawp over the roofs of the world.

—Walt Whitman, *Leaves of Grass*, 1855–1881

INTRODUCTION

One cannot leave a record of another without leaving a record of oneself.
—Elizabeth Hardwick

He looked upon his whole life as a ceaseless entertainment, which somebody
for some reason had taken it upon himself to arrange for him.
—Leo Tolstoy

The global empire being forged before our eyes is not governed by any particular state or ethnic group. Much like the Late Roman Empire, is ruled by a multi-ethnic elite, and is held together by a common culture and common interests. Throughout the world, more and more entrepreneurs, engineers, experts, scholars, lawyers and managers are called to join the empire. They must ponder whether to answer the imperial call or to remain loyal to their state and their people. More and more choose the empire.
—Yuval Noah Harari "Sapiens; A Brief History of Humankind," 2011

SOME OF WHAT FOLLOWS is based on fact. Some is fiction. Some is a mix of the two. These are tales written over a fifty-year period, some excerpted from novels and stories that were never published. Each offers a perspective of the time in which they were written, as well as my own thoughts from those times. There are two overall themes:

First, the issues, challenges, and values of those who struggled to bring about change and improve lives in lands facing extraordinary barriers over the last fifty years. The efforts of those, like my fictional character Walt Whitman Stein, with good hearts and intentions, who worked to stabilize newly independent countries and lands freed from the yolk of tyranny, lawyers that created legal frameworks for democracy, engineers who developed infrastructure, economists who created networks with local officials to further development and tens of thousands of others in health and education who roamed the Earth in those years so that today there is little question that most peoples of Eastern Europe, Africa and Asia live with greater freedom and in better economic conditions than heretofore.

Second, is my own personal growth, how a lad filled with dreams and ideals evolved working in academia, development, government and the corporate world, each with distinct values, consulting in dozens of countries about the world with so many issues, profit, loss, efficiency, risk, famine, civil war, corruption and bureaucracy. It is a quagmire that these pages try to put together.

Two types of development, the one economic, the other personal, the two weaving their way on a long and twisting road, an epoch fading into the past, its soldiers already forgotten.

This work is published in a limited edition, the commercial press not deeming it worthy to compete with mysteries, science fiction and celebrity biographies and gender, race and political tomes and the works of literary giants and emerging talent from hundreds of writers' programs.

While memory contributes to the stories, all characters in this volume are fictional and any resemblance to anyone alive or dead is in the soul of the reader.

And finally, a word from Walt Whitman:

> *Do I contradict myself?*
> *Very well then I contradict myself,*
> *(I am large, I contain multitudes.)*

MILES WORTMAN

WASHINGTON

(1966)

Vietnam War — Cultural Revolution in China — Leonid Brezhnev becomes Soviet leader — Indira Gandhi becomes Prime Minister of India — Coups in Argentina, Burkina Faso, Burundi, Central African Republic, Ghana, Indonesia, Nigeria and Syria — Civil War in Chad — Florence flooded — John Lindsay becomes New York Mayor — New York Subway Strike — Riots in Watts and Chicago — "Is God Dead" Time Magazine cover — First artificial heart — Black leader James Meredith killed — Star Trek

I ENROLLED AT AMERICAN UNIVERSITY to pursue a Masters in International Relations, even though it was not a particular interest of mine. I was twenty-two, immature, and drifting all about, but I needed a student deferment to avoid the draft in the Vietnam era.

My professor was Elspeth Rostow, an elegant, Radcliffe- and Cambridge-trained economist and academic administrator once described as never having "a hair nor a thread nor a word out of place." Eloquent, proper, quietly intense, and continually self-deprecating, she was a wonderful teacher who, at a later time, would have been more successful and be far more recognized. A familiar story.

Perhaps it was her husband who held her back. Walt Whitman Rostow was one of the prime architects of the Vietnam War. At the time, I knew him as the author of a notable work on international development, *The Stages of Economic Growth: A Non-Communist Manifesto*. His book theorized that economic development occurs in five steps until "take-off," followed by mass consumption. It was one of those books latched onto by the mass media. Only later did I find out that Rostow's previous life was involved with the OSS, the CIA, and other intelligence organizations. He had advised three presidents—Eisenhower, Kennedy, and Johnson—to steadily increase foreign aid together with military activity to Southeast Asia.

One evening, Elspeth Rostow invited her class home for dinner and to meet her husband. I was naïve and searching, like all twenty-two-year-olds, blithely unaware of his importance and the growing tensions in the White House. My views on Vietnam were in flux, having thought originally there was logic behind the American presence but now unsure of any benefit. Should America send more troops? How deeply should we be involved?

In fact, it was a critical moment. Ex-President Eisenhower accused the current administration of being weak and called for sending a half-million troops to the war. Opposition to the war was growing in the streets and on the campuses. President Johnson had to decide whether to withdraw from the conflict and face certain defeat in the next election or plough deeper into what increasingly seemed like a quagmire. It called for courage on his part and that of his advisors. The "hawks" in his cabinet who favored increased involvement won out, and Rostow was their leader. Of all this, I was ignorant.

It was late in the evening when Walt Rostow came home. He spoke to the group for a few minutes, but he was clearly tired and tense. When I asked innocently how we were able to support a Vietnamese government that was so weak, he stood and screamed at me. Didn't I know what we were doing? What the consequences were? That there was a war out there and there was no alternative but victory? He yelled and yelled, like a madman. I walked out.

This was my first brush with "development" and those who form policy. Rostow was a creature of Washington, a government official who devised and implemented theories from his desk. He had the air and looks of an intellectual, very much like Henry Kissinger who was soon to advise Nixon on the Vietnam War effort. Everything he advocated came not from experience "in the field" but from a mixture of what was then called "political realism" tied to what seemed to be sophisticated, academic ideas. A colleague once remarked about Rostow: "I finally understand the difference between Walt and me. I was the navigator who was shot down and spent two years in a German prison camp, and Walt was the guy picking my targets."

We tend to appreciate simple solutions: quick weight loss, the power of positive thinking, instant salvation. Simple solutions sell books and appeal to the media. Their authors are lifted onto pedestals and proclaimed as prophets. Both Karl Marx and Walt Rostow offered simple—though diametrically opposed—solutions to the problem of economic growth. Yet to postulate a unified theory in a world of complexity and constant change makes little sense considering the issues of newly independent nations. The rules of the game change constantly in lands without economic resources, where corruption is rife, and commodity prices continually fluctuate.

The pattern of smart and seemingly logical academic and bureaucratic theories raising havoc throughout the world can be seen in every administration, Republican or Democrat, since America emerged victorious in World War II. International development agencies like the World Bank, the I.M.F. and USAID stumbled from unified theory to unified theory, some contradicting others, some favoring financial and corporate interests or corrupt government agencies, all the while fundamental problems persist. Graham Greene saw this in his prophetic novel *The Quiet American,* his eponymous character advocating a "third way," much as Rostow had under the Eisenhower administration.

It may be trite to say, but we all are ruled by humans, ministers, advisors, military experts and the like, with all the frailties we all possess, egotism, self-righteousness and myopia, all swayed by the survival instincts of bureaucrats, saving their own skin, and political realities. The Vietnam War was a choice made by humans based on flawed information from the front and a failure to exert courage at home. That conflict, together with the failure to achieve racial justice, scars my generation. It burdens our souls.

I began my professional development being thrown out of Walt Whitman Rostow's house. I ended my professional life with the unfortunate drone killing of my friend and colleague in aid, Warren Weinstein, he out in the field and working in development. During these years, I came to understand that, rather than follow the dictates of straightjacket policies like Rostow's "stages" of economic growth, it was and is important to have non-ideological flexibility in policy and implementation for the different issues which each nation faces in trying to grow.

I achieved my degree. The next year I entered the Peace Corps and began wandering a long and winding road into the mountains of the world.

OBREGON'S CAT

(1968)

Tet Offensive in Vietnam—Martin Luther King, Jr. assassinated— Prague Spring—President Lyndon Johnson does not seek reelection— Robert Kennedy assassinated—Riots and strikes in France—Intel founded—Chicago Convention riots—Student riots in Mexico— Richard Nixon elected President

I AM IN THE BACK OF A CARRETA, a wooden oxcart, laying prone while the body on top of me seeps blood onto my clothes. My head is propped to one side, and my legs are scrunched like a fetus to keep dragging on the road. This is neither a desirable nor comfortable position. But here I am. The bleeding man on top of me is bent as well except for his wounded leg. We wedge our grimy selves as best possible. A soiled horse blanket covers us. The jogs and jags of ruts and mud bounce our bodies back and forth.

Stars light our path, highlighting dark, grasping trees overhead. A slight mountain breeze brushes our faces. We proceed slowly; the silhouetted driver up front yells to the oxen as he has done ever since he removed their genitals. He sticks a silver metal point at the end of a long stick into their sides, first the ox on the left, then the one on the right. The two beasts move in tandem, a heavy wooden yolk binds their course. They snort and grunt loudly.

The cart pulls and pushes on the uneven path—into soft mud, out onto hard surface, then a quick drop back into the mud on a road that scarcely merits the name. With each jolt, I hear the plea in my head that has been cried ever since my arrival: *We need a new road. It is impossible to get our crops to market and if someone falls ill, the hospital is too far away. The government promises to build it, but it never happens.*

The carreta, the national symbol of Costa Rica, is not meant to carry bloody six-footers. It hauls bags of rice and beans, cases of beer or soda, crates of saltines, canned tuna, detergent, machetes for clearing fields and axes, hammers and nails, pots and pans, firewood for cooking. Usually the cart has four sides, but now the rear slat has been removed to allow our legs to dangle. I stare at the path falling behind us, shaking my head to ward off mosquitoes that sweat attracts. Two postal butterflies flit by. Rut after rut jerks our bodies, as the sea tosses vessels.

I pray for a moment of ease and sleep for my alcohol-soused soul. It has not been a good night. It has not been a good year. It is 1968. King and Kennedy are dead, friends killed in Vietnam, riots in America's cities and romantic anguish torments my soul and despite glorious stars above and a quiet contemplative village life filled with nature and self-fulfillment, I lay in blood, moving about to find any comfort, releasing and retying this guy's tourniquet, listening to him bemoan his fate. Meanwhile, the oxen shift direction, tossing my head all about as we proceed towards the main road where an ambulance awaits this poor son of a bitch.

Just two nights ago, I was dead asleep in my damp, hard bed, drugged by guaro liquor, when I was awakened by a sharp knock on the door. One thing about alcohol: dreams and reality tend to mingle back and forth. You never know which is which until it's too late. I mean, look at this poor son of a bitch bleed on me now, drunk, half-alive, half-dead, not sure of his fate.

The knock continued, and I yelled "momento" and stumbled out of bed. Obregon's cat, the thief that softly and quietly stole my warmth, jumped from my chest up to the roof and out through the rafters. I grabbed muddy pants crumpled on the floor, shook out the roaches and felt my way to the door. In dark shadows stood two young men, rough types, machetes drooped to their side, taut, scarred faces, cowboy hats, soiled clothes, fresh from the fields. But they all look alike don't they? Strong, skinny machos, every one of them. In this age of Che and Ho Chi Minh, who knows what fate awaits me?

They grabbed my arm, pulled me out the door onto the grass and pointed to the sky.

"Suya," one of them said to me.

I replied, "Que?" It was hard to know what's going on in a place like this, especially with my limited language ability and their mountain Spanish.

"Suya," he repeated. I understood that much. Something up there in the sky was mine. And all that was up there were stars. *These guys need to dry out*, I thought.

They pointed up and guided my head. And then I saw it. A little spot, speeding across the heavens, like the star of Bethlehem.

"Suya," he repeated, smiling and patting me on the back. It was one of those new, big balloon weather satellites the States put up at the dawn of the space age, easily seen from the ground. Surprised they didn't paint an American flag on it.

"Suya," he repeated.

I nodded my head. "Si, mia. Mia. Gracias."

They shook my hand in that polite way they have and returned into the night, their boots slouching noisily through mud. A horse neighed in the distance as my star passed over the mountain. Here I was, 1968, at the end of the American frontier—or, rather, the mountains of Costa Rica—under a circus of constellations, so distant from the crime-ridden streets of my New York home, talking with cowboys about weather satellites.

❧

But my star isn't circling tonight. No, instead a fierce headache rounds my head as the ox-cart yawns and bounces to the highway, my patient heavy on my torso. He sleeps, then jerks awake, jamming my hips into the cart's hard corner.

Tonight was not supposed to be like this. Tonight was to be La Fiesta de San Carlos, a party, a rare time for fun in a place where television has yet to arrive. They pushed burlap bags of rice and beans to the side of Obregon's storeroom, strung an electric wire from his generator, hired a mariachi band, slaughtered a cow, and invited neighboring towns to mount their steeds and come by for a drink, to dance with their daughters, perhaps to marry, if they were lucky. Country folk having fun. It happens once a year in each pueblo, half a dozen times in the towns in the outback.

Felipe Obregon owned the town's only store, a long, wooden building on the main road that offered the basics of life, rice, beans, crackers, cans of evaporated milk, aspirin, bandages and such. All were given credit, repaid with the year's harvest. In the evenings, men played pool and drank there, seeking peace from the day's heavy labor. He was a businessman, neutral in the town's conflicts, be they political or religious, and cautious in all his views.

The fiesta began. A mariachi band played old, romantic Trios Los Panchos numbers, "Solamente Una Vez." The musicians jumped up and down striking the marimba; two played melody, the third hammered rhythm. Husbands and wives danced an awkward one-two, one-two on the wooden floor. Young guys lined against the wall, hands in pressed, tan work pants, hair greased with brilliantine, some with white cowboy hats and fancy leather boots, showing off for the pretty young girls garbed in flowing flowered dresses their mothers made from the cloth Obregon sells by the bolt.

My Spanish was poor, so I studied faces and poses. The women all had the same hair and makeup and wore the same cheap perfume. I ignored the style and focused on their eyes, their expressions, their smiles and glances, searching for essence. When I first arrived months earlier, these mountain farmers were convinced I spoke Spanish since I smiled and nodded when they spoke. Of course, I couldn't understand *mierda* but they were not convinced. So I looked straight at them, searching for any meaning, like a newborn babe.

That's the way you get to know people, through eyes, head movements and facial expressions. It works frequently. Sometimes it gets you in trouble, like that time in Tirana with the cops at the roadblock, but that's another story.

Outside the barn beside the hitching post, men drank coke bottles filled with guaro, laughing and jostling. Horses moved about nervously with all the pushing and shoving and yelling. Not usual for these parts.

You have to be careful with guaro. A narrow wooden plank was the entrance to the dance, over a thick pool of mud, A little slip and down you go. Everyone laughs. Good fun.

Not everyone was at the party. The Evangelistas don't dance and certainly don't drink, and they were half the population. It was their town, actually, the Evangelistas. They had arrived twenty years earlier, cleared the scrublands in this valley between two volcanoes, and erected their homes, a school and a church. Lacking enough believers, they had sold parcels to Catholics and allowed a Catholic Church to be built.

The lines were pretty well drawn. The Evangelistas, all of whom were once Catholic, met and prayed and talked about how the Catholics ruined their lives by dancing and drinking. Nothing like a convert for real faith. Anyway, Obregon was Catholic and offers credit to all until the crops come in, so there wasn't much argument about the party tonight.

The Evangelistas may have a point. Guaro is evil. It's a clear drink, like American moonshine, suggesting purity, but grabs your head and shakes it real bad and makes you another person and gets the best of you, which is what happened to this guy bleeding all over me in the oxcart.

The fiesta was going strong and the guaro was flowing like water and I'm standing around looking about, observing and saying, "ola, como esta?" to passersby and trying like hell not to dance when Don Zacarius Ruiz ambled over and put his hand around my shoulder, hugging me real tight—as in, "I've had too much to drink and you're my pal." His weathered, cracked face nestled into my chest. He pushed a bottle toward me and I took a swig. He teased me about dancing with his daughters, which I would have loved to, but I also didn't want to find myself at the wrong end of a shotgun.

The Ruiz daughters were something to behold: quiet, shy pretty peasant girls, gaunt bodies with tan hair rather than Latin black and with piercing green eyes they got from their mother. *Inocentes.* The five looked alike, from the little, cute child to the womanly sixteen-year-old, wearing the same dress cut from the same cloth. They stood against the wall looking like a time-lapse picture of evolving beauty. I stared intently at the eldest, which was probably why Don Zacarius kept telling me that I should choose one.

Maybe I was as drunk as Don Zacarius because I didn't see the fight at first. Through the din of the mariachi, I heard a commotion in the corner of the bodega and saw a circle form. The crowd pushed back and forth, and I saw the heads of these two guys in the middle moving about, like fighting cocks. Slowly the music faded and then stopped. I pushed to the front and saw the drawn machetes. The young studs were sparring unsteadily, guaro tripping their intentions, blades flying here and there. They swung their knives, each one missing wildly and falling off balance and quickly jumping up. They swung again and then again and then one guy fell to the ground.

Just like that it was over, the flash too fast to see, the fellow on the ground tossing and turning. The blade had sliced from the top of his thigh down towards the knee. The thigh dangled and blood gushed out, turning his tan slacks bright red.

They carried him outside, and I grabbed a cloth and a stick and applied a tourniquet, holding it until slowly, the blood ebbed. The fight at the OK Corral was over.

The victim was dark-skinned and the crowd kept talking about the Nica, which is what they call people from Nicaragua in these parts. Doesn't matter if you're from Nicaragua or not, they still call you by hue. If you are white, that's a Tico, a Costa Rican. If you are dark, a Nica. That is, unless you are from the Caribbean and speak English. Then you are a Negro. But there aren't any Negros living in these parts. The law didn't allow them into the central mountains until a few years earlier, and they wouldn't think of coming up to this part of the world anyway. No welcome at all. Nicas live in mountain shacks high above the village, doing chores for Costa Rican peasants. Refugees from Somoza's paradise up the road, these Nicas. They don't vote, send their kids to school, or hang out at Obregon's. They have no money. Like ghosts, they roam about, heading to and from the fields.

In the background, the marimba started up again. No sense ruining a good evening. Couples joined together on the floor. The victor of the fight pranced about, cock-of-the-walk, laughing and pointing at his downed victim. The town policeman ambled over, a nice young guy who got the job because of his family's political connections and because he's big and strong. A pistol dangled from his side. Not much for Wyatt Earp to do around these parts. If there's a crime, people handle their own justice. No questions asked.

As town cop, he handled the telegraph line, the only immediate contact with the outside world. It was not really a telegraph, but a singular telephone line. The telegraph waystation on the highway translated the Morse Code and read the messages to the policeman in the hut that was also post office and jail. The cop jotted them down, more or less, and delivered them to the right people, more or less. If the name was foreign, he came to my door — Angelina sent me a message just a few weeks earlier that he delivered as: Hapy Birtday and all that Jass - Otherwise, he took it to Obregon's. Obregon knew everybody. That's because they owed him. Until the harvest came in. The policeman also farmed, of course, but he was the law in Rio Naranjo, in a matter of speaking. So Wyatt Earp grabbed the drunken, grinning winner of the fight and escorted him away. We didn't need any more sliced meat this night.

A loud voice of the carreta driver commanding his oxen announced the arrival of the cart. A tall skinny fellow descended and pulled out the rear wood panel. Didn't take long to figure out that I would be going with the victim. Someone had to cradle him in the cart, to loosen the tourniquet from time to time, and make sure he didn't fall out. I had the least to do, so why not?

I climbed into the hardback limo and the men lowered the Nica into my cradling arms. Doing good for humanity sometimes isn't the most comfortable chore.

We head down the road, crossing the stream they call Rio Naranjo, a stream that is more a river these days with the wintry rains. I hear the slush of the oxen hooves followed by the bumps across the riverbed, announcing our departure from our little Brigadoon. We bump along, settling into a rhythm, and I begin to drift off into a guaro sleep when the guy starts to move about. I shift my weight and then he moans and cries. He is young, sixteen or seventeen with a dark innocent face, marred with tears. I tell him he's going to be all right, that maybe he should get some sleep. We'll be getting him to a doctor and he'll be good as new. But he keeps sobbing and shifting, and I'm not quite sure he's going to make it even if he makes it to the highway because the blood keeps seeping. Even if he lives, he may require amputation, and people in these parts don't do so well on one leg.

My pants are soaked with blood, part dried, part moist. I shiver in the night mountain air. The guy keeps crying for his "mama," and I'm trying to be compassionate but I have a horrible hangover and it's hard, very hard. Then, he turns quickly and starts slipping out of the carreta.

I grab him and yell to the driver. The driver shouts a command to the oxen that trudge to a stop. An owl hoots in the distance.

Oxen are castrated after their first birthday and paired with one driver. The driver yells "para," the beasts stop together. "Vaya," and they stomp forward, eight hooves in unison. They work in tandem. Should one of these 800-pound muscled beasts keep going while the other stands its ground, you've got a lot of spilled rice and beans. A lesson in cooperation and teamwork. A thick brightly-painted yoke binds the oxen's heavy, muscular necks together and the sharp metal jab from the driver helps the cooperative spirit. *En Union Hay Fuerza*, they told us in development training. With Unity comes Strength.

When one ox dies, the other becomes dogfood, useless for anything and when the driver passes on, both are slaughtered because the oxen only understand his voice and commands. A marriage for life. For centuries, the carreta has been rolling through the Costa Rican campo and all of Latin America. But these days, oxcarts are fading out. Except in the outback and tourist shops.

I get the guy back into the cart and we jostle into the night to the tune of the driver: "left ho," "right ho," "easy," "push there." Once in a while, a horseman passes and yells a brief "adios." The guy on me cries quietly, and I'm near sobs from the throb in my head and the pain in my cramped legs. A chorus of cicadas erupt in a loud scream. Dogs bark in the distance.

"He called my mother a puta," the guy says.

"No," I say, not because I don't believe him but who wants to have this conversation?

"Si. Si. I swear. He called my mother a whore. I couldn't let him do that, could I?" My Spanish may not be too good but I understand this.

"No, of course not. You did what is right but you must get some sleep." He's shaking his head back and forth. I'm holding onto him as best I can but my arms are weakening and I'm not too good at consoling a drunk who may soon lose a leg because of some insult.

"Mi madre, mi madre," his voice lowers.

"Duerme," I say.

"Sleep. Sleep." He exhausts in my arms. I feel a slow warm liquid on my leg. Things could be worse. It could be raining.

❧

Rain is a constant in this part of Costa Rica. The problem, the way Don Zacarius Ruiz tells it, is that Costa Rica sits at the center of Central America, and Rio Naranjo lies in a volcanic mountain chain that runs right down the middle. We are the crux of the matter, you might say, the United States to the North, South America to the south. We get the rainy season from the Atlantic first, and when that's over the Pacific rains start up. The weather passes through the cordillera mountain range, dousing verdant volcanic peaks and then Rio Naranjo.

A metaphor, this centrality. The nations to the north, El Salvador and Nicaragua, suffer harsh poverty and waves of civil wars; those to the south, Colombia and Panama, drug trafficking, coups and more conflict. This ox cart travels in an island of peace called Costa Rica, with universal literacy and medical care. Peace, that is, except for an occasional theft or the flash of a machete.

But nothing is perfect. The rains go on for months at a time. As the heat builds, they commence at midday just as I am walking back from lunch. One such afternoon a few weeks back, Dona Ana, Zacarius' wife, had made me a plate of fine rice and beans and fried plantains and beefsteak. The steak comes from the town matadero that slaughters a cow each week and salts it for preservation making it as tough as can be. Dona Ana pounds and pounds it to make it palatable. Dona Ana has hands like hammers, big, strong and marked by years of toil. Sometimes she puts a fried egg on top of the meat for flavor. She makes coffee by pouring hot water through beans she grinds by hand into an old, stained cotton sock that hangs from a piece of metal. But oh, what coffee! Rough coffee, like guaro, that burns the tongue and wakens the senses, as rough as Dona Ana's hands.

Dona Ana doesn't smile much. She doesn't rest either, what with rearing five children, carrying water from the river, swabbing wooden floors, scrubbing clothes, grinding coffee, grinding corn meal into *masa*, flattening tortillas, beating meat and all the rest. She looks on me with disdain, as if to say "who is this guy who comes to our town, who doesn't work from dawn to dusk like the rest of us." Or so I imagine. Her only joy, it seems, is her parrot, Lorita, guarding the front porch, screaming "*hue puta*" at all who pass, language learned from passing workers.

Over lunch that day, Zacarius and I talked about the world, the war in Vietnam, the killings of Kennedy and King, the riots in the cities, and all such. With my poor Spanish, I wasn't sure how much was getting through. Still, he taught me what was going on in town, who to trust and who not to. We talked politics carefully. He is literate, as are most Costa Ricans and reads the national conservative newspaper. He hates the liberals in the capital that seek to tax his hard labor. He relies on markets to survive, corn, wheat and beans. Zacarius told me he is sure that the rain will end with the new moon, a prediction that has failed for three moons now. So much for the wisdom of the campo.

Zacarius is my crutch, my support, the man who quietly led me through the ways of Rio Naranjo. He, who from dawn until sunset, farms his hardscrabble patch, works on hacienda lands, trades rice and beans, machetes neighbors' land and does whatever it takes to make ends meet. They all labor, these men and women of Rio Naranjo. Carlos, the Evangelista minister, caters to his flock and is the town carpenter and barber. He farms his small plot. He built the school's new outhouses, digging through the dense volcanic soil and installing cement blocks to meet health regulations. Obregon runs the store, gives credit, hauls rice and beans and drives a makeshift bus when the weather allows. The others, hundreds of them, survive at hard labor. They are strong, these men, with spindly strong arms and legs, gaunt, rugged and serious faces. Mountain men.

After lunch and full of energy I strolled home. Despite the heat and humidity. I was content, watching the bright southern sun illuminate the hillside village. Glistening ferns and orange helicons lined the front of small houses together with hyacinths and brilliant yellow corteza trees. I passed a green lime tree in the schoolyard, and gazed over at the tamarind and avocado trees in the two church yards, the Catholic and the Evangelical, as if they chose their denomination by taste.

Passing the school, I listened for the teacher's voice in the school. He is the reason I came here. He had read about the Peace Corps in the newspaper and sent a letter asking for a volunteer. I was due to work for a government agency setting up credit unions in the city but when the agency was shut down for corruption, Peace Corps officials panicked, went to the mailroom and pulled out the teacher's letter. Just like that, the fates intervened and placed me in the middle of the mountains in the middle of Central America to cradle an injured drunk in the back of an oxcart and do whatever a twenty-two year old can do for a small, poor town. Fate is like that. A bureaucratic decision. The cut of a machete blade. Life changes.

As I walked home from lunch, I watched the rain descend from the north, forming idyllic triple rainbows that drifted onto Volcan Tenorio on the other side of the valley. A sight to behold—but not for too long, as a deluge follows.

The winds picked up and the rain arrived. Nobody left their homes, not even to Obregon's for a nip of guaro. I remained in my hut, under the loud, pounding tat-a-tat-tat on the tin roof. I spent the afternoon reading, writing long letters, pacing back and forth and trying to pick up Voice of America on the radio. The rain went on and on and I started the old backandforth, pacing, counting black slits in the dark floor, picking roach buds from the walls, tat-a-tat-tat, laying down, reading, flitting around the radio crackle, outhousing through the muddy grass, toothbrushing, standing and peering out into the dark gloom as shrouded horsemen clomped by heads down with no sign of life except a plaintive "adios," me, pacing again, talking to myself, to others not there, arguing with Angelina, why did you leave me? When are we going to see each other? What went wrong? Pledging love to a distant soul long gone, repeating Walt Whitman's plaintive cry:

Sullen suffering hours! (I am ashamed—but it is useless—I am what I am.

Hours of my torment—I wonder if other men ever have the like, out of the like, out of the like feelings.

All alone, troubled and heartbroken, agonizing and staring into space. What to do? What's next? Tat-a-tat-tat. Listening to passing hooves,

"Don't let them think you're a vago," they told me in training. "That's bad. Keep busy. Keep going. If you get the vagabundo label, then your credibility's shot."

Don't shoot. I thought to myself. *Please don't shoot.*

Just then, Obregon's cat jumped through the rafters and stared at me, checking the scene. I didn't move. It waited, turned and jumped back out.

Three o'clock. Children screamed as they scurried from school, yelling through the rain, and kicking mud drenched soccer balls. Desperately bored, I threw on a raincoat and headed up to Don Carlos, the teacher. I touched a few kids' heads and they yelled "hello" in English, giggling on their way past. Humanity. An aged dark-skinned woman swept the school porch. Carlos sat at the end of the singular long classroom, papered with Costa Rican flags, math tables, portraits of patriots and posters, a Grand Canyon here, a Disneyland there, gifts of the US government. The school desks were all clean and books carefully piled on shelves.

Carlos wore a cardigan sweater over a neat, freshly pressed open shirt. The teacher's uniform. He likes me. He likes America, he said. America fights for freedom. America hates Castro. America is so big. Someday he wanted to visit America. He was young and alone in this town like me, except he's got a full-time job. All six grades. Papers to grade. Reports to write. Sensing that I was a distraction, I let him be.

At dusk, Obregon's generator kicked on noisily, lighting the bare electric lights, a signal for men to come for dominoes, pool or a tip or two of guaro after their harsh days in the field, before heading to their homes, wives and kids.

The rain kept falling. Tat-a-tat-tat.

"Felt needs, that's what ya' gotta find out in community development," they said back in training. "Find out, then you get the town together and you fix it. That's what development is all about."

Fix the felt needs. They never mentioned who pays for these needs, the water systems, and the roads. The harsh struggle of earning a few pesos a day while supporting their growing families. Tat-a-tat-tat. "Fight the good fight." In the mountains. "Feel their needs." When will this rain end? Listening for moving shapes. Face washing. Situpping. Tat-tat-tating. Reading. Pacing. Waiting.

Community development was the catchword of the age, the American liberal response to communism, although the common root is obvious. Bring together the townsfolk, find out when they feel they need and work to fulfill it. I wonder now about the felt needs of the guy laying on top of me, a drunken peasant spending his life in the fields although that work may well have been shortened by a machete's blade.

Each decade, government policies and academicians propose paths to end poverty to counter the "commie threat." First, Walt Rostow's "Five Stages of Economic Growth," then, "Community Development" and "the Alliance for Progress," later "privatization" and "globalization" and every few years, new prescriptions: "The Third Way," "The Asian Model," "Building Capacity," and "Transformational Governance." New concepts spring up with innovative catchwords, strategies and goals that well-paid bureaucrats and academics develop in their cubicles, ignoring the yolks that bind the oxen pulling the global load: wage slavery, trade protectionism, capital domination and power politics.

When I first arrived, I was treated politely by all concerned. Zacarius took me in and showed me about the town. A few weeks after my arrival, he came for me. We walked over a hill and joined a group of mourners at a graveyard. A tiny casket was lowered into the ground.

"She was eight months old. The water got her."

The water. The river is the only source. As it falls, water for drinking and cooking is fetched, in the middle, the laundry is washed and further down, feces are dumped. But roaming cattle obey no rules and so the water needs to be boiled by all.

Zacarius led me up the mountain to a spring that would serve as the source for good, clean water. Together with the teacher, we held a meeting to organize a campaign. We went to the county seat, hours away by horse, to ask the public engineer to develop a system. The townsfolk wrote the governor and its representatives.

This was what "community development" was supposed to be all about, to amass the combined strength of a town of 300 people to fix its issues. We were promised a survey, when the budget allowed. Nothing happened.

At midnight after a long day of unending rain, there was silence for a brief moment. Then a dog barked, then another, and another. Roosters cawed. Owls hooted. A flock of parrots flew by overhead, screeching away predators. Deep into the night, horsemen rode by, talking softly.

In rural darkness, you see everything by feel, cockroaches falling from the rafters onto the bed or the wispy hair of Obregon's cat who crawls onto my bed night after night, seeking my warmth. When nature calls, nature inspired by bad drinking water or food or too much drink, I run naked and shoeless across coarse grass and mud to the outhouse behind the house. As I enter, creatures scurry about and jump into the hole, frogs enjoying the bugs feces attract.

In the few evenings when skies are clear and all earthly lights are extinguished, I would leave the house and stand naked in the grass, under a celestial paradise, shooting stars, bright constellations and passing planes, amazed at my great fortune to be in this peaceful paradise.

Tonight in the carreta, we are lucky. There is no rain and me and this bloody Nica are out for a ride under the stars, holding each other closely, like lovers, listening to creaking wooden wheels and grunting oxen. But the aches never cease.

I calculate the distance to the highway, oxen not being the fastest means of transport. In the summer, when the road is dry and they've ploughed the carreta ruts, the bus comes in, a Volkswagen van Obregon engineered with a Chevy engine mounted in the middle of the cab and four-wheel drive running off it. Everybody sits around the motor, eating smoke, and puffing on cigarettes and five-cent cigars. The ride lasts five uncomfortable hours with twists and turns past ruts and boulders and stops and starts, jostling around nature's obstacles. From time to time, a sudden jerk and the axle snaps. Then, oxen are brought to tow the bus back to the highway and the garage. Passengers proceed onward afoot.

The horse is reliable, of course. Winter or summer, always available. Sure, you have to catch the animal in the potrero, saddle it, make sure it's fed and washed down every now and then. But the beast is always there. Seven hours by horse to reach the road. Straight and non-stop. No problem. But tonight, by ox-cart? I guess ten, maybe twelve.

This is why everyone wants a new road, a macadam strip that would offer an hour's ride in a bus and provide the means for heavy trucks to come in and extract farm goods easily. The road will bring progress and wealth. As with the water, we all worked to pressure the government. We visited ministries and wrote letters to the provincial authorities. Nothing happened.

We trudge on. Dawn brings the sweet songs of chattering birds followed by screeching flocks of parrots. Peasants pass and chat with our driver. The cart hits a deep rut. A wheel falls off. The driver dismounts and pushes it back on.

With the sun, my patient starts wailing again. Riders come upon us and glance at the victim. We stop for a moment at the hacienda to pick up buns and coffee and then descend into the Pacific lowlands and heat and dust. On horse, there is the air of movement. In this casket, there is dust and sweat. But now the cart is moving faster. The road is drier and more level.

Hours later, we plod from dirt path onto the Pan American highway. Passing motorists zoom by this anonymous road on their way to Costa Rica's famous wild and virgin beaches. Beaches that will not remain virgin for long.

An ambulance awaits us. Wyatt Earp had telephoned ahead. The Nica is transferred and the driver asks if I wish to go along. I look at my clothes. I have little money. Perhaps I might run into another gringo or gringa in Liberia, borrow some cash, get drunk or get laid. Not this day.

I decline the invitation, turn and head inland. My legs ache but the pain disappears as I concentrate on the rugged path, hopping from place to place. The sun is burning hot but the trek is enjoyable. Rice fields spout a sea of new grass tuffs. Herds of cattle turn in unison to watch me. Bright and gaunt *garza* cowbirds walk about them, picking their droppings.

Afoot and light-hearted I take to the open road, wrote Whitman. *Healthy, free, the world before me. The long brown path before me leading wherever I choose.*

Nobody is about. Only mad dogs and foreigners go out in the midday sun. I scuff from rut to rut, warning sleeping lizards of my approach. A grapefruit tree provides refreshment.

I might have rented a horse, but I have been challenged. A young high school student who lives up the road jogs forty miles each week through the mud, crags and streams to the high school in the city. Every Friday evening, he returns home the same way. If this kid can run all this way, I certainly can walk home.

I must do what everybody else does. I am determined. I may be a gringo, my Spanish poor, and I may be ignorant of farming rice or herding cattle but me, a twenty-two year old manchild, can adapt, ride a horse, shit in outhouses and walk this mountain path to return home.

I look down on the twisting brown road, watching for rocks and ruts and snakes. The heat is rising fast. Mosquitoes buzz and bite. Cacti grow in the pasture. The earth smells of dust.

My shirt is drenched with sweat. A distant crow's caw distracts me. I glance up and my foot slips. I turn my ankle. I instinctively reach out to catch myself and brush my arm on barbed wire. Burrs dig into my arm, making deep scratches across it. Thin lines of blood spurt out. I kneel to the ground in momentary agony. It is not serious but messy. Salted sweat burns the wound. Not a big deal. I inspect the rusted and dirty wire, wipe blood on my shirt, and head on. Condor vultures circle nearby.

I'm exhausted. It is early-afternoon and the heat will not ebb until evening. Unless it rains but then walking would be impossible through mud, deep pools and a swollen Rio Naranjo. I need rest. I look for shade and spot a tree across a field. Brahma cows stand about, their heavy humps resembling hunchbacks. I duck through wire and collapse under a tree to a chorus of muffled bovine cries. The cattle move about nervously. I fall into a deep sleep.

Cold water awakens me. A boy stands above me, a shrunken image of all the campo men in campo, with open shirt, torn pants, cowboy hat and muscular arms. He offers me water from his plastic canteen.

Don't drink the local water, I've been warned. Water must be boiled. Beware of parasites. Be safe not sorry. Parched, I guzzle it down.

"*Vamanos*," he says, holding out a hand to help me up and lead me off.

We chat the usual conversation: What is your name? How old are you? How many brothers and sisters do you have? Why aren't you in school? He is Miguel. He is ten and has eight siblings. He goes to

school in the morning and chops firewood at the hacienda the rest
of the day. He is happy to meet me.

We enter the grounds of Hacienda Tenorio, a ranch with small
houses, a sawmill, landing strip and a butcher. He guides me to a
large rustic house at the top of the hill. An elderly man greets me.
"Ah good. You've been saved," he says in accented English.

"Saved?"

"Yes, I was told there was a foreigner struggling down the road.
I sent Miguel to look for you. Please come in."

"I didn't realize I was lost. News travels fast."

"Juan Fernandez," he holds out his hand. "I am the administrator
of the hacienda." I introduce myself. "You need to wash up. I'm
sorry," he hesitates, "Your clothes are a mess."

"Yes," I say. "I've been through hell, sort of."

"But I don't think I have any clothes for you. You are too large,
you Americans."

"Oh, I'm all right," I say, glancing at the ghoulish fluids covering
my body. "I must have scared Miguel."

He takes me to a spigot in the rear and I wash as best I can and
return. A pot of hot coffee awaits. The living room has plush sofas
and a thick mahogany table.

"Please, please, sit down," he says.

"I'd better not," I say. "I am quite dirty."

"Not too bother. Much dirtier peones have sat here, believe me.
Tell me, what brings you to these parts.

"I'm with the Peace Corps," I say. "I'm working in Rio Naranjo
in community development."

"Rio Naranjo? Why there? Not very much happening up there."

"I think they need help."

"Everybody needs help. Why don't you come and live here on
this ranch. Many more people. They need education, skill-training,
nutrition."

"You speak English very well," I say. "Where'd you learn it?"

"Tulane University. I'm an agronomist."

"So, how's the land?"

"The land? The land is wonderful. Centuries of volcanic ash, the best type of fertilizer. What we have is bad weather. One year it never rains. The next, it never stops. Hard to plan. Hard to produce. When the weather is good, the price we get for our crops is too low. When it is bad, it doesn't matter the price."

"Your people in Rio Naranjo are suffering," he says. "That's why so many come here for fieldwork, but they don't earn nearly enough. They are all in debt. I hope you can help. They certainly need it. But what are you doing?"

"We are trying to get the government to build a new road," I say.

"Ah, the famous road. The government has been promising one for years. Yes, that's a very good idea. If you need any help, we'd be happy to assist. A new road would do well by us."

"And I suppose, the people of Rio Naranjo," I say.

"Oh yes," he says. "A good road would bring down the price of food, make access to schools and hospitals easier and increase the value of the small plots of land and houses. For us, here at the hacienda, it doesn't matter so much. I fly my avioneta into San Jose and the guys haul the stuff out on ox carts. But for the poor, it is very tough."

He offers me a horse for the remainder of my journey. I cannot refuse. As we walk to the steed, he says, "I am serious about what I said. If you come here, I will let you have resources, a jeep and a house. You can use my plane. Whatever you want."

"Let me think it over and talk to my bosses."

I head into the hills, my horse bopbopbops me along. I nod off with the rhythm. The sun falls behind the mountain, the wind picks up and with it, a slight drizzle slaps my dazed face. At the river, Rio Naranjo, my horse stops quickly, fearful of the rain-filled stream. I kick and urge her on. She reluctantly moves into the waters, feeling her way, one hoof, then the next and then a slip, a bump, and its knees buckle. Over I go into the river. My elbow smashes into a rock. The horse splashes from the water and pulls violently and I release the reins.

There are times when you feel enough is enough, that you're just gonna lay there because you're too darned tired and the world won't leave you be. After all, how much can one man take?

This was not one of those times. No time for thought, the freezing water shocks me into a quick run up the embankment.

The lights of Obregon's store shine brightly. Too tired to mount the steed, I grab the reins and lead it into town. A few guys play pool, others drink guaro and Obregon is fixing to close up. He is a slight serious man with a thin mustache. He does not drink or play pool. He buys and sells, runs the bus and loans money to the locals. He sees me approach.

"Eh, gringo, you look a mess," he says.

"I feel worse," I say. "How'd the fiesta go?"

"Not bad. We made a little. We could have done better. Where'd you steal the horse?"

"From the hacienda. They lent it to me. Are some of the guys going back there tomorrow?"

"Sure, at dawn. They gotta work. I'll have them take it back."

I have a slice of local white cheese, a packet of saltines and a couple of shots of guaro and wander to my shack. It smells of musk. I light a candle and hear rustling from the bedroom. I peek inside. Obregon's cat jumps into the rafters and out of the house. On my bed is a dark spot. I touch it. Blood. I look closer and see little blobs. They are kittens, complete with afterbirth. I carefully gather them up in the dirty linen and carry them up to Obregon.

"Your cat left me a present," I say.

Obregon looks at them. "Dumb cat. She's supposed to chase mice and all she does is fuck." He takes the kittens from my hands and goes outside. In a flash, he dashes one against a rock.

"What are you doing?" I say, incredulously.

"Do you want them?" he asks, offering them back.

"No," I stutter. "no, I can't take care of them."

He turns and, one by one, smashes the remaining furry blobs.

I return home and head to the outhouse. The frogs scurry about the hole, my little family who live off my shit. The outhouse is dark, damp and putrid but here I feel comfortable, sitting on the wooden shelf, my eyes closed, the sound of life beneath me, the rain tat-a-tat-tat on the roof.

It is beautiful, this life, innocence and ideals, frogs, cattle, machetes and snakes in the grass. I may not accomplish much here but I see and feel. Depression gone. Romanticism ended. I am home.

❧

Ten years later, the civil war in Nicaragua erupts with Socialist forces pushing to victory. Rio Naranjo is just sixty miles south of the border. An all-weather road is built. The jungle is cleared for rice production and Costa Rica prospers from new exports but just for a time. The nation joins the World Trade Organization and industrialized American farm production swamps local markets, bankrupting small farmers.

Fifty years later, I return for the first time and make the one-hour drive from the highway. I pass a teenage bicyclist zooming down the paved road garbed in Tour de France spandex. Obregon's store remains but he is gone, moved to the City with his earnings. I drive around what is still a small village and ask a passerby for Zacarius. He points to a house by the school.

And there he sits, the old farmer, now ninety-seven years of age, rocking on the porch, and watching children kick a football. We embrace and he leads me to a spigot and turns it on. Fresh and clean mountain water.

"We did it," he says.

BROOKLYN

(1969)

Richard Nixon becomes President – Vietnam War — US bombs of Cambodia — Woodstock — Stonewall Riot — Beatles Last Performance — Arafat becomes PLO head — The Godfather — Golda Meir becomes Israel PM -- DeGaulle resigns — Chappaquiddick incident — First Man on Moon — Charles Manson murders — Coups in Libya and Somalia– Chicago Eight trial — Sesame Street

WHEN I RETURNED AFTER TWO YEARS in the Peace Corps, America had changed. The ideals and dreams of the sixties were fading quickly. Tie-dyed shirts, long hair and beards, afros and dashikis were the new uniforms of my generation. "Give Peace a Chance" had given way to "Hell No, I Won't Go."

I found work at Brooklyn College. Lyndon Johnson's Great Society initiatives included a major federal financial aid program for students. In previous years, Brooklyn College had offered $30,000 annually in assistance. Now, it had a budget of three million. An office was set up to handle the immense bureaucratic chore of distributing the windfall following federal guidelines, determining who needed what. I was hired along with three young African American women and a young man named Desmond Cartey. A Trinidadian and brother of Wilfred, the noted poet who taught at City College, he later served as a minister in his nation's government.

The times, they were in turmoil. Martin Luther King Jr. was killed the year before. Urban riots caused massive destruction in black neighborhoods; Newark and Detroit have yet to recover. The Nation of Islam, Young Lords, the Black Panther Party and a dozen other "black power" militant groups challenged Dr. King's non-violence message and were exerting greater influence over the civil rights movement. Opposition to the Vietnam War became widely prevalent and increasingly violent. The Woodstock festival was held in what was to be the climax of the decade; the music lingers on in malls, airports and elevators, anthems of faded dreams.

That year, the City University implemented a policy of "open admissions," providing all high school graduates with admission without taking traditional exams. This was revolutionary. While it always had minority students, the institution was still predominately white and middle class. Almost overnight, it was transformed into a working-class haven, and the new impoverished students brought with them all the social issues that heretofore the ivy towers avoided.

Financial aid was crucial for students on welfare, single-parent mothers, or wage workers trying to earn a degree. They all came through our office. We, my colleagues and I, surveyed their requests and interviewed them. With time, we evolved into a counseling department. Some students had issues at home; abusive parents and spouses, psychological problems, drug and alcohol addiction. Our office became a center for minority rights.

Some of those who applied and received help did not make it. Some were poorly prepared and others could not adjust to the campus life. They sunk back into the morass that is American poverty. But many did. They were not the famous and much publicized minority students at ivy league schools who went on to run corporations and governments, but they gained a liberal arts education and went on to good jobs and raised families with the dignity that all Americans deserve. Progress

When I arrived in 1969, I didn't know Brooklyn and certainly did not know the African American community. My colleague, Desmond Cartey, became a friend, and together we visited churches and community halls. Many places were in terrible shape with abandoned lots, burnt buildings and closed stores, the combined scars of riots and the daily toll of life in urban poverty.

For eighteen months, I lived with the issues of racism and inequality. To be sure, I was not "integrated" into the Brooklyn black community, but I was treated as a friend. I was that weird kid who danced and played with the "brothers" and "sisters" to the sounds of Stevie Wonder, Motown and the Supremes. Still, there was a barrier between us that I could never breach. In America, there is always a barrier.

It was not that I had lived in a sheltered, white world. My high school was half black and my father practiced law attorney in Harlem, in the Bishop Building right next to the Apollo Theater. 125th Street was a part of my education. Dad and I ate at Frank's, Club Baby Grand, Sweets, and Chock Full of Nuts. But Brooklyn was different, and the emerging African American militancy changed relationships with whites.

Writing about racism is always fraught with danger. The subject stirs the passions unlike any other. And to write about "solutions" here is absurd, given its complexity. Nevertheless, these years at Brooklyn showed me that there is not one divide in America but two. The first is the separation of peoples by their skin color, history, and class. But the other is experiential. Most of the nation has no experience with "the other," however one defines it. Many live isolated in suburbia, gated communities, and rural areas; they may appreciate African-American personalities, singers and sportspeople and support civil rights reforms but they are in different nations with an imagined sense of the other. Most New Yorkers, though, rub elbows with other nationalities on the streets, in the subways, in bars and in stores, in government offices and businesses. We hold doors for each other. We are neighbors if not communities.

Where is the greatest level of integration in America? In the military, where all groups fight and die together. Major universities may be the center of liberal activity for social justice, but they can never erase the differences students bring with them.

Brooklyn College was no exception. The campus was in constant turmoil. Students ran amok, electing radical student leaders, seizing academic buildings, and holding teach-ins. Sex was everywhere, on the lawn, in the stairwells, and in administrative offices. As an "adult," I patrolled the halls, once encountering the head of the nascent Jewish radical organization, Meyer Kahane, with a group of young men. He claimed he was there to protect Jewish students. I ushered him off the campus.

In the meantime, as the impact of "open enrollment" took hold, the faculty revolted and insisted that "weaker students" be given a separate campus. Many saw the word "weaker" as a racial euphemism and it enraged the situation further. Once liberal professors became conservative. The "neo-con" movement emerged, becoming an ideological basis for the Reagan presidency.

What we believed in earlier and more idealistic times about reform through law was shattered into disillusionment, militancy, nihilism or indifference. The dreams of the sixties, the simplistic belief that deep and complex problems can be solved in a few years, or with vain "hopes" or with "demonstrations," all vanished. In these eighteen months, I came to understand that economic class was as important as color and that invisible barriers remained, despite changes in law.

Moreover, I recognized the emerging "blame game" that still rages in our politics today. Increasing black fury towards *all* whites disappointed me, to say the least, although I agreed with the scorn directed towards "concerned" Americans who would do anything to help minorities except share their standard of living, neighborhoods, and schools. Other movements, such as gay rights and feminism, disconnected me from activism in general, regardless of my feelings. A trend towards ideological disintegration fragmented liberal opposition—who was "pure" and who "sold out." Self-righteousness and victimization became the rule of the day. Identity politics emerged with a fury that rages still today.

I was burnt out and left for Europe. I was paid well helping the poor in Brooklyn, some $80,000 annually in today's dollars. I used the money to gain an education in France.

This was one more step in the odyssey, from city streets to rural Central America to Black Brooklyn to Paris and Morocco to academic teaching in rural America to consulting to major corporations on international risk to consulting on international development in forty countries around the world.

In Brooklyn, the white boy's development continued.

MOTHER INDIA

(1979/1984)

Excerpted from the novel *The Shadows*

1979: Vietnam conquers Cambodia deposing Pol Pot—The Shah flees Iran—Idi Amin is deposed in Uganda—Margaret Thatcher becomes Prime Minister—Iranian militants seize the US embassy and take hostages—The Soviet Union invades Afghanistan—Three Mile Island Nuclear reactor releases radiation

1984: Virgin Atlantic founded—the AIDS virus identified—Iran-Iraq War—Amritsar Golden Temple attacked—Tetris—Brighton Hotel Bombing—PEMEX explosion—Indira Gandhi assassinated –Bhopal chemical explosion—Reagan reelected President

OH, HOW I MISS INDIA! Fresh mango, guavas, and papaya at breakfast, dosas at lunch, and lavish tandooris, kebabs, biryanis at dinner. The scents that filled our days—curry, cloves and cardamom, lilies, freesia, and incense. Elegant and friendly people, so polite and a joy to be with. A life filled with servants and sycophants. And Mr. Singh, how I miss him most of all. I have never found anyone quite like him.

It was 1979. American firms were expanding around the world. I had prolonged my education and earned degrees in chartered accountancy from both Britain and America, figuring that school as a draft-dodge was far better than fighting Commies in Asia. I also had a hunch that dual certifications would serve me well—a calculation that hit the mark, if I must say so myself.

These were the days of Mother Theresa, Ravi Shankar, the Beatles, and of the Maharishi who came out of the Himalayas, it was said, to relieve the world from suffering through Vedic knowledge. His disciple George Harrison proclaimed, "Imagine all the workers on the Ford assembly line in Detroit, all of them chanting 'Hare Krishna, Hare Krishna' while bolting on the wheels."

We in India lived a different reality, peoples whose hunger never ceased from birth to death, as Ruth Prawer Jhabvala then wrote. Children kidnapped, maimed, and sent out as beggars. Girls sold into slavery. Millions killed over religion, ethnicity, or sect. The day-to-day fight for survival. The rampant corruption. The ostentatious wealth. Indira Gandhi declared a state of emergency, imprisoned hundreds of thousands, destroyed the legal system and installed Congress Party partisans in all areas of government. This was India, far from Hare Krishna chants in automobile factories.

Bombay was different then, not the overbuilt mess that today is called Mumbai, before the ethnic riots produced so much ugliness and before the crazies bombed the Taj Hotel. Contacts. Handshakes. Understandings. A few families and corporations ruled the national roost while one party dominated everything. You could get things done back then without fear that some politician would come along and disrupt the established order. The Brits were there, of course, and the Arabs; both had been there for centuries. Now there were Germans and Israelis and Dutch, each trying to sell their goods to the monopolists.

I had been in Bombay for a year, hired by American Foods Corporation. AFC, the multinational that provides the world with everything from corn flakes to diapers. The firm opened an office in Bombay with the hope of introducing Orangilla, claiming the dried juice drink provided all the essential elements for child health. Vitamins C and D with a healthy dose of coloring, sugar and artificial flavorings, perfect for a nation of 800 million consumers. AFC meant well, although its idea was to use the drink to establish a beachhead for other products: cereal, paper goods, candies. Overconfident, like so many American firms, it ran into the usual archaic rules and protectionist roadblocks of the Indian bureaucracy. Approvals were delayed, applications went missing, and Indian officials demanded access to the secret Orangilla ingredients. Frustrated and about to give up, they passed the assignment down to me. And when I say down, I mean all the way down to the junior accountant in the corner.

It took some time to sort out tax and import issues, the rights to sell an American product in India, and a name change into Hindi. But all the time spent cutting red tape helped create the alliances in industry and government that would ensure AFC's future success— and my own.

It was the numbers that mattered most: the cost of inputs, the freight, the local profit, and the division of the spoils amongst our various friends. I did the calculations and passed them around. Young, energetic and idealistic with that smiling "save the world" personality, I didn't pay much attention to what were called "informal barriers," feeling that capital paves all roads.

The local business elite took to me. They invited me to their clubs and introduced me to their families. I was the "nice young American" who was "trying to help India." They nurtured me, taking me through the rather arcane world of Indian business. Other AFC execs fought the bureaucracies directly; I dined with the powerful players. Over plates of biryani I sold them on the health benefits of Orangilla, the ease of transporting the powdered citrus drink, and the lack of any national competitor. I pointed out the large profits to be earned for the right people who could make this business happen. The Indians bought the story, became silent partners and took over the approvals. Soon Orangilla was in every household.

Overnight, I became a legend. The largest and most important firms had failed miserably. Coca-Cola had been tossed from the country and IBM had its technology stolen and reproduced. But AFC prospered, serving hundreds of millions children who urgently needed good nutrition. Despite my success, AFC managers still thought me too young for promotion. Success in a third-world country didn't count for much. The whispers in the staid corporate offices in America told the story: "One lucky success;" "Others did the ground work;" "He's just an accountant;" "Very young. Too young."

It was clear corporate life was not for me. Other firms offered me jobs but instead I set out on my own. I rented a small office in the prestigious Nariman Point neighborhood, around the corner from the Tata Group and near the best restaurants in town, figuring an American with contacts and a great reputation could not fail. I was not wrong. The same companies that sought my employ took me on as an outside "accountant," not just for the numbers but my ability to make deals.

Life was good. I was young and independent and with a steady income. I was a loner, not anti-social, mind you, but preferring to work rather than suffer the endless evening cocktails that other expats loved. What is it that Sartre said: Hell is other people? Then July 4th came around and Mr. Singh pushed me to attend the annual bash at the American Club. Mr. Singh was my "Man Friday," as they say in old black and white movies, recommended by an AFC lawyer who also was the brother of the Governor of Bombay. Singh was a man with high standards, he told me, impeccably honest in a way that's "so scarce in these times."

Mr. Singh ran the household, overseeing and directing the maids, cooks, drivers and those dabbawalas who brought me succulent lunches each day. He provided tailors and shoemakers, maintained my clothes, suggested the finest restaurants and made sure I didn't end up on the wrong side of town. It was he who suggested I begin my own business. "A young man like you," he said, "cannot fail."

Tall and domineering with a deep and powerful voice, Mr. Singh was insistent: "July 4th? This is your day of independence. We here in India cherish our independence from those bloody Brits. We have a common history with you Yanks. We both fought them and our ancestors died for our freedom. You must do your patriotic duty! That's what one does."

When Mr. Singh commanded, I obeyed. It was a scorching day, the monsoon had yet to descend and the American Club was crammed with locals and foreigners seeking to escape the heat. I am not much for mingling. Small talk bores me and I would rather leave business chat to others. Give me a spreadsheet anytime. But I mingled as best I could, exchanging pleasantries and business cards, avoiding dinner invitations and golf outings.

An hour of mumbo-jumbo and I had enough. Claustrophobia hit. Desperate to escape, I pushed past extended hands and feigned illness, although truth be told I did feel weak. Nobody escapes the Bombay heat. I stumbled towards the door when I spotted four young women sitting in the corner in blue jeans rather than dresses. Certainly not the business set. They seemed happy, laughing among themselves. They had to be American or European.

I was not particularly looking for romance, a feeling that would come when it would come, I thought. I was far too busy making money. An introvert, yes, I admit it, but I did not see myself as attractive. Short and premature balding with what they call poor self-esteem, life at a desk and too many dosas had added a bit too much weight around my waist. An occupational hazard. At college, the alpha guys did booze, drugs and sex and went on demos for all sorts of causes. While they were fucking, I did formulas and algorithms. No, I did not see myself as a "catch."

But as I approached, the women fell silent. "I was just wondering," I said rather nervously, "are you Americans?"

They were. Volunteers teaching English at the local Catholic seminary. English was the *lingua franca* of Indian business, the legacy of colonial rule, but only 10 percent of the country spoke it. Any Indian seeking to climb the social scale needed to be fluent. So their work was invaluable, as I then commented.

"What is your name?" one of them asked.

"Virgil."

They couldn't control their giggles. The party was quite noisy.

"Virgin?" one of them spouted, barely able to control herself.

"No, Virgil," I insisted. "You know, the Roman."

"Yes, yes, Virgil," she said. "Dante's Virgil, no doubt."

"If you say so."

We fell silent and I moved to leave but a voice said in faux-mocking British, "I say Virgil, this party isn't very interesting. Would you like to come have dinner with us? We were thinking of the Taj, weren't we girls?" The others turned in shock.

"The Taj," I responded. "I didn't know they paid volunteers that well. I guess I'll have to treat."

Amazing, how things happen. This was not like me. Looking back, I guess I was lonely, not feeling loneliness, mind you, with all the well-wishers and glad-handers about, but lacking, what? Companionship, I guess.

And, suddenly, she touched my hand, inviting me to help her up. I was amazed. She was taller than me and she looked down with deep, piercing blue eyes, like a mosaic of blue porcelain, with a tenderness and confidence that seemed so gentle. Her look transfixed me, saying "don't worry, you can trust me." Me, a nervous and weak-kneed child, had no choice. My defenses crumbled and, involuntarily, I smiled back. I took her hand and pulled her to her feet.

And that's how I met dear Ellie.

I became a bridge, a conduit, connecting the high and mighty foreign corporations to the Indian elite, trusted to keep confidences and made sure everyone got their piece of the curry pie.

It was a great time for business, during this Gandhi "emergency." The government may have been autocratic and oppressive, forcing sterilization on the nation's males, but the ministries were controlled by a small group from the ruling party, a group that could be counted on to complete deals. Still, this was India where one person's "yes" became another person's "maybe" and then a few ministries' "need for more study." Agreements were made and then forgotten. Contracts were signed and then revoked as competitors stole the business.

But India was a huge market, so the world descended with their products: The French with their cheese and jet fighters; the Germans, sausages and generators; and the Americans, cornflakes and tanks.

But to make it happen, "to seal" the deal in the lexicon of the day, the word was out: Call the Kid. That was me, the innocuous fellow in the modest Nariman Point office around the corner from Tata. In the sporting clubs and drinking holes, the suits advised, "See him. He may not look like much but he gets the job done." They descended knowing I would work through the mazes of licenses, permissions, and ministerial authorizations that blocked so many deals. I brought in the right partners and monies needed to grease the right palms.

Of my rapid success, I have no explanation. Luck? Fate? Perhaps it was my youth that avoided a foreigner's haughty attitude. German engineers needed everything signed hard and fast. American MBAs thought Indian businessmen naïve or ignorant, an attitude they could not hide. The Brits assumed a common understanding with the elites through shared history and language, a belief the locals nurtured for their own profit.

I knew what worked and what did not, what was worth the effort and what was too small. I knew what India wanted: hydroelectric dams, steel mills, locomotives, mining equipment, all good; toys, radios, shoes and school supplies, not really worth the time. I ran the numbers, developed the projects, went back and forth showing all what was possible and what was unreasonable and then divvied up the profits between the ministers, their friends and families, the local partner and the foreign corporation. And of course, a little for myself. Just a little. I was always scrupulously fair. That was accepted. "You can trust the Kid. What he says goes."

There was also chemistry, me a modest young fellow who admired the Indian elite, not kowtowing, as the Brits used to say, but with a genuine respect, me, ready to learn, to understand how things worked and what didn't. I got along with the Mumbai upper crust, confident in their position, with subtle humor and civility that I've never found elsewhere. The men were direct and to the point. Yes, they exaggerated to prove their status, but that was part of the game. Their wives moved so gracefully in their silk saris with their "so pleased to meet you" that seemed so genuine. More agreements were reached over a sweet lassi at a small Nariman Point milk bar than whiskeys at the Taj.

They all wondered who I was and from whence I came. I was a loner and the more I kept to myself, the more curious they became. Rumors had me as an illegitimate son of a Rockefeller, the boyfriend of a Gandhi cousin, or a CIA operative. Truth be told, I was nobody from nowhere who lucked into the job. The fates and the gods were behind me.

"You really have a great deal going," one German businessman once remarked, "playing both sides of the street."

I didn't respond. It didn't matter. I didn't engage in idle chatter. I just ran the numbers and figured out what was possible.

It all went so fast, so easily. Ellie wanted to travel to explore India, tired of her American girlfriends and of being cooped up in a school dorm. She had to *smell* India, she said. She wanted to see the nation, not just the big city. I am not much for touring and tried to satisfy her with dinners at the city's best restaurants and cruises on the Bay. We even took a weekend on Goa's beaches. But this was not enough. She wanted the *real* India.

I was at a loss, I told Mr. Singh. I had a business to run with no one to share the chores. He laughed. "A business? You have your own business to take care of."

"That's what I mean."

"That is not what you mean."

He was tall and imposing. Like all devout Sikhs, he sported a large beard and a bright orange turban under which his unshaven hair was tied, a walking stereotype. He was as regal and elegant as I am short and wonkish. His English was impeccable. He possessed a confidence that I had never known. He looked at me with an imperious and unflinching gaze saying, in effect, "you'd better listen to me." How did he do it, those dark, unmoving and dominating eyes?

"That is not what you mean," he repeated.

"I don't understand."

"Do you like this woman?"

"Of course."

"Of course. Don't you have any sense of yourself, Sir?"

"I'm not understanding."

He scoffed. "Sir, it's time you take care of your life. Go away with her. Take two weeks off."

"But my work...?"

"Your work will wait. In fact, the more those chaps wait, the more they'll come begging. People are like that, grabbing at what they cannot have until they get it."

"I don't know."

"You leave it to me. I will hire a car. Go to Ajanta."

"Ajanta?"

"Yes, the great caves. A national treasure."

"Caves? Why would I want to go . . ."?

"You want to go, trust me."

"How far?"

"Not far. Twelve hours."

"Twelve hours? Can't we fly?"

"Don't fly. You want to get to know her, don't you? If she is going to live with you for the rest of your life, you should get to know her."

"What are you talking about, the rest of my life?"

Mr. Singh laughed, loud and boisterously. "Oh Sir, you haven't the faintest idea, do you?"

This was absolutely true. I had no idea. Did Ellie? I wonder now. I was an innocent. Or perhaps just so focused on business, the numbers and deals that cloud your actual life. So we took a car, Mr. Singh driving, and headed out beyond the city onto narrow, potholed roads crammed with roaming cows, trudging ox-carts, and weaving bicycles. Dust blew in our faces. We rolled up the windows and the heat withered us. We rolled them down and roadside beggars and hawkers assaulted us.

Foreigners go to India to visit the Mughal Forts and the Taj Mahal. They hire guides to lead them through squatter hovels to see the poor cooking on coal stoves and ragged but pretty boys and girls running about them, smiling. Poverty tourism it is called, all very predictable and safe for the visitor, taking in the lives of suffering and starving souls and then, with deep, deep concern, returning to their hotel in a luxury limo for a few G-Ts and a curry. Eye candy of despair. There's something attractive about misery.

This was different. If Ellie sought experience and to "smell" India, we certainly achieved it. In heat and dust, we drove through masses of people struggling to survive, picking at garbage heaps, hauling sacks of dung for their ovens, men beating clothes in dirty streams, women in ragged saris balancing sacks of cloth towering above their heads, skeleton beggars wandering and pleading for alms. The sun shined across a bronze earth sprinkled with small ponds of water and spare banyan trees. Small and barefoot children not more than seven or eight harvested rice from the fields. Aged men and women with crooked canes limped alongside water buffalo.

A bicycle piled high with bales of straw cut across our path, forcing the car to stall. A beggar thrust his hand through the window. Ellie reached into her purse.

"You should not do that," Mr. Singh said.

"It is just a rupee or two."

"No, it is not that. You give to one, others will descend and soon we'll be engulfed. Charity can be dangerous here."

"Just this once?"

"I would prefer if you didn't. It would only lead to trouble."

Ellie frowned and said nothing.

Singh drove on, weaving through and around the hordes of crowds and beasts that mindlessly crossed the road as if we didn't exist. He never sweated. He seemed the perfect stoic. He turned back to Ellie.

"A few years ago, this woman, the wife of some French executive, visited Sabarmati Ashram in Gujarat State, the famous spot where the Mahatma lived for many years and where he founded a school to teach manual labor and literacy. He famously said 'this is where we carry on the search for truth.' It is a national shrine, a beautiful spot on the banks of the Sabarmati River. Tourists like to visit, walk about, see the students, have lunch and donate some money."

"Maybe we might visit it sometime," Ellie said.

"If you wish, we can arrange it. But on the way home, this Frenchwoman passed through a rural village. Gujarat is very poor, its farmers always suffering from something or other, drought, disease, bad crops, and corrupt landlords. Just a poor place. They die young in Gujarat. The government doesn't give a damn, regardless of the Mahatma. Anyway, she asked the driver to stop as school was letting out. The school had just one room, six grades, two teachers, you know. She reached into her bag and took out a few pens, some crayons and pencils, things she brought from France. The tiny kids came running. Indian children are beautiful with dark piercing eyes and smiles that break your heart. She responded as foreigners do, handing the stuff out and smiling back and the kids, they saw her hands in the bag and pushed their hands into it. She pulled back saying gently, "no, no, no," but then bigger, tougher kids joined the fray. I'm not talking about teen-agers but boys of ten or twelve, farm boys, big and strong. They seized her bag, stole her money, and threw what was left onto the road. Others jumped into the car.

The driver screamed but could do nothing except beat them back. Hands groped the woman, tearing at her dress and grabbing for her shoes. She fought to get into the car and if it wasn't for the teachers who came running, I don't know what would have happened to her."

"Very sad."

"Yes, ma'am. Very sad. It's not that I don't believe in helping people. I don't know how it is in the rest of the world, but here in India, when people are desperate, it is dangerous."

Ellie made a slight sob and shook her head. I took her hand.

"If I may say, there are people who come to see starvation and despair, others see the same scene and promise hope and change, even if there is no hope, and then there are those who recognize the situation and pay no attention. That is not wrong because in India, this is reality, it overwhelms us all and we understand that the best life for each of us to live is a righteous life that leads to a better life in the next world."

I think of that trip frequently. Certainly, Bombay had its share of poverty and beggars and homeless, but alongside them was glittering wealth and beauty, the thin veneer of what we call civilization. The city was saffron, its color, odor, and opulence. Women in vibrant silk saris and businessmen in bespoke suits sipped tea at waterfront restaurants. Uniformed children playing cricket in neat schoolyards. Bookstores. Movie theaters. The beach. The veneer of wealth. As a numbers man, I knew the equation. One man's addition is another's subtraction. The poverty around us paid for the prosperity we enjoyed.

On that rough road, Ellie and I knotted and entwined, bumping back and forth, viewing the strugglers of the earth. Our fluids combined, she wiping the sweat from my brow and me, hers, like monkeys in a zoo. For a lifetime, we endured the ailment contracted living in far-off and alien civilizations, a curse suffered alike by missionaries, aid workers and businessmen: a deep skepticism at the righteousness of the self-righteous, of those who fight for *their* inherent rights without concern for the consequences for those without power who slave to survive every day out there in the invisible world.

❧

We drove through the forested Sahyadri Hills and out of nowhere, seemingly, we arrived at the Ajanta caves. Mr. Singh dropped us off. A crowd surrounded us hawking bracelets and bangles, postcards and wood carvings.

To be young, falling in love and exploring an alien land along a narrow, treacherous path and under a scorching sun between ancient stupas and monumental Buddhas, looking about in ignorance and amazement at the carved stones, ancient, intricate paintings of the lives and stories of the Buddha and of his followers. Every image brought joy to her face, a smile, even a laugh. She strolled about in a state of astonishment, not conscious of my stare. "Look at that," was her mantra as she pointed here and there at giant statues and tiny, ancient rock drawings of shipwrecks, ogresses on flying horses, and the great Lord's reincarnations. "Those colors, those shapes, can you believe they carved all this so long ago. How did they do it?" She looked into my face, starry-eyed. Yes, that's the word. Starry-eyed. That was always her, finding the best of everything and taking it in with zest and without restraint, a force so strong that time and again it shook me and shakes me to the core.

Did I share her appreciation? Yes, I thought the caves interesting and intriguing, although then as now I never experience absolute joy. I looked into the beatific smile of the Buddha and saw the peacefulness it promised. Interesting, I thought. An idol for others? Certainly. Not a goal I might attain.

Truth be told, as we wandered the uneven and narrow paths. I could not believe my luck. From cave to cave, painting to sculpture, I kept thinking: Why me? Why did she choose me, a smallish and not very attractive numbers guy, so much her opposite, a yang to her ying?

The heat was intolerable, the sun causing my vision to blur. I tried to keep up with her pace and enthusiasm. We came upon a drawing of a prince seducing a lover with wine. I leaned towards Ellie, again an involuntary gesture which I never understood. I put my hands on her shoulders. She leaned towards me. I kissed her.

"You inspired?" she asked.

I looked at the prince and whispered, "I guess I am."

She was so active and curious while I withered, the Indian heat choking the air from my lungs. Sweat poured from my body. I could barely move. We sought relief in a dark cave, dropped to the dirt floor and huddled. Our legs brushed, our hands sought each other and we fell into a deep, long embrace. I moaned. No idea from where that came. I certainly could not account for it, but there it was. She pulled back and looked at me—or at least I believe she looked at me, for the room was pitch black. She broke into a joyous laugh. And her laugh sparked my own. Our bliss echoed through the rocks. A guard entered, shined his flashlight on us and withdrew.

"Love, that loosener of limbs," she said softly, "that bittersweet and inescapable, crawling thing, seizes me."

"What?"

"Just a poem."

I didn't understand and she let it pass.

♋

A few weeks later, Ellie's time as a volunteer was coming to an end. She was heading home.

"So?" Mr. Singh said.

"What do you mean, 'So'?"

"You're letting her go?"

"I don't see what I can do to stop her."

"Sir, let me suggest that you consider this problem a little."

"There's nothing I can do short of marrying her."

"So?" He looked at me imperiously, his dark eyes piercing my weak subservience.

Was it a good idea? I knew so little about her. She seemed a typical Midwestern American, positive, self-assured and idealistic. Idealism has its attraction, despite my disdain for the non-factual. But I couldn't put two and two together. I couldn't figure the pluses and minuses, the risks and rewards. I was as dizzy as in those caves. Yet somehow I knew from the first moment we met that she was for me.

Was she on the level? Was this a youthful fling? If she rejected my proposal, that would be a big minus. A major minus. Why would she marry me? I am such a dullard. I don't play sports, I can't even catch a cold. Cards and board games bore me. I am not a social animal, as I've said. And she? So pretty and enticing. How her skirt swayed. That dazzling smile. She could marry anyone.

I didn't think I could stand rejection. Then again, I didn't know whether I could stand anyone so close to my soul. I measured my situation. I was alone in India with no one to talk to or be with, surrounded by businessmen with their clubs and bad jokes and conniving. Of course there was Mr. Singh but he was more like a father than a companion.

"So?" Mr. Singh asked in his strong and demanding manner.

She did thrill me. There was no accounting for that. In Ellie, I might have a wife and a partner — that is what it added up to. If it worked, that is. If she accepted. Retaining her was to be my life's ambition.

I took Ellie for lunch at Corniche, a quiet and hidden spot on the bay frequented by politicians and Bollywood types. It was not particularly convenient to my office, a bit away from the center. What with Bombay's horrible traffic, it was going to take some time to get there, but Mr. Singh insisted and I obeyed.

We chatted for a while about the weather and a book she was reading. We ordered prawn cocktails, a lamb saag, vegetable sabzi, and some chapatis. I don't particularly like prawn cocktails smothered in mayonnaise the way they are served in Asia, but it seemed fitting for an outdoor café on the bay and the occasion. As an afterthought, I ordered two glasses of wine.

She looked at me quizzically. "It's a bit early, isn't it?"

I smiled meekly.

We fell silent and looked upon the water. I inhaled deeply and said, "I was wondering…" My throat seized and I gagged.

She brought me a glass of water. "You alright?" She looked down at me, smiling as she always does. I nodded. "You were saying?"

I held up my hand, trying to catch my breath and gasped, "I was wondering if you would marry me?"

She shrieked. Very un-Indian. Diners turned and stared at the noise. I struggled to regain my composure. She leaned over and hugged me. "Is something the matter, ma'am," a waiter interrupted.

She shook her head back and forth and said, "No, no, everything is fine. I was just proposed marriage."

The waiter nodded solemnly. "Very good, ma'am. I wish you a good life."

She kneeled and kissed my lips. "Thank you," she whispered.

It was a small wedding, colleagues and students from her school, a couple of my clients and Mr. Singh. Ellie was radiant in her embroidered Kashmiri shawl. I wore a simple business suit. Of course, Mr. Singh was elegant in his formal Sikh robes. He diminished me by his presence.

The ceremony was held at the Church of St. Thomas, named for the apostle "doubting Thomas" who evangelized India. Neither one of us was Catholic, but the Indian priest was good enough to provide us with a secular ceremony and gentle words of encouragement. We pledged to love, honor, and be faithful.

He quoted an ancient hymn, about St. Thomas: "It was his mission to espouse India to the One-Begotten. The merchant is blessed for having so great a treasure."

1984.

Ellie and I had settled in. The year began well. India won the Cricket World Cup and jubilation swept the country. Muslims and Hindus celebrated together. One country, finally. It was as if its torturous history, the wars, ethnic violence and corruption no longer mattered. The mirage of sport.

I was at the height of my profession. A Danish firm, Magic, sought to introduce its famous noodles. In its distinctive aluminum foil packaging, the noodles appealed to mothers wanting to provide their families with a quick and healthy dinner. My Indian partners were interested as well; Orangilla was now ubiquitous and the small packages would fit perfectly in their trucks.

Successful in Europe, the Danes stumbled as they tried to gain approval. The government had a monopoly on pasta production and sold it at subsidized prices. Interest groups were blocking our path.

We followed the outlines of the earlier campaign, working our way through the health and trade ministries, developing partnerships with local officials and making deals with wheat farmers to pay high prices for the raw material. Magic launched a marketing campaign in connection with the Cricket World Cup using the tagline, "India Needs Magic!" When India vanquished the hated rival, Pakistan, the product was launched. We used a furtive strategy as well: we leaked reports to the press that dangerous pesticides were mixed in the government noodles while advertising Magic as produced under strict and clean conditions in modern factories. That did the trick.

It was a tremendous success and once again my reputation was enhanced. I decided to celebrate. Ellie and Mr. Singh organized a reception in the main ballroom at the Taj hotel with classical Indian music and entertainment from Bollywood actors. The nation's elite attended, the Gandhi family, government ministers, ambassadors and the most important Indian industrialists, all dressed elegantly, the men in their sherwanis and kurtas, the women in their saris and ghagra cholis. In the background, Rajasthani musicians played ragas on their stringed sarangis, flutes, and Nagari drums.

It was a glorious evening, the pinnacle of my success. From now on, I would be recognized in all the right circles. I had entered the nation's ruling circle.

⚜

Indians believe in fate. Everything in life is governed by karma from our actions and previous lives, astrology and the choices of the Gods. Personally, I always thought it was mumbo-jumbo. Still, within twelve months of that reception, all turned to dust. Maybe there is such a thing as karma. Who knows? But what happened that year still gives me nightmares.

Ellie and I were content with our lives. She continued her volunteer work but more and more we were in demand for social occasions. Custom dictated that she stayed with the women and me with the men. I sat on the side of the conversations, rarely disagreeing, as is the custom. Indians always agree, shaking their heads, "Yes, yes," they reply, "the sky is black but you must understand there are always interpretations." "Yes, Yes," there's much to learn from agreeing.

Then, one day, conversation turned to a revolt in Amristar, Punjab, home of the Golden Temple, the most important Sikh shrine. "Horrid business," my Indian friends said, "we must get rid of these fellows."

I asked Mr. Singh, who was of course a Sikh. "A complicated affair. Lots of bad people causing instability."

"I don't think I understand what Sikhs believe."

He smiled just a little. "We believe in a moral life, not taking too much from the world and giving as much as we can to those in need."

"But this violence?"

"We are not against violence to protect our own. Of course, there are bad people everywhere. I'm afraid we live in a world of vague morality where good and evil merge in confusing manners. We Sikhs seek knowledge and we reflect it. This creates righteous actions that culminate in benevolence. We seek virtue by aligning our mind, words, and actions with the teachings of our Sikh prophets."

"I don't understand."

He smiled briefly the way he did. "Don't worry about it," he advised and that was the last I mentioned it.

The violence escalated in the Punjab; police and political officials were assassinated daily. I assumed another sectarian battle and went about my business. But I was naïve and caught unaware, not that it was my problem, but still, one must understand the nation one lives in. The Sikh rebels seized the temple with heavy weaponry and called for an independent country. Madame Gandhi declared martial law. Tensions increased and finally, the army attacked the temple. The battle was fierce, the army suffered large losses but finally, after ten days, the rebels succumbed. The sacred temple complex was destroyed.

The assault was a disaster. Sikh army units revolted around the country. Word was leaked that the military high command had refused to attack and was replaced. "Mrs. Gandhi certainly made a mess of that one," my Indian friends said.

The nation mourned the loss of loyal soldiers and the destruction of a holy site. Bombay went about its business but we all knew that the affair had not seen its end. Then, in early July, Mr. Singh came to me limping with a young man at his side.

"I must take your leave," he said. "I made a bloody mess of my toe and it's badly infected."

"Of course, take all the time you need."

"Yes, I have a train booked tomorrow for Bangalore."

"Bangalore? Why don't you have your operation here?"

"Better hospitals there. I don't trust these buggers. Out to make quick money."

"Whatever you wish. Let me know when you'll return."

"I leave my son Balraj in my place. If that's OK?"

I did not know he had a son. I did not know he had any family. I wished him Godspeed and off he went.

A week later, Balraj came to me. "I have bad news. The doctors mucked up the operation. My father died yesterday."

"Died? Of a toe wound?"

"Yes, an infection, they say."

Ellie and I were distraught. We knew medical care was not very good for most Indians. Should we have insisted that he go to our private hospital? A second opinion? Might we attend his funeral? Better not, Balraj said. The tension in Punjab was too great, and we would be in too much danger.

Two weeks later, Indira Gandhi was assassinated by her Sikh bodyguards. All Sikhs were suspect. Balraj asked to leave and never returned.

The loss of Mr. Singh devastated us and the mood in the country, frankly, was not good. Much of my business was aligned with Congress Party officials and I feared retaliation. It was time to return to America. We shipped home the mementos of a brilliant life, Buddhas and Ganeshas, rugs and saris. I set plans to close the office. We would celebrate Christmas with our friends and depart. It was settled.

Then in December, a gas factory exploded in the city of Bhopal, releasing toxic gases into the surroundings. I didn't think much about it. In a land where thousands die daily from disease and malnutrition and lives are reincarnated over and over, you develop a certain Hindu stoicism about bad news. But I badly misjudged the situation. I was summoned to Union Carbide India Limited, a subsidiary of the multinational. I had worked for them and their managers trusted my judgment as well as my connections to Indian officials. I always thought Carbide to be a good and honest firm, producing agricultural chemicals that helped India increase production and feed its people.

Carbide's offices were in mayhem. Everyone was distraught and panicking. It was clear that in the densely packed city of Bhopal, thousands upon thousands of people were dying horrible deaths from choking, lung, kidney and heart damage. Being closer to the ground where the gas lingered, children were the most affected. Hundreds of thousands would suffer horrible symptoms for years.

There was little question that the authorities would soon descend upon Carbide's offices. Arrests were imminent and records would be seized. The Indian way.

The company needed an outsider to account for the damage on an ongoing basis, a calm hand to determine the financial situation, someone who would not be swept up by the inevitable rumors, accusations and indictments. How many people were affected? How would the accident effect the company's bottom line? What would be the long-term financial impact? Numbers. Facts.

Bhopal is a horror story, a Hiroshima and Chernobyl rolled into one. As the afflicted were gasping for breath in unspeakable dying agony, as thousands of children were crippled, and as tens of thousands of mothers suffered miscarriages, financial reports still needed to be made. What is the cost of a human life? A child? An unborn child? Pain? Agony? You may think this awfully cold-hearted in the face of massive suffering, but this is the law. This was my chore. This is what I was paid for.

If you work with average life spans and individual earnings, add some percentage for pain and suffering, you can come up with a figure that seems reasonable. I determined an average figure of $20,000 per person. Was this generous? Was this miserly? How do you recompense the dead? The survivors? Was this blood money?

In retrospect, I should have turned down the job. Recriminations and lawsuits flew back and forth and still persist today. In tragedies such as this, most problems derive from decisions made years earlier by politicians and businessmen long since gone. Before the catastrophe, Carbide had played a vital role in increasing agricultural output, feeding a growing population, venturing in a land where others avoided. The Indian government required production of the dangerous gas domestically rather than through cheaper imports, and it is clear that basic safety precautions were ignored. The factory was managed and run entirely by Indians, because government regulations restricted the employment of foreigners. There was little question that human error was, in part, responsible.

Furthermore, the Bhopal plant had been losing money and the Indian subsidiary reduced maintenance jobs. A hundred thousand squatters lived in a shanty town in the empty fields outside the plant. It was they who suffered the most.

That said, the majority ownership of the subsidiary was held by the American company, and the plant's design and procedures came from the United States. Activists and politicians had warned of the dangers and risks of the gas production, to no avail.

How does one ascribe responsibility? We spend our lives looking for guilt, books and studies are written, law suits play on for decades. Money is paid out, some to victims and some to others who use the opportunity to make a fortune, governments, lawyers and, yes, accountants. Politicians leap to accuse, currying favor with their constituents.

Where does guilt lie? In corporate profits? Poor government laws? Structural deficiencies? Cost-cutting? Poor judgment? Inadequate managers? Incompetent workers? Should any corporation manufacture a vital product needed to feed an overpopulated nation with inherent risks? Industrial accidents happen all the time, Chinese and American coal mines, Russia's Chernobyl, Japan's Fukushima, and BP's Gulf of Mexico disaster? Should banks take risks that finance global growth, prosperity and increased well-being but which also lead to financial crises that send people into bankruptcy and despair?

Don't ask me. As they say, this is way beyond my pay scale. Then again, in my head I hear the racketeer Harry Lime, looking down from a Ferris wheel in *The Third Man*: "Nobody thinks in terms of human beings. Governments don't. Why should we?"

Arrests were made and records confiscated. Communication with the Bombay office was restricted and calls to the American home office were certainly tapped. Ellie understood my late hours and tired efforts although it was clear we had both moved home, in our heads. Neither one of us were happy.

Then, late one night, there was a knock on the door. It was an American, from the embassy.

"You must leave the country, immediately," the stranger told me straight out.

"What?"

"Tonight. I've arranged a car and booked tickets to New York. The plane departs at 3 AM. You cannot tell anyone. Especially about me, the embassy and this chat."

"What are you talking about?"

"The police found your name in Carbide's accounts together with the nature of your work. They claim you're an employee and have to be held until judgment is made. That will take years as you well know. The whole business is before a magistrate as we speak."

My karma had turned for the worst. I thanked him. He put his hand on my shoulder and looked out into the crowded avenue. "Remember your friends," he said, "because your friends remember you."

I awoke Ellie. She was terribly upset, fleeing like thieves and not saying goodbye to our friends. Some people she just had to contact. No, I told her strongly. We were probably being watched. Any suspicion and I would be picked up. She could call from America. I was certainly not going to take any chances. Years in a Bombay prison awaiting resolution of Bhopal was certainly not attractive, especially for an American who was known to maintain considerable offshore accounts.

She cried, and I put my hand on her shoulder. She pulled away angrily ran into our bedroom and threw herself down. I poured a drink and considered the situation. What to take? What to leave? How to tell the staff? Ellie returned, looking drawn. She nodded to me her understanding and went to gather her things.

In the dead of night, we grabbed our bags and left everything else for the staff. I wrote a brief note of thanks. An embassy car hauled us through the darkened streets, past piles of burning garbage and beggars removing whatever they might. The car took us directly to the plane and we trudged aboard. Cool vapid airplane air replaced the dank Bombay smog. We were ushered into our first class seats and offered champagne. The flight attendant smiled, reassuringly.

While in flight, India issued a warrant for my arrest.

RASPAIL

(1972)

The PLO attacks the Olympics—Burglars break into Democratic Headquarters at the Watergate—British Miners' Strike—Northern Ireland Civil War—Idi Amin seizes British firms in Uganda—Governor George Wallace is shot—Richard Nixon Visits China—Richard Nixon re-elected –The Godfather—ABBA—Monty Python—Pong -"The Day the Music Died"

EARLY SPRING. April in Paris. Just like the song. The sun glistened through chestnut trees lining the Luxembourg Gardens allées, a faint warm wind scattered away leaves and the memory of a horrid damp winter. We sat silently looking at the pond and lads in shorts directing sailboats from the edge. It was time for me to leave. I needed to leave. I kissed Hélène on the lips, American style, as she grabbed to hold me back, a tear clouding her eye. I rose and slipped away.

I limped down the gravel walk admiring schoolgirls as they scampered about in their brief skirts, laughing innocently and thinking just like Maurice Chevalier in *Gigi*: Thank heaven for little girls. Something you can't say nowadays but back then was totally permissible. What was it from Montaigne? "All the world bends and yields to sexual desire." Something like that.

I strolled towards Boulevard Raspail, where Erasmus and Aquinas once rambled, a *flâneur,* "setting up house in the heart of the multitude," as Baudelaire wrote. "The spectator who is a prince, rejoicing in his incognito." Unlike any other city, Paris compels walking, observing and staring, with its quartiers, the Seine, the bistros and, above all the parisiennes.

I passed the staid Alliance Française, the school where Americans, Asians, and Africans stuttered their imperfect *accent aigu* and checked out the rusting, decrepit VW van I had abandoned the year before after a bunch of accidents along the road to and from Morocco. Why it hadn't been hauled away was beyond me. My shame, this van, its front mashed like the face on an aged boxer, a stack of wet and illegible tickets stuck on its cracked windscreen, its insides rummaged and burgled into an unsightly garbage heap. The plywood bed that had enjoyed so much pleasure was gone. The rear engine had been scavenged as well, its compartment open and naked. The smooth, aged tires remained, without value. My van: litter in a pristine city kept clean and correct like a bourgeois apartment. This van: a tale for another time.

Each week, I trekked to Raspail to meet my mentor and Professor, Ruggiero Romano, an Italian historian, former Communist and guerrilla partisan. Svelte, literate, and debonair, Romano was a model for the middle-aged continental bon vivant. Think Yves Montand. His rooms were lined with mahogany bookcases seized as war booty from Italian and French collaborators and now stuffed with journals and well-worn works in five languages.

Over whiskey, we reviewed my research and studies before falling into inebriated political arguments. These were the years of the Vietnam conflict, begun, as I frequently pointed out, by our French hosts but massively expanded, as he was fond to respond, by American imperialists. It was all good fun. He was a fine historian and intellectual, and I fear I did not take as much advantage of his mind as I did his liquid.

Romano's balcony overlooked the boulevard, perfect for drink, deep thoughts and spying on women passing below. Across the street, in a small park, was the American Center, an august nineteenth century structure that American Episcopals had turned into a home away from home. They sought to shield young Americans from the evil influences of communism, free love, and the other decadent trends of the twenties and thirties while offering teas and dances, billiards and all the social graces of good society. In the 1960s, the radicals moved in. Man Ray, Marcel Duchamp, Warhol, Christo, and Lichtenstein showed their works as Picasso looked on. Yankee hippie vagabonds followed, in flight from the military draft and taking advantage of cheap Parisian living. Black American exiles hovered about the building in the shadows of jazz legends, Johnny Griffin, Don Byas, and Dexter Gordon, and practiced what they called free jazz while picking up pretty young radical women who were "into" the cacophony. "You can't be free," Miles Davis commented at the time, "unless you first master the music." Or it might have been Roy Eldridge. Or Dizz. Bad music, maybe, but you certainly could get laid.

Having fled Hélène, I arrived at Chez Romano early. She was becoming a problem. Married and cheating to punish her wayward husband, we were playing a Deneuve movie. She pledged her love somewhat unconvincingly, but it didn't matter, it was unrequited by me and boring. The few times we made love, she refused to use the marital bed, forcing us to scrunch on an uncomfortable and unerotic sofa, screwing for vengeance and not for climax not my thing. Not that I was into romance. No, I was a bit too scarred by Angelina at the moment to fall into Venus' trap. Lust and experience were my goals. Henry Miller my muse. She, Hélène, was but an interlude, a little bit on the side for a poor man in Paris.

As I approached Romano's apartment, I spotted him on the balcony, a young woman on each arm, his hand resting suggestively on a thigh. They smiled and laughed and flirted oh so happily, he a middle-aged man, the women, young and beautiful. They all seemed so happy. Another French movie. Truffaut? Not wanting to disturb the scene, I hastened past and wandered to the Montparnasse cemetery. I wandered about the graves of Zola and de Maupassant, Baudelaire and Soutine and Dreyfus. Down the street, the monstrous Tour Montparnasse was rising from what was once the *terroir* of poets, now ploughed and cemented.

The day grew cool. I entered the café on the corner of Edgar Quinet and ordered an espresso. I sipped staring into space without thought when I spotted pretty young women sitting in a circle around an elderly man. I stared, but there was no way to avoid it. He waved me over. It was Sartre himself, the old ugly satyr. Unmistakable. He greeted me and I him. He asked if I were an American spy. I said absolutely and I needed to investigate what was transpiring with these beautiful girls. They smiled slightly, if I remember correctly, or maybe not at all. They were intense and serious, staring at each other, silently dismissing the unwanted Yank as women do, turning back to the master. *Tant pis,* I thought, and retreated.

I returned to Romano who was by now alone but well into his drink. Serious talk was out of the question. We spoke in Spanish, much better for me than French. I was writing on Francisco Morazan, the Simon Bolivar of Central America. It was a silly subject, he thought; old backwater politics not worth bothering about. But I had lived and loved in the mountains of Central America, ridden horseback over muddy, steep cordilleras, drinking and carousing, the echoes of marimba deep inside my soul. And Morazan was a national hero, his a fated and romantic tale not unlike my own. Well, not quite like my own.

"Waste of time," Romano said.

I didn't care. Morazan was unknown to the world and I was going to rescue him from obscurity. His story was just like my own.

Studying in Paris made romantic fights easy. The government allowed foreigners like me to obtain an education at no cost with subsided food at university restaurants—steak frites, vin rouge, and fromage for just a few francs. If my education was wanting, then experience would be the great teacher.

The whiskey gone, I bade farewell to my mentor and wandered home unsteadily to my garret room, seven flights up a winding nineteenth century staircase in a staid apartment house on the Rue de Staël, around the corner from the Pasteur Institute. If by now you detect my predilection for name-dropping, then you're getting the message. Madame de Staël! Napoleon's enemy and the first great liberal woman in France! And I, on her street! She the fighter of lost causes. She, the libertine. Just like me! Well, not quite like me.

My room was not really a garret but a chambre de bonne, a cold maid's room with just enough space for a bed, wardrobe and table, casement windows that opened onto the courtyard, a "Turkish" toilet down the hall for squatting with a sink for us peasants to use commonly. No heat and tired mildewed wallpaper, a victim of damp winters. Think Van Gogh's painting, Bedroom in Arles, the place where he had his breakdown and ear removal. With difficulty, I had hauled a large propane tank from my van up the stairs and installed it illegally under the table, attaching it to two burners also from my erstwhile vehicle. The mattress on the bed was terribly worn with a hole in the middle down to metal springs, a challenge to any Don Juan—one I readily accepted. I weighed 200 pounds and wore a scruffy 60s beard and long hair. On the mattress, one must be pliable, says Epicurus. The art of seduction was certainly tested here.

I was a poor man in Paris, as the song goes, suffering through damp Paris winters, coughing loudly as befitting La Bohème while struggling with frozen fingers to write my great doctoral work on a light-weight Olivetti travel typewriter (you don't know what a typewriter is? Look it up.). Yes, it was touch-and-go for a while whether I might fulfill my art and indeed, survive at all. Long and lonely nights, me staring across the courtyard into comfortable and plush Parisian dwellings, listening to spoiled children practicing Chopin or poodles yapping in the courtyard, odors of succulent French foods drifting up into my emaciated agonized existence.

It was horrible. Friends beseeched me to abandon my horrible existence and return home. Family worried about my health. Please come home, they pleaded, become a lawyer, an insurance salesman or a banker. But no, I would not give up. De Staël didn't give up. Morazan, neither. Simon Bolivar observed that he who serves a revolution plows the sea. I must persevere through thick and thin, plow the sea, whatever the cost, I coughed, in a fit of tuberculosis. Perseverance is the test of all men and women and so, so ......

Yes, it is a memorable story of survival. Alas, it is not true. Not a whit of it. I offer it as a sop to the literary world that defines life through suffering. But no, I did not suffer, unless heartbreak is included but that is another matter. Truth is, life was grand. My garret—for that is what I choose to call it—was filled with joy and music and sex and food. Music came first, the beat that kept me going, typing away, making love, stayin' alive. Ever since Bob Lee introduced me to R & B on a pristine Catskill lake, I needed my fix of Big Joe Turner, Elmore James, Johnny Otis, Chuck Berry, and all my soul brothers. Yeah, Rock and Roll fed into it, Clapton and the Stones stole the beat and all's fair in love and music. But those white boys didn't have soul like me and Bob Lee and Screaming Joe.

And the food! Terrines, pâtés, beet and potato salads, saucissons and jambons from the charcuteries. Fromageries with their fresh (and unlike in the US) unpasterized camemberts, bries, roqueforts, comtes, emmentals and yaourts. Vins de Nicolas offered inexpensive Chablis, Bordeaux, Burgundies, cidres and vins ordinaires. And the boulangeries, with their high-pitched clerks proclaiming "Bonjour Monsieur," their buttery croissants and crispy baguettes, and, on special occasions, tartes de pommes.

Not that I was incapable of preparing a fine meal for a pretty guest. Perhaps some nice mussels in wine sauce? Or a mushroom omelet? Ragout pasta? All were expertly cooked on my illegal propane stove, followed with some wild strawberries or sweet peaches set in crème fraiche, we sitting side by side on my sloping mattress, careful not to fall deep onto the springs and into sin before enjoying a nice cognac with fine chocolates.

The landlady was a sweet old woman. I did not trouble her about the rotten bed given the $20 monthly rent, and I certainly didn't wish anyone to see my little kitchen. And so I endured the mattress, suffering in silence along with periodic visitors who learned to adapt, adjust, push and pull into, around and on top of the life of a sordid artiste.

This evening, after Romano, I arrived a bit sodden, rang the button and saw the concierge's curtain move. He buzzed me in, opened his door and told me a friend was waiting upstairs. I trudged up the winding stairs to the top floor where, crouched at my door, was gorgeous Betty Sue holding a box of chocolates. She, always proper with her little house gifts, always so Right Bank, looked up at me woefully and asked if she might spend the night.

Before you jump to too many conclusions, women were not all over me in these quiet days on the Rue de Staël. They would come from time to time to be sure, but I was first and foremost an artiste, a writer, the savior of the forgotten Morazan! I needed to be alone and suffer the life of a solitary writer with so many bottles of vin ordinaire consumed to ease my loneliness. Vin ordinaire rather than Burgundy was my version of Van Gogh's ear deletion.

Not that I minded Betty Sue's offer, though. She was certainly not like Hélène, a chapter I wished closed. Betty Sue was an American beauty, southern, sweet accent, tall, a trim figure what they used to call lithesome, long black hair and slight hips. She was the picture of youth, always a slight smile with a dimple. Gorgeous and cultured, a product of one of those seven sister schools that produced America's ladies even during these halcyon revolutionary days. Think young Hillary Clinton.

Betty Sue was all culture. French culture. Her charming right-bank apartment off the Champs Elysees was filled with the latest *Le Nouvel Observateur, Le Canard Enchaine* and the in-journals of the Parisian intelligentsia. Think a literate Audrey Hepburn. I would have loved to have fallen in love with her but my psychic shield was raised high and hard thanks to Angelina, who broke my heart, and although Betty Sue and I played the Parisian scene happily and were, as they say, physically in tune, she clearly was of similar mind, a free woman in Paris. In fact, she was the freest woman I've ever met, making love with abandon and giving love with zest. She told of her life without embarrassment or bragging, of her teenage years, how she performed fellatio on every member of a biker gang so she might be admitted to their fold. That was Betty Sue: a sexy free spirit, literate and intelligent.

Her studies were on Louis Aragon, the French surrealist poet and a leader of France's literary establishment. "There are strange flowers of reason," she whispered his words in my ear, "to match each error of the senses." Her problem was not her intellect but her looks and style. This night she was in complete distress. Her professor at Nanterre was one of those veterans of '68, intense Marxist rebels who now held sway at their own Sorbonne. He told her quite directly that if she wanted to continue she would have to sleep with him. Another bad French movie. Jean Moreau, perhaps?

What could I say? After all, this was France where mistresses were normal and sexual peccadillos expected. I've frequently wondered if the suitor was Aragon himself. It would not have been beyond the old codger, then, as I am now, in his early seventies.

We meandered and murmured through the night, polishing off my best ordinaire and then another, napping a little, kissing, and finally collapsing in a loving yet forced embrace, because of the sagging mattress.

Betty Sue loved making love, but on her own terms and certainly not under the threat of academic exile. I suggested I'd visit the professor dressed as a Green Beret, military fatigues being all the rage among the rebels of the day, and threaten him with torture and dismemberment. Perhaps graffiti on his door. An American flag and a Clint Eastwood portrait. There was no room for graffiti, she said, the place was filled with it. And an American enemy would make his day, not hers.

There was nothing to be done, she bemoaned. These were not the days of political correctness or sexual harassment claims or victimhood, not that today it would bother the direct descendant of the Age of Enlightenment, a Parisian prof.

We left early the next morning and, like old lovers, walked arm in arm down Pasteur onto Garibaldi. Africans swept the streets, pushing refuse into rushing waters with long, straw brooms. At the marketplace trucks unloaded foodstuffs onto street stalls. A wide-eyed bronzini fish stared up at us from a bed of ice.

"Did you see it wink?" I said.

"It did not wink," she replied.

"It did, I saw it." She shook her head, smiled wanly and hugged me. We stopped on Grenelle for a tartine and espresso.

"You know they say a winking fish is the sign you've found you're life's love." She touched my cheek, gently and planted a little kiss.

"That fish is dead, mon cheri. It did not wink." She kissed me again and walked away.

Soon after, Betty Sue left France. I never saw or heard from her again. But I did recently come upon her love letters. This, scribbled on the back of a library book request form: "Schnook" (she called me schnook. Nobody ever called me schnook), "I have an almost uncontrollable desire to provoke a scandalous scandal in the BN (Bibliotheque nationale). Would you care to participate in the unleashing and appeasement of my most inner frustrations?" They don't make request forms like that anymore, I'm telling you.

To be an American in Paris in the early 1970s was to enjoy a glorious if movable feast (not including my poor, pathetic and paralyzed van). The Franc was dirt cheap and the French, still in shock from the Nazi occupation, the wars in Vietnam and Algeria, and the 1968 revolts. '68 was already a sentimental and mythic memory like fading graffiti on the walls of ancient monasteries, its veterans scattered to the ignored and ignoble Nanterre Sorbonne campus or, worse, into the ministries.

The soixantes-huitards had torn up cobblestones before fleeing *les flics* leaving the victors the spoils. They, a coalition of gauchistes, Gaullists, the aristocracy, *pied-noir* Franco-Algerians, bankers, real estate developers and once Nazi collaborators, razed the past. They drove truckers and merchants from the covered Les Halles market, the whores from nearby Rue St. Denis, and eventually bohemia from the Latin Quarter, Le Marais and Montmartre and Montparnasse. They raised monstrous monument, the Tour Montparnasse, the modern museum Centre Pompideau and, their great triumph, *La Defense*, a mega-corporate city in view of the Arc de Triomphe. A postmodern pyramid defaced the Louvre courtyard and the stately American Center, the building facing Chez Romano, was torn down, replaced by a glassed museum sponsored by the jeweler, Cartier. To be sure, La Closerie des Lilas still served its oysters and steak frites as it had to Hemingway and Fitzgerald, but now to tourists and the wealthy.

The times were changing. On the right were perfumeries, haut couture and corrupt state corporations. On the left were aging radicals. The *avant-garde* was dead or nearly so. The glory days of the twenties, of the Impressionists, with Cocteau, Zara, and Joyce, Fitzgerald and Hemingway, and *Le Hot Club*, they were the stuff of legends and academic studies. Aragon, Picasso and Nadia Boulanger, giants of the century, would die within a few years as would Sartre himself. *The Paris Review* moved to New York. The ideals of liberté, égalité, fraternité lingered as France remained a haven for Latin American exiles fleeing from harsh, military dictatorships, for Eastern European dissidents, Asians from repressive Communist regimes and war torn nations and for Americans, like me, exhausted and fleeing from interminable and unsuccessful civil rights and anti-war battles. The great Latin American literary tradition was in many ways born here: Vargas Llosa, García Márquez, Cortázar, Octavio Paz, Neruda, and Carpentier wandered Parisian streets. From a Parisian suburb, the Iranian Ayatollah Khomeini plotted a revolution.

Still, France's colonial adventures hung around its neck, and while Arab and African "citizens" were legally integrated into its society, the schism in language, culture and living conditions gave and gives lie to the civic ideal, plaguing France to this day. Business supplanted bohemia while an elitist society vainly sought to maintain its *grandeur* against the pressures of America, Europeanization and globalization. Paris lost its once proud global leadership in art, theater, poetry and, worst of all, food. The city became a museum as tourist buses crowded narrow streets in the place of poets and whores. Modern France became "prisoners of the heritage of their past," as Jonathan Fenby has said, searching for its old *grandeur*, maintaining a *Grand Illusion*.

To be sure, creativity was and is not dead. French film prospered. Jacques Derrida ignored Montaigne's adage that presumption is human's original infirmity, and advanced "deconstructionism" complementing while criticizing the postmodernist movement of Michel Foucault and others and influencing whole generations of cultural intellectuals in literature, art, architecture and music.

Today, we suffer the results. Academic theories fly high above the clouds, obscure and irrelevant while the general population engages in illiterate and illogical debates. Technological nihilism rules along with political and social anarchy, the collapse of rational thought and the rise of the mob in our daily lives.

I think of those days frequently. Paris may have been fading, like an aging Dame, with its cosmetic lights and faux-grandeur, but it offered me the opportunity to study, learn and prosper.

I completed my doctoral thesis and left Paris. The work on Francisco Morazan became a Central American history that is still published in Spanish. From time to time I return to savor the joys of the city, the markets and food shops, the boulangeries and cafes. And I walk to the Rue de Staël, still there, with the same buildings and shops. The stuff of memory.

NEW YORK

(1981)

I WAS APPROACHING FORTY, and my halcyon days in Europe and Latin America long gone. I needed work, but had no idea what sort of job to look for.

Education was not in the cards. I had published quite a lot, but academia was in recession and Latin American history was not the field most in demand in the early 1980s, to say the least. Truth be told, I was not eager to reenter the classroom in any case. A few years earlier, when I taught in upstate New York, a young co-ed asked me at the end of a lecture, "who is the President of Latin America?" Then a real estate agent told me that, with my meager bank account and small salary, I "might afford a trailer in a trailer park." This was not much encouragement.

Thankfully, a boutique firm had just formed to advise corporations on international issues and required a Latin American expert. I fit the bill, and they hired me.

The early days of the Reagan administration was a time for "political risk analysis," the trend to develop scenarios of what may or may not take place in a country in the future. Business schools taught it and, for their planning, corporations demanded five-and ten-year scenarios. What were the best and worst cases? Will there be political stability in Mexico? Will Australia experience growth? Will Spain integrate with Europe? An entire profession developed around this sort of crystal ball prediction. Forecasts might not work out, but managers could always pass the blame to the consultants who provided them.

The firm I worked for published quarterly reports on twenty countries, information derived from clippings of newspapers and magazines, like the *Financial Times*, the *Wall Street Journal* and the *Economist*. The writings were based upon the consensus of views on every issue. Controversy was avoided. All very unacademic.

Our clients were major international American corporations, agrochemical and pharmaceutical, automobile and technology, financial houses and government. As part of my job, I traveled and consulted to the business managers—all men—trying to understand the issues that informed their decision-making. It was a pseudo-MBA training. After half of dozen years, I came to realize that managers had little time to consider implications beyond their basic missions, to earn profits and limit risk.

I also came to understand that basic and current global information is prized most highly in the business world. Generalizations fail, of course, but the businessmen I met were engineers or generalists with only a minimal understanding of the outside world. They spoke no foreign languages and, indeed, viewed the rest of the world outside America as alien. They were hired for their intelligence, work experience, and middle-of-the-road backgrounds. They were married, had suburban houses, and went to church. Many were ex-military. They belonged to golf clubs and watched their kids play school sports. They watched television. They lived, by and large, in a Caucasian world (although IBM from early on had many more minorities in its ranks than all of the college departments I knew, but IBM had the pick of the best). They were literate but most did not have the time to read, what with family, sports and all the other trappings of American life.

And most important, they were not of the world I was used to, a ragtag mélange of the mean New York streets, of Paris bistros and Central America peasantry, of friends who read novels and went to movies with subtitles. Of vacations touring Grecian isles and French cathedrals.

Academics like to overwrite. Simple paragraphs and short treatises are treated as incomplete. Every statement requires long explanations. Facts, proofs, citations, "yes, but," "on the one hand," etc.—it is the nature of the beast. By contrast, the corporate world demanded definitive statements with no hedging and easy conclusions to be factored into spreadsheets. I had to adjust.

My first assignment was a consult with IBM to provide reports on Argentina, Brazil and Mexico. I wrote one for each. They were promptly rejected. Instead, I was given a format to follow:

- The first page should have no more than six sentences, each on a different line.
- The next pages should have the conclusions from page one on separate pages with another six sentences beneath each.
- Data should be simple: forecast inflation, politics, and currency with numbers that can be plugged into forecasts.

Corporate consulting needed to be simple and straightforward. This was not necessarily a failing, more a revelation of how limited even the most intelligent people are in their lives and professions.

"You always remember your first job," my friend Wally Stein said. Mine was a presentation in an IBM corporate facility in North Tarrytown, NY. My audience wore white shirts and ties, the uniform of "Big Blue." No colored or tinted shirts allowed. I stood at a long table, projecting brief and "snappy" slides that were to be the forerunner of PowerPoint. The men, and they were always men, took notes and asked few questions.

We went to lunch. A Norwegian sat beside me. We exchanged greetings and then he said, "I raise rabbits." I smiled, accepting the statement. "The rabbits are under my home."

I didn't know how to respond. "You have a lot?"

"You know rabbits."

"Yes," I laughed.

"There are enough of them to heat my house most winters. They keep my heating bill down."

He spoke with a thick accent. He was odd.

"I experiment with things," he continued. "I developed a system for IBM that puts sensors on Mexican volcanoes to measure rainfall and falloff. The computer then indicates which crops to plant, where and when."

Rabbits and volcanoes! This was my introduction to the business world which, so poorly presented in media as either villains or profit mongers, is the foundation of America's strength. My subsequent clients included Avon, Ford, Pfizer, Cummins Engine, Union Carbide, Eli Lilly, American International Group, and banks and financial institutions, and there was no one among them who I did not come to like and appreciate.

Whenever there was a crisis, I was called. Two years into my new job, I was sent to St. Louis. Monsanto was about to invest a billion dollars in Brazil when the Latin American debt crisis hit. Brazil's economy was falling apart. Inflation soared. Foreign investment and credit halted. Senior management needed to know if it should proceed, understanding that if the country fell apart, the corporation would be fatally damaged.

For a Latin Americanist, the answer was obvious: Yes. Brazil is a large and sophisticated country that has endured periodic economic shocks throughout its history but it had always "muddled through," the term of the period. Its large population and huge agricultural resources would yield major exports in the years ahead. I presented scenarios that, even in the worst case, showed that Monsanto would always profit. The company went ahead and is today one of the most successful American corporations operating in Brazil.

But what if I had been wrong and anarchy resulted? Then, the senior managers would point to my report and blame me. To be sure, they were dedicated officials not given to gambling their company's fortune. But their backsides were covered.

A few years later, I gave a speech in Union Carbide headquarters. My presentation was an overview of the global situation, but when I arrived the staff was running all about. Some were crying and others sitting alone in their offices. It was the day the Carbide facility in Bhopal, India exploded, killing and maiming tens of thousands of people. The tragedy revealed the fragility of industrial production as well as the risk of working with joint ventures and foreign partners.

I adapted to the world of business, its language and culture. After a few years, I realized that the firm that employed me was absorbing a substantial portion of the consulting fees I earned. Now with a good knowledge of what was needed, I founded the one-person Miles Wortman Associates.

My corporate work continued, but then Washington called. The government of Tunisia was overthrown and the new leader, General Zine el-Abidine Ben Ali, made overtures seeking closer relations with the United States. USAID needed someone who spoke French to talk with him and provide background on America. My life changed in an instant.

MOZAMBIQUE

(1988)

Excerpt from the novel *To Do the Right Thing*

**Perestroika begins—Phantom of the Opera opens—Collapse of
the Soviet Union—Iran-Contra affair—Soviet withdrawal from
Afghanistan—Al-Qaeda formed—Iran-Iraq War ends—First computer
worm—George H. W. Bush elected American President—Pan Am
Flight blown up over Scotland—the World Wide Web**

UNDER A BRILLIANT SKY and warm sea breeze in Maputo, I swam
laps, in a long azul pool surrounded by marble busts of Virgil, Homer,
and Plato. Just a few kilometers away, a decade-old civil war raged.

This was the Polana, the legendary hotel sitting high on a cliff over
the Indian Ocean, once a spot for dalliances and drunken vacations
when the Portuguese ruled and white millionaires from nearby South
Africa sought hedonistic pleasures. Graham Greene wet his whistle here.
Now the hotel catered to foreign military and charity advisers, journalists,
and a few business types racing to make a killing out of the war.

From the bar on high, "The Girl from Ipanema," clinking glasses,
and laughter gave background to my somewhat awkward but relaxing
strokes.

It was 1988 and I was out of work at forty, having run through
one marriage and a series of teaching jobs. A few weeks earlier, I
had received a call from a friend of a friend who asked if I spoke

Portuguese. When I replied in the affirmative, he told me about a consulting job with the Mozambique government, helping to develop their new investment initiative. Though I had no experience in international business, I was told that it didn't matter. I did speak Portuguese, didn't I?

And so here I swam, back and forth, under Thucydides and then Julius Caesar, clearing the cobwebs from the long flight, America to Lisbon to Angola and to here. As I climbed the steps out of the pool, a shadowy figure approached, and the lights from the bar blinded my view.

"Mr. Wolffe?"

My eyes slowly adjusted to the light. He was short and stout in a suit and tie, quite out of place at the pool. He might have been an accountant.

"I wonder if you would care to join me for a drink," he said.

I toweled off and threw on a robe. He led me to his table overlooking the Indian Ocean. Oil lights burned above like beacons for the fishing boats offshore. A bottle of Johnny Walker Black, a bowl of ice, and two uncorked bottles of Burgundy sat in front of us.

He lit a cigarette. "I hope this suits you. I've been told you like whisky."

"It's fine," I said, casting sobriety to the winds. My first resolution in my new job already smashed.

"I've ordered some tiger shrimp, if that's OK."

So this is how it begins, I thought. Was he CIA or military intelligence? Or was he working for the other side?

"Wally Stein," he said. "The company that hired you has a contract to deliver services to us at AID. That's me. I'm the guy in charge."

He poured his wine slowly and handed me his card. Walt Whitman Stein, African Bureau Director, AID. "This all must be quite strange for you," he said as he filled my whisky glass to the top.

"This all?"

"Your hire. This place. This world."

I nodded, slowly sipping the whisky, promising myself that I would imbibe with caution to keep my wits about me. I'd only have one drink, I thought. Or maybe two. The drunk's pledge.

"I wanted to meet you personally and since I was in Africa, arranged to fly in to have a chat and answer whatever questions you have." What I have learned since is that "answer whatever questions you have" means "I am here to tell you the heart of the matter."

We sat back, and I sipped while he puffed. "You're an academic, no? You've written quite a lot. Well received, it seems. Still looking for another teaching post?"

"Don't know. It's been a long slog and I'm not sure I like teaching or even my colleagues."

"I understand. I've been there."

A waiter brought the shrimp, the largest I'd ever seen—big and black with thick shells. He bowed, and Wally said something unintelligible to him. He nodded.

"I asked him to bring lemon and a bowl of rice. Too much alcohol without carbs is not a good idea."

"You speak Swahili?"

He lit another cigarette. "Yes, somewhat. He speaks Portuguese, of course, but I like to practice."

We started on the shrimp. "Mozambique's gold," Wally said. "Most of its production is controlled by the South Africans. Access to markets and all that. We're trying to get the locals to break into the world market without their rapacious neighbors. This job you have is to help the locals develop the right business environment for investment."

"I have no experience with that," I admitted.

"You have experience. You just don't know you do. You're an American. You've lived around business your entire life, unlike here where the Portuguese ran everything for five hundred years. And what you don't know you'll learn. For the moment, you won't give advice, you'll just listen. We set up interviews with the ministries, embassies, and the few private businesses operating. You take notes and then provide us with a report with all the right words."

He began speaking in Portuguese, describing the history of the country, the civil war, the Russian, Cuban and South African involvement, all of whom were now withdrawing with America moving in to guide the road to democracy. I responded equally in Portuguese that I had done some research and found the situation quite challenging. He was checking on my Portuguese. I passed the test.

He returned to English. "So, about promoting investment."

"Yes, about investment," I replied. "Isn't Mozambique in civil war? Isn't this a bit... well, silly?"

"Ah, the academic speaking. Analyzing critically before you hit the turf running, are you? Let me ask you some questions. Who is the President of the United States?"

I snickered and took a drink.

"Well?"

"Reagan," I answered.

"Yes, and what is his view of business and government?"

"He wants to promote business."

"And if you were developing a program for the US government right now, would you emphasize health or education or business?

I nodded. "I get the point."

"I don't think you do. Here we are in a country with an unstable and insecure government that has been fighting rebels supported by the Boers in South Africa and getting arms and soldiers from the Russians and Cubans. But the Commies have given up the fight and the government is adrift."

"And we are here to take up the cause?"

"We are here to end the civil war, push the Boers out of government in South Africa, and establish a presence here. Now, why would we want that?"

I filled my glass. He was treating me like a child. "Tell me," I said, chastened.

"China. We need to establish a firm foothold here, make the right connections, sign the right agreements. This is Africa, and what happens in the future is unpredictable. Mozambique has tremendous wealth and resources, but all that is secondary to where we sit. Look out there. That's the Indian Ocean, where grand navies will maneuver for power."

He finished the first bottle of wine, staying steady. I noticed he still had half a pack of smokes to consume. "I am being straightforward with you because you are smart and need to know the lay of the land. Especially since you are moving into this business," he told me.

"Am I moving into this business?"

"Yes," he nodded, "you are. You're a good fit. Smart, good with languages, and you write well. That's all you need. You're adrift in life and need a handle."

"So I'm to become an expert in promoting business?"

"Sure," Wally said. "This time."

"This time?"

"Next time, if the Democrats win, you'll become an expert in health, education, that sort of stuff. And then when the other side gets back in, you'll brush up on grain markets and trade policy. You're a professional responding to the Washington merry-go-round—the business types leave, the social do-gooders come in, each with new ideas about how to save the world."

"You're a cynic," I said, slurring my words.

He ignored my comment and began his second bottle. "You're a historian of what?"

"American history."

"What exactly?"

He knew the answer, of course. He had read my bio. "The frontier."

"Yes, the frontier. Frederick Jackson Turner, wasn't it? Turner and those ideals."

I nodded. I was growing tired. Everyone knew the Turner thesis, that America's ideals were formed on the frontier as the country moved west.

"How real are those ideals?" he asked me.

"What do you mean?"

"I mean democracy and equal justice on the frontier. How real?"

"Yes. Yes. Slavery. Indian genocide…"

"Mob violence," he interrupted. "Imperialism."

"What's your point?"

"Myth and reality. Every nation has it but in this business the myths are created every day. How to help people. How to change societies." He took a drink. "Do you know what America's flaw is?"

I shook my head.

He stood up. "Time for a break. I have to go pee. Why don't you jump in the pool and splash around a little? That should wake you up."

"I need to get some sleep."

"I know you've been traveling and the jetlag and all that, but I am flying out early tomorrow and I need to finish our conversation. Go take a swim. I'll order up some coffee for you. Would you like cognac?"

The whiskey bottle was still a third full. "No, I better not."

He left and I plunged into the water. That was Wally. Always on the move, never stopping, never showing signs of too much wine, travel, or talk. Always enthusiastic. I did a sidestroke down the pool, looking up at the bar where a few stragglers remained. A statue blocked my view.

"Hello, Herodotus, how ya' doing?"

I heard a loud laugh, looked about and saw an African woman smiling at me. "You talk to yourself while swimming, do you?" She was swathed in a bright yellow capulana, and the sarong emphasized her svelte figure. Her hair was carefully coiffed. She was very attractive, her smile seductive.

I threw on the robe and returned to the table. She sat in Wally's seat. "Buy me a drink?"

"I can't. I'm having a meeting."

"A meeting," she said, mockingly. "Everyone has meetings. What's your name?"

I stammered. Wally approached and said something in Swahili. The woman stood angrily. He pulled out twenty dollars and she withdrew, haughtily.

"That was not gentlemanly. What did you say?"

"I said we didn't want to be disturbed and would thank her for making sure no else comes. We've reach the time of night when devils descend and offer spurious joys."

"You're religious?"

"Not at all but there are still devils about, not all of them offering sexual favors. Where were we?"

"America's flaw."

"Yes, of course. America's flaw is we need to do *good*. We're convinced of our moral rectitude, that we're a force for God, freedom, democracy and prosperity. The world's 'last best hope.' It's in every politician's speech. We keep armies to advance our lofty goals. Our businessmen provide investments in the name of positive growth. Our churches send missionaries to save souls because it is the Christian thing to do."

"And, what's wrong with that?"

He lit another cigarette, tossed his head to one side and looked into the sky with a wisp of a smile, a whiff of condescension as if to say *Is it so obvious that you cannot see?* That was Wally, ill-mannered and disdainful, an offensive style that hurt him throughout his life.

"It is naive," he whispered. "Naive. We ignore the realities of life, the world's cultures, ancient histories and myths and beliefs that each land is the most sanctified and each God is the legitimate divinity and they are God's children. We believe our values are the right ones, divine, biblical, righteous and all the rest. We ignore the unintended consequences of our actions, the ancient grievances we unearth when we disrupt the status quo. And I am not talking about napalm but such things as giving free food to countries that competes against and destroys local production or advocating free speech in nations without any basis for democracy who live in fragile peace with rival and angry groups holding ancient grievances."

"And try as we like, we can't avoid it. It is in our genes. Send the Marines, give free food, and break up bloody squabbles. The national flaw is as ingrained as our drive for sex and power. The rich fund charities for distant lands without any understanding of what they are doing or the havoc they cause. We sponsor local chieftains because they speak English and parrot our beliefs and when they turn out to be tyrants or worse, we shrug. When we flop and destroy lives, we don't do penance, maybe we write a check or apologize and move on to the next chore of saving the world."

"So why are we here? You and me. "

He smiled. "Because we work on the margins, we avoid the silly mission statements and programs that come from Washington and try to help the people we meet. We try to understand each situation and each point of view. We work with our counterparts, offer them advice, and give them hope where there is no hope. We do what we can and nothing more. We don't exaggerate our value or undervalue the others' existence."

"You are not offering much incentive for my new life," I said wryly.

"What is it that Leonard Cohen says, 'There is a crack in everything, that's how the light gets in.' You do what you can within the limits of what is possible and you ignore the rest. That is what life is about."

He waved to the waiter and said something. "I ordered us a nightcap."

"I'm really too far gone."

He ignored me and reached for another cigarette.

"Those things are going to kill you."

"Maybe," he said, prophetically. "Unless something else gets me first. Do you know how many people do the work you are about to begin?"

"A few thousand?"

He scoffed. "Hundreds of thousands. Perhaps millions. Maybe tens of millions. Bureaucrats in every major nation, all very well paid, planning programs, academics studying the impact of this and that, tens of thousands of officials in the United Nations and all the other international shops, think-tanks developing new strategies, consulting firms that profit by sending people like you to implement the well-thought out studies that have gone through choppers of committees after committees, changing goals to fit political needs, committees filled with the naïve, liars, connivers, fools, with zealots, the obtuse, the depressed, the manipulators, drunks, missionaries, romantics, martyrs, and the self-righteous. The quality of each of these experts—and that is what they call themselves—varies from genius to certifiably idiotic, and you just need a few, just a few, of the lesser beings to warp an effort and destroy years of work."

He took a long drag from his cigarette. "Your program, the one you're about to begin, took over a year to develop. Experts were hired to write it up and then AID squabbled about it, moved it to the next fiscal year because someone in some department had a favorite he or she wanted to hire while the situation on the ground here changed. But no matter, the inertia was there and so here you are."

The waiter arrived with another bottle of whiskey and glass of cognac. I looked askance. "Not to worry," Wally said, "a little present from me to take to your room for medicinal purposes." He tilted his glass. "To a successful career."

He continued. "Think about the sort of person who is trying to change the world right now. Most grew up insulated in lives of well-being, with corn flakes, sitcoms, and cars. They played football or baseball on suburban lawns. Their parents were professional, sent them to private schools where they were indoctrinated into free-market or public policy ideologies by professors who wrote the books in their private offices, ideas cemented by their peers who took power. They live in the richest land ever in history at the center of empire, in Rome itself, and they believe they have the understanding and theories to bring the peasants on the tundra up to their standards.

"You don't make it sound attractive."

"Attractive? You want attractive? Go back and teach fat, dumb, and happy schoolchildren about your American frontier. Spin your tales about dead Indians and cowboys, about which they don't care and will soon forget. You have the opportunity to use your initiative to help a few people. If you go back to a cushy, tenured post, your work will be done by somebody less competent than you, someone who is trying like hell to earn a living who couldn't make it as a bank teller or selling insurance. By your presence and your qualities, you will contribute. And I'm not flattering you one bit.

But to succeed, you will have to forget everything you know about language and logic. You will need to learn words with no meaning, concepts that make no sense whatsoever. You will have to parrot back to DC what DC wants to hear. You will make it sound sophisticated, of course. You will offer proofs and data to defend indefensible words. You are in Washington's world. Washington pays you and controls you. But what you do outside this Wonderland is what will matter to you and to the people you will serve."

"You know I drink."

"Doesn't everyone?"

"A lot."

"Probably a basic qualification for this work." He didn't blink an eye.

"And I tend toward depression."

"Better still. Nobody likes a Pollyanna. I know your history. You lost jobs and a wife and you're a little lost. But you have a sense of morality and goodness as well as an analytic mind. All that adds up to is a drunken cynic. And as long as you can control your impulses, you'll be perfect for all this."

I sighed, looking out at the marble giants before us, at Virgil, Caesar, and Herodotus. The moon rose over the ocean, casting a brilliant gloss on the water. My eyes closed.

"You'll be fine." He rose and touched my shoulder. "I made an appointment for you to fly up to Mafimbese to see my friend Polkinhorne. No myths at Mafimbese." He made to leave and then said, "Enjoy your first assignment. You always remember the first time, isn't that what they say?"

I nodded. "That's what they say."

"Yes, they do. Welcome to Africa."

❦

Johan Polkinhorne, the chief engineer of the Mafimbese Sugar Works, greeted me warmly at the front gate of the sugar plantation, his calloused hands rough against mine. He was not a big man but had large shoulders, strong arms and a solid, thick neck, handsome for his years with a farmer's weathered, determined face.

We toured the grounds. The cane was high and tasseled, ready for harvest. We passed through a grove of palm trees, a smoking refinery, and workers' huts where children played out front. His aide, Gary Spinola, arrived and we went to his home, a Quonset hut with a netted porch. We ate thick fried potato slices and drank dark, local rum. Under a brilliant star-lit sky he spoke of how he had come to this farm in the middle of Mozambique, the music of mosquitoes, eagle owls and night herons playing behind his strong voice.

He had retired from running Transvaal plantations in South Africa when Wally approached him to take charge of Mafimbese. The Russians and Cubans had pulled out, leaving the plantation and the rest of the country half destroyed and scarcely functioning. The farm had lost its labor force, vanished into the bush, and was exposed to constant Renamo rebel attacks.

The Americans financed the plantation's recovery. Polkinhorne was well known. He knew African soil, he said, and how to "handle" Black Africans. Wally offered a good salary as well as a share of the profits and deposited a bonus in a Geneva bank. "But it was not the money. It was the challenge, to get this thing back on its feet."

Maps and plans covered the walls of his hut, announcing that this was his factory, his organization and his creature. "The place was a mess," he continued. "The Portuguese had destroyed the refinery when they fled after independence. The Cuban machinery was run down and unfit for the tough African cane. I restored it all using old steam engine parts, rusting East German control instruments and makeshift pipes. I took everything apart, cleaned and reconstructed it. At first I was all by myself, but I drafted workers from the resettlement camps to which the locals had fled to escape Renamo. I taught them how to cut cane, showed them the right temperature to refine bagasse and the recipe for sugar, molasses, and rum. I gave them plots and seed to farm their own *shambas*. I lent them trucks and tractors, built the school and a clinic and brought in the teacher. I gave them work, shelter and food. Most of all, I gave them peace, if just for a moment.

"I trained them to fight, to form militias to defend against rebel attacks and I got rid of the government army, a useless bunch, filled with raggedy and beggaring peasants who fled at the first shot.

He spoke with so much pride, I couldn't get a word in.

"And then I studied the old accounts to figure the production we might get. You wouldn't believe how well these plantations worked in the past with luscious bagasse from the well-watered fields, an ample supply of cheap labor and a railroad straight to the Ocean. Back then, nothing could stop production, except politics."

"But then the tax collectors came," Gary Spinola chimed in, "and tried to take everything we had."

Polkinhorne laughed. "So Gary and I said 'Go ahead, take it all. You run this place. We quit.'"

"That's when Wally interceded," Polkinhorne continued. "The ministers got all angry and nationalistic and said it was their country and they'd do what they want. My guys, the workers, left and wandered back to the resettlement camps because there was no work or money. Wally came down and gave them a lesson in business. We negotiated a face-saving solution with the government. They got twenty percent of the profits and we got left alone."

⚜

The next morning, I awoke to a dank odor of decaying palm leaves and wood fires. I looked through the haze into a tight grouping of small, wood-frame houses with ashes glowing. Colored cloth hung like flags on tree limbs to dry. Two soldiers ambled through the hamlet, puffing on cigarettes and kicking at scraggly chickens crossing their path.

Daybreak, the best time in the bush, birds awakening, chirping and fluttering, a coolness that gives the feeling that all is right in world, before the heat grows and shrinks the will of men and women. For a brief moment, the sun shot through the trees presenting an idyllic scene. A door opened and two children emerged, breaking the peace. They wore bright white shirts that contrasted with their black faces. The boy giggled, pushed his sister gently and ran ahead. The girl gave chase.

"We all forget the joy in living," Wally once said. "In the harshest lives, children play and people love and that is life."

The children ran towards a roundhouse in the center of the clearing and as they approached, a short, gaunt man emerged, limping markedly. He patted them on their heads but did not smile. He peered into the fog in search of other children. He was the teacher, a strange man who spent his nights alone, reading and writing under dim candles.

Soon after, their mother and father came out and turned onto a brown dirt road through palm trees, vanishing in the haze. Men clad in dull blue and gray work shirts and dark trousers followed, along with women, taller and broader and sheathed in African yellows, blues and reds.

I trailed the parade, through the palm woods along a large chain fence crowned with barbed wire arching outwards. It was by no means a grim procession. They spoke quietly, laughing as they went. They came to a paved road, then the factory gate and a parking lot where a herd of brilliant yellow Caterpillar tractors sat beside black Mercedes cars.

The line divided, the women to the north, across railroad tracks built by Cecil John Rhodes a century earlier and past the irrigation ditches that brought water from the Zambezi River. They faded into the sugar fields. The men entered a large dark refinery that towered in a hazy illusion, like Babel itself, over the grounds.

I returned to see Polkinhorne behind his desk, puffing on his cigar and on the phone. In the background, the coughing ignition of the refinery engines announced the start of the day's operations. The time of harvest. "Would you please raise Quelimane and find out when the train is due in? Also, get the numbers on last week's shipment to Maputo."

The pops came faintly at first, seemingly a part of the usual factory noise. Polkinhorne, however, knew right away.

"Shit," he said to himself and then, in a much louder voice, "Renamo!" He reached for a set of keys, opened the door and ran into Gary, his assistant.

"They're hitting the settlement," he said. "Get the guns and raise Beira." He looked at me for a moment and waved for me to follow. "Come on, come on. Where's the fucking militia?"

Beneath the din of factory machinery, I heard the sound of running cattle, first softly and then louder and louder. The beasts poured through the gates, Renamo fighters hiding between them. Polkinhorne yelled, "Grenades. Get out the grenades!" He pointed at me and three workers, "You and you and you. Get in." We climbed into his Mercedes and sped to the gate, honking, carefully pushing the cattle to the side.

He passed through the gate, jumped out and sprayed the bush with machine gun fire. Two Renamo guerrillas fell immediately. Others jumped for safety. He called to the men in the car. "Close the gate." They hesitated. He pointed the Uzi into the car. "Get the fuck out and close the fucking gate."

They jumped and ran towards the gate. Polkinhorne stayed in the middle, shooting at the bush while I cowered in fear in the rear seat, confused and looking out at the chaos. The guerrillas returned fire. A worker fell. The gate slammed shut. Polkinhorne sprayed the stranded Renamo fighters caught within the compound. He picked up the car microphone, "Homebase, homebase, I'm heading towards the settlement. Tell me, what else?"

"The choppers are coming," Gary responded, "but it's still too foggy to get much support."

"I want two cars in the settlement and three men at the gate," Polkinhorne ordered. He waved to the trembling Africans to return to the car. The Mercedes turned off the pavement onto the path.

"You've got that?" he yelled.

After a delay, I heard Gary's voice. "Roger that."

We returned to the township. The mist lifted, replaced by smoke from burning homes. Guerrillas ran from house to house, carrying children in their arms. The body of the schoolteacher lay in front of the roundhouse, his face gone, his body riddled with bullets. Two women were beside him, machete-hacked corpses pouring scarlet rivers onto the hard earth.

I sat in a daze, immobile, staring at the burning houses, the roundhouse and corpses strewn all about where, a few minutes before, children ran and played without care. Tears came to my eyes.

Polkinhorne jumped from the car and crawled. He motioned for his men to move alongside the path. Two guerrillas came out of a hut, carrying children. Polkinhorne fired a short burst into the air. The rebels dropped their prey and fled toward the trees.

All fell quiet. Then a large burst shook the ground, sending black smoke skyward from the refinery. He grimaced. We returned to the hamlet where the wails of men and women had replaced the sounds of gunshots.

We walked through the village, surveying the charred remnants of what were once homes. Out of the morning mist an African man approached, walking with fear. "Sr. Polkinhorne," he said, "this is very bad. All our preparations and then this. And the children. And the teacher. The poor teacher." He began to sob and shake.

"I'm very sorry. We'll do what we can." Polkinhorne looked at the African, both knowing there was little to be done. His face dropped and he shook his head. "Next comes the Renamo counterattack. They'll return with the captured children and force them to shoot their parents. Then the little kids will be too afraid and ashamed to return to their homes and will become Renamo fighters."

His assistant Gary drove up. "It's all over. The choppers have arrived. They got the power station. Doesn't look good."

"Great," Polkinhorne said to no one in particular. "Without the generator, the electric controls don't work and the oven won't ignite. And without the refinery, we can't cut the cane. And if we cannot bring in the cane on time, it will go to seed. The harvest is lost."

"I don't know how many kids they got, but we've lost six men," Gary said. "We got twelve of them at last count. A bunch of houses were blown. There's quite a few dead cattle to clean up, too."

I was still trembling. My arms crossed my chest. A procession approached, villagers carrying their dead to a hollow beyond the fields. Soon, friendly and enemy corpses were dumped into a pit and covered with lime.

Exhausted and shaken, I returned to Maputo and retired to my room. I got drunk. The next day, I got drunk again. My mind kept wandering back to the lost children, those dead and kidnapped and the mangled body of the schoolteacher, innocent in the dust. In the years ahead, I would think of other children who played briefly before the demons descended, Sunni and Shia, Srebrenica Muslims, Mauritian Fula, Hutu and Tutsi, Azeris and Meskhetian Turks, Syrian Christians, Egyptian Coptics, and of all the other political and ethnic horrors that would come forth as Wally and I and others of our ilk labored on to keep the world in balance.

"You always remember your first time," Wally said.

Then, one morning, I went to the hotel pool and swam laps, washing Mafimbese from my soul. I swam until exhaustion and dragged myself to a lounge. I stared at the hot, tropical sun and fell into a deep slumber.

A cool evening breeze awakened me. I returned to my room, ordered a pot of coffee and wrote my report on the climate for investment in Mozambique. As I checked out of the Polana, I reviewed the charges. They were all there, Wally's wine, the two bottles of whiskey, the shrimp, his three packs of cigarettes and the cognac. It was the first of many times that I picked up his bill.

WHITEY

(1991)

Czech Velvet Revolution—Tiananmen Square protests in China—First
GPS satellites—Exxon Valdez oil spill—Seinfeld—Internet service
begins—The Berlin Wall falls—Communism collapses in Eastern
Europe—The end of the Cold War—The US invades Panama

JERRY FLETCHER? White shirts, that's Jerry, neat and starched, collar perfectly in place. Jerry rode for hours in an open Jeep on rugged, dusty roads under scorching tropical sun and arrived with the same clean, well-pressed shirt, as fresh as when he donned it that morning. How he did it, nobody knew. Why he wore them, impossible to understand.

It certainly risked confusion. If you wear a white shirt in Africa, you're either a Mormon or an oil magnate. He just liked it, he said. Denoted neatness, a position in life, a formality. To this day, amongst the stripes and dark colors in Washington or the leisurewear in Maryland supermarkets, Jerry wears those shirts, neat and tightly tucked near his slim waist.

Jerry was class. He came from money and spent it without regard. He showed contempt for any white man or woman who might mention such mundane matters as salary, retirement or the cost of a good meal. True to form, he also kept his money neat. His dollars, naira or CFA francs were organized and separated into stacks. Jerry would have his house boy Eduardo press his money each morning. It gave Jerry a sense of regalness or so he said. In the local markets, merchants studied the money closely, because in Africa, new meant counterfeit. Jerry liked that.

After a while, the shopkeepers recognized the crazy American in the white shirt with the neat money. They called him Whitey—not as pejorative, but because he was the only man in Africa wearing starched white shirts with no signs of wilt under the tropical sun. He had been on the continent so long, everyone just thought that was his name.

He was a presence, a man who walked, talked and slept neat and clean. "You have to set an example for these folks," Whitey said. "Show them the proper way to act." He sounded like a Baptist minister, which he was anything but, given his love of liquor and women and the African high life.

The last time I saw him was at the Maputo hearing in 1991, the inquiry into irregularities in the Mozambique food program, the disappearance of a food aid worker in the north, and, ultimately, Whitey's future in the aid business. He was still a noble figure, so erect and well groomed, like pedigree. Only his aging face showed signs of wear.

Whitey Fletcher was *the* Africa hand of all of the thousands who came and went, businessmen, bureaucrats and do-gooders. For most people, the place was something you had to endure, depressing given all the illness and corruption and difficulties in getting anything accomplished. Whitey? He enjoyed the easy, slow pace that fit his *que sera sera* style. He'd wander into Lagos dives, tall, white-skinned and seeming to shine in the darkness on the dance floor. He'd buy drinks for the guys at the bar, exchange jokes and then wander about looking for an available young lady. Life was good in Africa for a white man.

Before I went to see him, I spent a week looking over his dossier, reviewing his security clearances and supervisors' reports. I called on his colleagues. I like to cover the whole case, the personality, what makes him go, his weaknesses and his tastes. His past was pretty well laid-out: upper-class Episcopal and Dartmouth. During the Vietnam War, he did what other loyal and patriotic, white Americans. He joined the Peace Corps. Two years in Senegal teaching English, good work, agreeable to his buttoned-up Bronxville parents. Maybe that's where Whitey got the white shirt thing.

While he was in the bush, his father abandoned his mother, ran off with his secretary, and started a new family. Perhaps that's why, when the USAID people came around, he accepted the Africa posting.

The AID decision set out a life that fit him. In Africa, a few dollars buy a cook, a maid, a nice house, a garden and a chauffeur. International clubs offered grass courts, cheap GTs (gin and tonics), and a fast social life with eligible, one might say desperate, young women and lonely wives and, if that failed, the downtown bars.

True, the work was tedious. After all, what did he do but push paper, approve food shipments, locomotive parts, machine tools, college scholarships and emergency flood relief, prepare forms in triplicate for approval by one bureaucratic layer after another? In bureaucratic battles, Whitey was as unflappable as the neat tucks in his shirt. He swayed and ducked, avoided confrontation and if some money happened to be diverted to the friend of a Congressman or an African politician, he didn't know.

And really, the advantages of this life far outweighed the negatives: trips about the continent, conferences at Victoria Falls, training sessions in Cape Town, and retreats in game parks. Whitey's *bon vivant* and stylish way suited Africa. It recalled the good old days when European colonials played at clubs and hunts. He became famous in his own way, the man who knew the best sites, bars, and adventures. When dignitaries came by, it was the guy in the white shirt to whom they turned for a fun time. Everyone knew Whitey, Washington types, AID officials, US Senators, and businessmen all had stories about the cooler crammed with GTs, the jars of cashews and the Land Rovering about the back country to tribal ceremonies and lion hunts.

Then he met Jeri, a tall, striking Australian blond working on food relief. Whitey and Jeri became a thing. How could they not? They were both so relaxed and happy. Whitey took to Jeri's looks and body, Jeri with his lifestyle. They were together for a decade. They lived the good life: no children, trekking through the bush, sunning at the pool, drinking the night away. Young lovers in paradise.

Until love faded. Jeri grew tired of the African expat life. How many GTs can one drink, being left at home or at the club by a husband who was, more times than not, out in the bush or hitting the bars? Jeri began going out on her own. Her demeanor became less than acceptable, drinking and dancing and flirting with the staff. Her reputation plummeted, a tragedy in the expat world where gossip is the manna of survival. First, there was the Italian ambassador. Then the head of American security. And then the tennis coach.

If Whitey knew, he never let on, too cool to let it bother him. Still, the plot was as obvious as a sordid soap opera. One morning and carrying a nasty hangover, Jeri wandered downstairs, saw Eduardo the houseboy ironing Whitey's money, and broke into uncontrollable laughter. She called for a cab and flew home.

I am with the Office of Special Interests. OSI handles delicate matters delicately, to be settled without publicity that may cause embarrassment to the President, the Congress or the officials of the international aid agencies. Africa, in particular, suffers more than its share and the general rule at OSI is: keep African problems in Africa. Our work has become more challenging with the internet and international e-mails, do-gooding missionary groups, charities and the academics. They all muddle in the muck, raising questions about complex matters that have huge implications for governments. The academics are the worst.

Doing evil is easy but doing good is hard. Assistance is jumbled by Washington politics, African corruption, diplomatic needs, ideology, antiquated laws and regulations, political correctness and bureaucratic squabbles. Wherever money is, vultures descend, they fight and scratch so that at the end of the day if some funds gets to those in need, it is a miracle.

Most aid workers do not look at implications. They look for quick and easy successes for their personnel files to move up the ladder. Implications be damned. What is left behind is only explored in the most dramatic failures: build a power dam in West Africa to solve energy needs and spread river blindness or import cheap food and drive local farmers out of business.

The issue at Whitey's hearing was food. The numbers didn't add up. For every hundred tons of wheat and rice arriving at the Port of Maputo, sixty went walkabout. Poof! Trainloads of food evaporated into the sweet African air.

We love to give food to the world because there's far too much in America's silos. When the market is glutted, prices drop and Midwest farmers turn to the government to give them top dollar for grain they cannot sell. Farm senators get reelected while city senators claim they're helping the starving in Africa.

Everybody wins except the African farmer who tries to sell crops for which he has scrubbed and toiled at the local market for a reasonable price, competing against free Iowa grains, especially when the Iowa stuff is stolen at dockside and sold for virtually nothing. The farmer quits his land and moves to the city, increasing the need for free Iowa wheat.

Managing the US food program is like herding cats. Everybody wants the free stuff, the local military, hospitals, and schools. Everybody wants to distribute it, the ministries, the NGOs (non-government organizations), or the missionaries. Food is power, after all. Whitey's job was to coordinate it all, to make sure there was no "leakage." Leakage is defined as having food sacks bearing the US flag being sold in markets from Johannesburg to Cairo.

Leakage always happens. A local stevedore who earns a dollar a day for hauling food sacks in hundred-degree heat has more than a little incentive to stash a few behind the trash can. If he loads a couple of hundred sacks into the wrong truck, say, of the local customs agent, he can retire for life. It's a matter of degree, and, anyway, nobody is going to make a big deal out of missing wheat, neither the Iowa farmer nor the Senator from Chicago. The game proceeds without notice.

But then, an American food agent went missing. That changed everything. His Tennessee church raised the alarm, the local newspaper investigated and his Congressional representative called for an investigation. What were once a few drops of missing grain became a scandal. Leaked memos suggested skullduggery or incompetence. How could millions of dollars of food evaporate into thin air? And what about this aid worker who was taken from under the nose of the Mozambique army?

The day before the hearing, Whitey and I went for beer and tiger shrimp at the Copacabana, the local beach hangout. We looked out from the verandah onto the Indian Ocean under palms swaying from the cool sea breeze. African women stood at water's edge watching their children play in the calm water.

"You know," I told Whitey, "you have nothing to worry about. This hearing is all *pro forma*. A few questions and clarifications and we'll set the record straight."

"OK, no problem," Whitey said, smiling. He'd been around government too long to know that nothing is *pro forma*. My little speech was procedure, written down in some manual as standard approach.

"But there are a couple of questions," I said.

Whitey sipped his beer. "Yep. Glad to help."

"So, this consultant who went missing, what was his name?" I asked

"Stouder."

"Yeah, Stouder." I pulled out a small pad and took a note. "There's a suggestion that you transferred him upcountry on purpose."

"I transferred him," Whitey said. He picked up a shrimp and delicately bit off its head, dropping it onto the floor for the waiting dog. "He was poking around and we all thought it best to get him out of Maputo."

"Why was that?"

He paused and sipped his beer and picked up another shrimp. "These are good, aren't they?"

"Yes. Very good."

"Tiger shrimp, the specialty of Mozambique. The Japs drift offshore with their vacuum cleaner boats and suck them up from the bottom. We try to stop them, but you know how it is. Our allies."

"Yes," I said, waiting patiently. I motioned to the waiter for more beer. Whitey's reputation for drinking crammed his personnel files.

"I don't know your clearance," he said.

"My clearance?" I said.

"Yes, your security clearance. What level?"

"Me? I have the highest security level. It was in the memo I sent. It's OSA procedure."

"Was it?" he said, with a slight English affectation. "I wasn't sure."

"We could go back to the office."

"No need. I guess it was there," he said.

"You've dealt with OSA before, haven't you?" I asked, knowing full well.

"Yes, of course. This is Africa."

"So, why did you have to get this guy out of Maputo?"

"Because he was poking around, asking too many questions, learning too much."

"Or not enough," I said.

"Of course," he said. "But we couldn't tell him, could we?"

"No," I said. "I should think not." The waiter brought more beer, their outsides sweating in the heat. "There seems to be an indication that when you sent him upcountry, you sort of cut him loose, didn't give him the usual protection."

"No," he said. "I don't think that's true. We stationed him up near the Beira garrison. I understand the brigade was ambushed as well. Suffered losses, they did."

"Was he aware of the risk?"

"He was happy to go. At least it was a job. These consultants, you know, they'll do anything for a paycheck."

"So you didn't cut him loose?"

"I don't understand what that means," Whitey said.

I let it pass. The bowl on the table began to spill with pink refuse. I waved off the flies. "How much did he know?"

"Not much, I don't think."

"What do you mean, you 'don't think'?"

"Not much. He couldn't have known much. But he was asking questions, getting in the way, became a real pain in the ass. You know these guys."

"What did he see?"

"Look," Whitey sighed, staring at the sea and drinking his beer. "Stouder got nosey. At the docks he saw food being transferred from the ships to the rail cars. He asked where it was going and the dumb fucks said South Africa. He found that curious. Why would a poor African nation struggling to feed its people ship food to one of the richest countries in the world, a country that exports food? Cops were standing around holding ledgers, checking invoices and bills of lading. The longshoremen were working openly. Nobody was doing anything. Everyone knew that corruption was rife. But this was in the open, in daylight. Surely there was a logical answer. That was his question. So I told him the world was complicated and there must be an explanation but, rest assured, I would look into it. I advised him to let it pass. After all, it wasn't his job to check on corruption. It was mine."

"But did he let it pass?"

"No. He kept returning to the docks and seeing the food heading to South Africa while the newspapers screamed about starvation up north. He came back to me, so I told him again that I was looking into it, that it was best he not say anything."

"But he kept bringing it up?"

"You know these consultants. They're a paranoid bunch. They work for themselves and fight like cats for contracts. They're weird. We don't know where they come from or where their loyalty lies. I mean, I knew he was a Christian. He didn't drink. He was serious. Very serious. These dedicated religious types. They're the worst."

"Did you threaten him?" I asked, matter-of-factly.

"I asked him if he liked his job. He said of course, good, tax-free wages and real work, dealing with real wages and helping humanity. So I asked him if he really wanted to risk getting in trouble for a few specks of grain. That's when I put a tail on him. We didn't want him getting in too deep, did we?

"No, I suppose not,"

Whitey sipped his beer and nibbled at the shrimp. He was so neat, carefully cleaning his fingers after picking the shells off. "But he kept on, like an obsession. He took notes of train numbers, numbers of sacks sitting on the sidings. Estimates, you know, nothing serious, but still he had numbers."

"Why didn't you have him stopped?" I said. "Have our friends keep him away from the port?"

"Impossible. The port's a sieve. If they tried to keep him, a white guy, out and who knows what he'd have done?"

"Originally, he was brought in to help keep the records in the embassy. He's a numbers guy, ya' know. He keeps the ledger arrivals, shipments and how the resettlement camps are supplied, stuff like that. He fills out the forms that go back to DC. But he was supposed to do the counting in the embassy, not in the yards, work with papers, not with sacks."

"Why didn't you send him home?"

"He was on the seventh month of a three year contract," Whitey said. "These guys don't have rights, but they do have contracts. And what excuse did I have? The guy was boring? He couldn't take no for an answer? He was doing his job? It would have taken six months to get him home. There was no time."

He downed a beer and waved for another round. He sure liked to drink, but it didn't seem to faze him. While I sweated in the afternoon sun, Whitey sat coolly with his white shirt, calm as could be, here in the midst of a civil war, a starvation zone and, perhaps, the end of his career. He didn't know that yet, of course, but he must have suspected.

"Look," Whitey said, "you have to understand. It's the nineties now. Things are complicated. Some of the Mozambique brass is getting nervous. They saw the guy asking questions. They told me to keep him away from the ports. I was afraid they'd kill him so I thought I'd ship him upcountry for a while, have him handle the food relief in the hinterland. It'd be safer. Anyway that's where the real starvation was taking hold. He'd like it up north, I told him."

Crows sat in the trees above, inspecting our food beneath. "Anyway. We can't muck up," he said. "Our entire foreign policy may be at stake because of this guy, and our cousins in Virginia told me that these shipments were critical. What do you think?"

"Me?" I said. "I wouldn't know."

"You do know, though, don't you?"

"Know what?" I said.

"About the food? Our little arrangement."

"Whose arrangement?"

"The USG and our friends in the Kremlin."

"Let's take a walk," I said, "down to the beach. Check out the lovelies."

We weaved our way through palms and laughing children to the waters' edge. "How shallow is this?"

"You can head out a kilometer," Whitey said, "before you have a fall-off. I wouldn't do it though. Too many sharks around here."

"Really?" I said.

"You have to be careful in this town. You forget you're in a civil war. It all seems so peaceful with the lovely water, the beer, and the nightlife. You head out too far, a shark will get you."

"Sharks, huh," I said. "It all looks so peaceful."

"Ask the kids dragooned into the army," he said. "You should go to the war zone and see the little ones hobbling around, victims of land mines and then go to the resettlement camps and see the creatures who were rounded up and forced into filth and squalor, doing nothing except waiting for their daily food rations."

I ignored the invitation. "OK," I said. "Nobody's bugging the beach. What's this arrangement with the Russians?"

"I'm surprised you don't know," Whitey said.

I was sweating profusely, my white shirt drenched. The heat and the beer were getting to me. Whitey remained calm and stoic, his shirt dry and pressed.

"Tell me," I said.

"I don't understand it all, but the way they told me, Washington has this problem: the Soviets want to give up and end the Cold War but they can't afford it. Their armies, the upper brass, these guys are powerful. After all, they've got the fucking bomb. They're willing to throw up their hands and go home but not if they're gonna starve. They have no place to live. You've got to keep the military happy, you know?"

"So?"

"We need to get the generals out the door without pushing buttons, right? They need pensions. They need places to live. Most of all they need to go quietly. But Uncle Sam can't let it be known that we're paying off the Red Menace. Wouldn't play in Peoria, would it? I mean, we can't feed our poor in Appalachia and we're sending aid to the Evil Empire?"

I was growing impatient.

"So they figured out this scheme. We'd give lots of food to poor, starving Mozambique, and then we'd ship it to South Africa where it would be sold at very low prices to our Russian friends. You know, like a bad commercial deal. They'd turn it around and sell it at market prices. The Russkis get the food low and sell high and then they get their pensions. It's not as messy as Iran-Contra. Nobody gets hurt except taxpayers, and we're gonna save them money on defense spending down the road. Everybody wins."

"So we're paying off the Soviets?"

"Yeah. You can say it like that. But this consultant Stouder runs right into this deal and cries foul."

"Let's go back to the restaurant," I said.

"Getting hot, isn't it?" he said.

"Yeah," I said.

"You knew this about the Russians, didn't you," he said.

I nodded. "I just wanted to make sure your version matched with what they told me, just so there won't be any problems later on."

"Should we have one last beer?" he asked.

"You go ahead. I think I'll have a Coke."

"I've done a lot of jobs in Africa," Whitey said. "But this is the strangest."

"You've put in over twenty years."

"That's right," he looked sentimental. "You know what Africa is? Beer and music. Wherever you go, there's a radio blaring a sweet South African or Senegalese tune and guys stand around drinking beer. It's the joy of it all."

"It's a lot of suffering from what I can see."

"What else is new? You go back a hundred and fifty years, every place had the same suffering as Africa—the illness, the disasters, the wars. They're just behind the times. They'll catch up eventually."

"That doesn't make it easier now," I said.

"When a man dies here," Whitey said, "everyone goes to his funeral—his family, his neighborhood, his fellow-workers. Everybody. And between AIDS and the wars and every possible misfortune, there are plenty of funerals. Eduardo, my houseboy, he was gone ten days last month."

"It's sad," I said.

"Is it?" Whitey said. "I'm not so sure. Someone dies, they call in the trucks, everyone piles on and everybody catches up. It's community. We may live longer back home but we live lonelier."

"It must be lonely for you out here," I said.

"Me? Not at all. I have my work and I get out every now and then. You know I met this guy. He's a doorman in a hotel in Lome in Togo. Ever been to Togo?"

"No."

"Togo isn't bad, if you don't mind the government. They don't like what the newspaper writes, they draft the editor and journalist into the army and send him to the outback. An easy way to get rid of problems."

"I guess so."

"Anyway, this chap is a hotel driver who is taking me to the airport. And I'm making conversation, so I asked him if he had any brothers and sisters. He said, 'From *my* mother, I have eight.' He emphasized 'my,' so I asked him if his father had other wives. He said, 'Yeah, my father had sixteen wives and 92 children. He was a Chief.' Isn't that incredible? You've got to figure that the previous Chief had about the same number of kids, and the one before that too. If you go back four generations, how many kids is that?"

"It's like that chess board puzzle," I said. "You put one grain of wheat on the first square, and double it each square, and you get enough food to feed the world."

"That's right, something like that," he said. "Say about two-thirds of the Chief's kids survive, which is about standard here. So the first generation has 60 kids and their offspring has six kids each on average, except for the next chief with 60 more and you keep going like that for four generations. I figure four generations produces about 115,000 people. Five generations is 700,000. Now they say there are fifty tribes in the country. Fifty times seven hundred-thousand is thirty-five million which can't be possible unless a lot of guys left for Paris or died or never had kids or the kids died. And then you figure that's the level of life, births, disease, and suffering. All those funerals. What should be a country of 35 million only has four million today."

Whitey was excited but lost in his world. And drunk.

"In the end, isn't it wonderful?" Whitey said. "All that family? Some place to go home to. It's humanity."

"But no family," I said.

"What?"

"You have no family," I said.

"I had a family in New York, growing up," he said sharply. "I don't need family." His mood dropped.

"Are you ready for retirement?"

"Me? You must be kidding. Look at all this, the beautiful water, the children, these shrimp, the warmth, the music, the agony of it all, and the passion. This is life. Why should I leave this? I like it too much. I was born for this."

I kicked aside a dog scrumming for shrimp shells. We looked out upon the flat and peaceful sea. The picture of a tropical paradise.

"Retirement has its benefits," I said.

"Yes," he smiled and waved his hands about. "But can you give me one reason why I'd want to? By the way, another beer?"

"Who's Francoise Leclerc?" I asked

He looked at me. "Who?"

"Francoise Leclerc of Abidjan."

He sipped from his beer. I detected a slight smile. "A friend," he said, quietly.

"A friend?" I said.

"Yes."

"Interesting. She says she's your wife."

"You spoke with her, I see."

"Yes," I said.

"Well then," he looked into my eyes. "I guess she must be. When did you speak with her?"

"Two days ago, in Abidjan," I said.

"You were in Abidjan?" he said.

"Yes."

"I didn't know."

"I was."

He said, "I like Abidjan. Nice restaurants, interesting people. A warm, French paradise."

"Do you love her?" I asked.

"Of course. She's my wife. She is a wonderful woman, don't you think?"

"So I guess you're not so lonely, with a family," I said.

"She's far away," he said, "but it helps."

"Who's Ima Mboko?" I asked. His eyes closed and I paused. "You've got one in every port, don't you?"

"Did you see Ima too?"

"Yes, as a matter of fact."

"When?"

"Yesterday, in Nairobi."

"You've been travelling a lot," he said.

Whitey was cool. He kept the banter going without any emotion or any sign of desperation.

"You still married to Jeri, that Australian woman?'

"Am I going to be arrested for bigamy?"

"No," I said. "Bigamy isn't against the law here."

"So it's just a little detail for the file," he said.

"What turned us on to these women were your irregular travel patterns. A week in Abidjan, a week in Nairobi. That, and your telephone calls."

"I missed them," Whitey said.

"Yes, of course," I said. "But you can't expect the US taxpayer to support a global orgy, you flying about the continent on business that's really pleasure, can you?"

"I'll refund the money," he said.

"It's not that simple, Whitey."

He chuckled, sipped and looked at me. "You really are a son of a bitch," he said. "You've been playing me."

"It's just a job, like yours." He knew what I knew, that the food problem and the disappearance of the food worker needed a scapegoat.

"I can't believe it," he said. "You're in a place where aid money vanishes, lands torn by mines and grenades and you're taking me down for this? A little joy on the side?"

"Yes."

"I keep my pension?"

"That depends. You admit your errors in the food program. You describe how you were negligent in not keeping better records that show how local officials sold it abroad."

"You want me to fall on my sword."

"It's up to you. You can work with us and keep your pension and the investigation will close."

He looked straight into my eyes. "The investigation closes?"

"Yes."

"What about that missing consultant?"

"Who gives a shit about him?" I said. "Yesterday's headlines. A war victim."

"I see the point," he said. "I can consult for AID after retirement?"

"Maybe after a couple of years. I think you should take a vacation, maybe to Abidjan or Nairobi or someone else we didn't look into?"

"No, that's it." He sighed and walked to the edge of the verandah. "So how do we handle the hearing tomorrow?"

"No hearing tomorrow, Whitey. This was the hearing."

He smiled again. "Good work you do."

"I have a lot of practice. You'll submit your letter of resignation and sign a confidentiality agreement and we take it from there. You have any problem with that?"

"Problem?" He hesitated. "No, I don't think so."

After it all, the shrimp and the beer, the sun and the interrogation, Whitey stood, the sun in his face, his white shirt still neat and tidy, looking as comfortable and laid back as could be. I wondered how well he would do at home. We don't much brook middle-aged men married to four women, do we?

"Want to have a last beer?" he said.

"No, you go ahead."

"How about some more shrimp? They're awfully good. I'm gonna miss them."

"Yeah, why not," I said. "OK, I'll have a beer." My willpower is quite poor and I liked this Whitey, his style and coolness.

"I was thinking of heading to Johannesburg," I said. "I understand it's quite beautiful. Maybe spend a couple of days hanging out. What do you think?"

He shrugged. "Johannesburg? I wouldn't recommend it. Too big. Dangerous, too." He turned and faced me. "Unless you have business there, it's not worth the visit."

"Business? No, not that I'm aware. I guess I'll head north to Lisbon. They say that's nice."

"Yes," he said. "Lisbon is preferable. Quite pretty."

Whitey did have a fourth wife. I did not ask him about Lucy da Sa, his Johannesburg wife or friend or whatever you might call her. We discovered she was his business partner in a little company that assisted Russian traders to sell grains on the local market. It wasn't too prosperous a business. They had maybe half a million in the bank.

But I said nothing. After all, I needed to control the situation, keep it quiet and avoid the embarrassment. If Lucy came out, the IRS would get involved. So would Treasury, Commerce and Agriculture. Congressional hearings would be called, wasting a ton of time and then, around election time, a major fracas. Who knows what else they might uncover? Who knows who might be next to fall on a sword? Best to leave it lay. Whitey's South African bank account would give him an extra bonus for taking the blame.

I took the pre-dawn flight from Maputo, scheduled early to avoid the risk of missile attacks from the guerrillas in the outback. The plane headed north up the East Coast of Africa. The red, rising sun reflected off streams and rivers draining from the highlands, the Limpopo, Zambezi, Luanga, and the hundreds of other rivulets that fall from the central plateau and casting an image of thin blood veins running across the earth's blackness. Short flashes of sunlight reflected up from the water, blinding the eye.

It was a sight to behold.

Africa is so beautiful.

RACE

(1992)

**Yugoslavia dissolves—Bosnia War—Peace in El Salvador—End of
the Cold War—The European Union founded—Power-sharing in
South Africa—John Major becomes Prime Minister, UK—Civil War in
Afghanistan—Bill Clinton elected President—NAFTA—End of Civil
War in Mozambique**

IT WAS ONE OF THOSE MISSIONS you don't give much thought to. Everyone in government knew apartheid was ending and the Boers were passing power peacefully to Mandela. Wally Stein called and asked if I wanted to do a quick trip to South Africa, to develop a strategy to support small business under the incoming government. Very Wally, wanting to get into the action first.

Wally introduced me to Pierre LeMay. African-American, mild-mannered, Yale-educated, a Democrat with a capital D and a Brookings Institute fellow. He specialized in Africa, Wally said, and was close to Mandela's African National Congress.

Pierre was good-looking with a slight body and a jaunty way about him. Quite personable, he was the darling of the DC liberal establishment until they realized that trust was not part of his portfolio. Wally named me head of the mission with Pierre as my subordinate. He trusted me.

Nothing is ever simple in DC where bureaucratic gorillas are always ready to pounce. Wally was a Republican hired by Bush the First to promote private sector development, foreign investment, that sort of thing—policies antithetical to the Democratic hierarchy that had just taken over. He had a solid contract that ran years into the Clinton administration, but the new liberal boys and girls on the top floor of Foggy Bottom kept Wally cornered in his office, ideologically and personally, treating him as a contagious alien. But there was little they could do. He had his contract.

Pierre and I spent two weeks in Joberg. He was polite but there was always an edge, a permanent stand-offish attitude which I ignored. In matters of race, best to let the great divide pass. At first, we interviewed all the usual suspects, ANC officials talking of new and hopeful policies to transform South Africa and create an African heaven for the Black majority living in poverty and despair. We met with civil rights activists and black businessmen champing at the bit to gain control of corporate wealth. Hope is such a lovely and romantic feeling. Amazing how we fall over and over again for the same dreams.

As the project progressed, Pierre failed to show up. He missed meetings and then would reappear in the evening, mentioning something about Winnie Mandela or ANC affairs, even as he made clear it wasn't my business. Then, one weekend, we were invited out to the home of Sue Lakely, a petite blonde, slim and well-kept with a bright and cheerful personality. She was a leader of the whites fighting to end apartheid, married to an insurance executive. Her house had a long lawn, a swimming pool, and a tennis court.

Pierre and I hit a few balls, and Sue did not hide her admiration for my opponent. After tennis, we dove into the pool. While I waded about, Pierre swam laps with a well-trained crawl and then turned to backstrokes. He waved at Lakely. We had gin and tonics and cold-meat vetkoek, and we spoke about the coming transition. She gushed about how the great man Mandela was going to handle the ANC divisions, reveling in the optimism in the air for the new age. It was a beautiful, sunny day, a touch of paradise in the white, well-manicured Joberg suburbia, just a few miles from Soweto hovels. I dozed off.

When I awoke Pierre told me he was staying. Would I mind taking the car back to the hotel? He would join me the following morning. I am not a puritan, so I said of course. Pierre was married to Karabo, a tall and elegant woman from South Africa, with two young kids back home in Virginia. She spoke with a gentle lilt, a hint of Dutch and English. A fling on the road was certainly not unique among foreign workers and I certainly would never blow any whistle, discretion being paramount for professional survival.

I continued on with the interviews and he reappeared a few days later. Nothing more was said. We returned home and I wrote a report. I passed it to Pierre for comments before submitting it for review. The usual procedure. He never responded. A couple of weeks later, I was called to a meeting with the new Clinton appointees. We sat at a round table with a dozen men and women in their thirties, perfect suits, the latest fashions in ties and shoes. Very expensive and very white, except for Pierre.

They attacked. Why was I leading the mission given that Pierre was black and me, white? And he an African expert? A dozen bureaucrats, all young and strident, were essentially calling me a racist.

I played dumb. "That was Wally's call. He's head of the African department bureau, and he made these decisions." I gave Wally cover, though: "My understanding was that he wanted someone with years of experience to run the mission."

This enraged the mob. "But Pierre knew South Africa and was friendly with all the leadership of the ANC. Didn't you think it would look bad having you running the show?"

I shrugged my shoulders. "I wasn't running the show. We worked as partners."

The interrogation went on. I did not mention Pierre's fling with Mrs. Lakely on "company time" or how he begged off our Joberg interviews claiming he wasn't feeling well. Too much exertion that he wasn't used to, he said at the time, the entendre understood. I did not mention any of this. Wasn't worth it. The ambush was well organized. But I did pull out my calendar with the interview notes that detailed who participated and which showed the days Pierre went missing. I offered it to the lynch mob. They were not interested.

"Well, I'm going to xerox this and pass it on to all of you so you can judge what and what did not go on." I stared at Pierre.

For two hours they cross examined me, the contractor with no authority whatsoever, the contractor, always the one to crucify when things go wrong and they, the newly-appointed senior officers of AID, men and women garbed in Brooks Brothers, delighted in their authority and freely deploying the race card, the ultimate bludgeon, although their skin was lily white.

There is no defense against implied racism, the subtle "uh-huh." These suburban Ivy League elitists accusing me, a subway-riding New York public-school boy of racism. That bothered me to no end.

I kept thinking back to Bob Lee. It was 1959 and I was fifteen, working as a waiter at a kid's camp. I didn't fit in. The other staff came from the same suburban school and saw me, a city boy, as a nerd. Worse, I was a clumsy waiter and the target of angry rages from the cook, a huge, angry Irish woman.

Bob Lee was the dishwasher, a black veteran of the Korean War and a drunk. Who knows what horrors he suffered for his country? After one particularly bad day he invited me to go fishing on the mountain lake. It was a lovely day. The lake was nestled amongst the Catskill pines. We dropped our lines, he lit a Camel cigarette, pulled out a flask and took a drink. He offered but I turned him down.

We sat quietly and then he said "Hey, you got soul?"

"What?"

"Soul, you got soul?"

I didn't know what he was talking about. "You know Robert Johnson, Chuck Berry, Nat Cole, John Lee Hooker."

"I don't think so."

"No, man. You from the city. You got soul and don't you forget it."

"Yeah, I guess so."

"Yeah man. You got soul."

The following week I dropped a jug of cocoa, causing a huge mess. The Irish cook screamed and Bob Lee ran to my defense. She turned and threw him out. And with that, Bob Lee disappeared from my life.

As I sat before this Washington witch trial, I couldn't believe that I, the city boy, was being accused of racism, me from the city where ethnic colors flowed freely, in the subways, on the streets, in the parks and on the beaches. My high school was public, not an upper-class private school. Half the students were black. Good fellows, young and optimistic in a generation of hope, hope that was to shatter for African-American men in Civil Rights riots, as draftees in Vietnam, as drug addicts and as jailed criminals. Not all mind you, but enough to make me mourn for the country and race.

I shuttered before my accusers. Orwell had nothing like this, I thought.

Wally sat quietly next to me, saying nothing. The meeting had reached a dead-end. Finally, I sighed and said, "I thought we were here to discuss the final report."

Didn't I know that Pierre had submitted his own report? they responded. I was surprised. No, he never showed it to me. "Might I see it?" I asked the tribunal. No, I might not, they answered. If I had been given such a report, I said, I would certainly have integrated his findings.

I never saw his report and doubted either its existence or its quality. But that was not the point. The knives were out for Wally through me, just another DC civil war fought among and between lower level officials who deemed their new jobs critical to the world, ideological children playing at a reality that scarcely mattered.

Don't get me wrong. The Republicans do the same when they take charge. It's called "cleaning house," hiring political allies and children of their patrons. Burning the opposition at the stake. It's the nature of the beast.

"Don't worry about Pierre," Wally said that evening. "He's like all these new kids on the block. They come with such high hopes, ambitions to save the world, young and ambitious, then they end up in a tight cubicle, tied to regulations and red tape and their frustration grows. They want power. They want influence. They want to move up to the next level and, if they are successful in their quest, to the next and then the next and if they are not successful they do horrible things to their families and friends and colleagues. They cheat, they drink, and they growl at their so-called failures. And if they are successful and move to the next level and then the next they eventually go over the cliff and find there is nothing left in their lives. They're vipers, sitting at desks, judging others, plotting personal gains and, at AID, all in the name of humanitarianism."

It was the DC game; just roll with the punches and move on. You see it every day in hearings where Congressmen fry low-level bureaucrats for carrying out policies the same Congress enacted. I knew it wouldn't affect my life or career; Wally would see to that. But for days I kept fighting at that round table, muttering to myself, drinking too much and pacing late into the night.

What is the defense for being attacked publicly by sinners for sins that you have not committed? What is the cure for the sense of powerlessness we all must feel at some time or another? Especially in this age when shouts of racism permeate every part of the nation in one form or another. I don't know the answer but I do know that accusations of all sorts are bandied about by those seeking advantage. And that continues to make me tremble.

I didn't go quietly, though. A couple of weeks later, I purchased an Omega watch from a high-end Georgetown jeweler, carefully choosing the largest and most ostentatious one, and drove out to Pierre's home in mid-afternoon. It was a typical, split-level house, with a large backyard and an in-ground swimming pool. African masks decorated a living room with modest, white furniture. I sat and spoke with Karabo, his wife, laughing about the good times Pierre and I had in Joberg. She was enticing, personable, and sympathetic, unlike her husband. Her kids ran about, showing off. A large, tan Rhodesian Ridgeback, watched me with a suspicious eye, protecting the family.

Pierre was late, so we enjoyed lots of whiskey and cashews. We were having great fun when he finally arrived. He looked at me and then at his wife. "What's going on?"

"Good to see you, Pierre," I said. "We were just going over the fun we had on our trip."

"Yes?"

"Yes. Good times, they were." I was laying it on a bit much, but whiskey and a beautiful woman do that.

"OK," he said, suspiciously. "Can I help you?"

"Actually, I'm helping you." He looked bemused. "You left your watch in my office."

I pulled out the Omega. It gleamed what with the jewels and the gold watchband. Karabo glared at Pierre. Something was not right, I thought.

"That's not my watch," he exclaimed, somewhat guiltily.

"Yes, I'm sure you left it."

"No. I wasn't in your office."

"You weren't? I was sure I recalled you dropping by. Soon after our return. To discuss the report."

He yelled. "That's not my fucking watch!"

"Pierre!" Karabo exclaimed. "Your friend is trying to return something and you treat him like this." The Ridgeback sprang to its feet and ran to me, snarling. I sat back while she grabbed the dog and put him in the corner. She turned, angrily.

"Are you sure it's not yours?" I said.

"No," he began to shake, looking at his wife. "It is not mine."

The thing about sneaks is that no matter what they do, they always seem guilty. There was no need to prolong the fun. The damage was done. "Well, I must be mistaken. I was sure but if you insist. It is a very nice watch. I guess I'll have to keep it as a souvenir of good times.

"You do that," Pierre said.

"Well, it was great speaking with Karabo." I turned and kissed her on the cheek. "You have a wonderful family. You take care of them Pierre, ya'hear?" Yes, I put on a southern drawl. Liquor does that to me sometimes.

As I drove home, Brown and Roach played "Green Dolphin Street" on the radio. "I sure love the human race," I thought.

I returned the watch to the dealer for a refund. I certainly couldn't afford anything like that. Pierre hung on in Washington for a few more years until Clinton left office. He was quite influential in running projects, determining their goals and hiring South African consultants. When Bush Junior took office, he migrated to South Africa. He teaches American studies at a University, I'm told.

I never saw him again.

JOHN BASS IN TIRANA

(1993)

European single market formed– Sri Lankan Civil War—Bosnian
War—Bill Clinton becomes President—World Trade Center bombing—
Windows OS—US defeat in Somalia– NAFTA

"You've never heard of John Bass?"

"No," I said.

"The great American guitarist?" He was astonished.

"No, never heard of him."

*"In the darkest days of the dictatorship, my cassette of John Bass kept
me going. You sure you never heard of John Bass?"*

This is Nestor, the energetic twenty-seven-year-old Albanian Vice-Minister of Finance, a survivor of the tyrannical dictatorship of Emir Hoxha and my guide to the depths that perverse ideology wrought.

Here I am, once again on a prop airplane, circling Albania, a nation recently freed from a tyrant's terror and renowned for its backwardness, isolation, and skullduggery. Roughly the size of New Jersey, it is said to be poorest nation in Europe. Three million people live here, mostly rural, most in desperate need. As we approach, I look into darkness and see a few faint glows. Landings are usually filled with light from cities or cars or streetlights. Not here. What waits ahead? What to do when I arrive?

It's early December, and my boss Wally asked me to do a job for the Italians. The Italian aid agency was under a cloud, something about the government subsidizing the sale of a frozen food plant from a bankrupt Milan firm to the Central African Republic, where frozen food is absurd given the lack of electricity. The Italians needed someone clean, someone beyond suspicion. Like Caesar's wife.

I met with the Italians in the Palazzo della Farnesina, the gigantic and ornate Mussolini creation that now serves as the Ministry of Foreign Affairs in Rome. We lunched at the Ministry club, along the banks of the Tiber with swimming pools, tennis courts and children scurrying all about. In aid there is profit.

On the plane to Tirana, I am seated next to Richard Cleveland, a gruff, grey-suited American businessman who carries evidence of the good life bulging about his waist. Cleveland is an engineer who has spent his life engineering in Ohio. Two kids. Two grandchildren. Pictures. A dog, too. First time in Eastern Europe, he says, although he was once in Paris with his wife on one of those two week tours. Didn't like it much.

George Soros asked him to check out the Tirana water system which is in terrible shape, leakage, bacteria backing-up from sewerage into the drinking water. New machinery needed. Chemicals too. The country too broke to pay. Cleveland was approached because he knows water, pipes and reservoirs and sanitation and could afford a few days and do some good. Won't do it too much, he tells me. Doesn't like to leave home.

We land roughly, chump-chump-chump-ing along the cobblestone runway. The airport is small and worn, chipped paint, broken windows and a few dim lights. Gangs of men mull about, looking tough, unshaven, old clothes, grim faced. I had faxed the government to send a car, but there was none. No expectations, no disappointments.

Cleveland is met at the airport by a Soros' employee, K, a handsome young man in jeans and a stylish ski jacket. He speaks English. The driver is not happy about me, a stranger, coming along for the ride. In these circumstances, everybody is suspicious. Of everybody. The driver directs Cleveland to the front. K and I are sent to the rear. From time to time the driver turns to K and says something in Albanian. I look at them as they speak. The driver looks at me. I have often been accused of understanding foreign languages. I look into eyes and at facial expressions and my face responds in kind. I smile at people laughing and stare at their serious faces. I look for their meaning as they speak incomprehensively, a tradition borne from an eternal and frustrating search for understanding in the Babeled world.

The van moves into the darkness. I see nothing. No lights, a few lorries, from time to time, a brief halt at a police checkpoint. Flashlights shine about the van and we are waved through. K is, like me, from the Bronx. His father is Kosovan who fled to Italy in 1945 and then to America. He worked as a handyman but returned home to smuggle out family, bringing them to America and arranging work. Haven't you heard of Abdullah? K asks. He is very famous. He manages large apartment houses in the Bronx and has done so well now he owns four of them. Employs many Kosovans.

I know about what is called the Albanian Kosovan "mafia," not pejoratively. The doorman in my building as well as the building superintendent next door and the carpenter who redid my kitchen the year before are all Albanians. The owner of the pizza chain, Famiglia, is Kosovan, as are most cooks in Italian restaurants.

After a half-hour of bumps and curves, we arrive in town. Cleveland stays at the Soros facility and, sorry, there is no room for me. I am dropped at the Tirana Hotel. It is full, I am told. Absolutely no space. K says not to worry. Just wait. We stand silent, out of small talk. The hotel is cold and I am fading from the long day's journey. The clerk appears more interested in chatting up a woman than finding a bed for me. The electricity is out and he reads the scribbled roster using a fluorescent flashlight. He mumbles in Albanian. I hate people who mumble.

This is not Africa; it's worse. Everything is dim. No lights on the road and none in the city. No emergency systems. No room at the inn. K talks to the clerk who turns the pages on the ledger back and forth; he pauses and moves back to his friend down the counter. They laugh. He wears grey, worn sweaters, layered on top of each other. She is in a heavy coat. She leans towards him seductively. He lights a cigarette and hands it to her. He lights another for himself.

Never get impatient in developing lands. Impatience only hurts the self. Ignore the headache, the exhaustion, the grim perspective before the eyes, and just wait and observe. Let time go by. Hum a song. Write a mental letter. Think of todos. Have an internal conversation with the wife.

The clerk and woman end their flirtation. He wanders back, looks at the log again, mumbles, turns the pages and looks up. Yes, there is a room. 604. Only for one night, mind you, just one night. Yes, that would be greatly appreciated, I say. But just one night. The next day, I am to move out. Is that clear? Certainly.

Before departing, K tells me not to worry about leaving. Just stay on. There is no system and the night porter will not talk to the day man. I have a bed. A glorious bed.

I glance at the key and then realize there's no electricity. How do I get to the sixth floor? I point upstairs and the clerk shrugs. Some language is universal. Shrug = Not my problem. He lights another cigarette and drifts away. I grab my heavy bag and head to the dark stairs. I feel my way up, one step at a time, one hand on a banister, pausing to catch my breath, awaiting a glimmer of light. I arrive panting and sweating in my overcoat, the bag dragging behind me. The floor maid comes with a flashlight and lights the candle.

The room is small and barren. It is cold. Bitterly cold. No hot water. An old shortwave radio sits useless by the bed. A thin towel hangs in the bathroom, brown lye soap on the sink. Much more than I hoped. The sweat on my body quickly chills. I undress, jump into sweatpants and throw a sweater over my tired, fetid white shirt, the product of a day's pilgrimage from the height of civilization to the depths of Europe. Deep sleep.

But then I awake. The blanket is thin, and the room is like ice. I need to pee but am too paralyzed for the hididdydiddy scamper. The bathroom faucets drip continuously. The cold permeates the building, the walls, the floors, the bed and enters my body like a virus, grabs my bones, my nerves, and takes hold.

The year before during a harsh winter, Albanians took to the mountains and cut down trees for warmth, deforesting most of the nation. I now understand why. I shiver constantly. This year, the Swiss donated electric heaters. But, as the cold descends and the heaters are switched on, the power surges through fragile lines and the city blacks out and the cold returns.

I sleep in heavy layers. Two pair of sweatpants beneath a crumpled wool suit. I drink whiskey. "A good schnapps to stay warm," my grandmother used to say. The next day, I take a Mercedes taxi and have the driver turn on the heat. We drive the city in the good German artificial heat. The joy of warmth returns.

I work for the Ministry of Trade. It's not an easy assignment, but that's why they call it work. Two years ago, the present government took power, throwing out the Communists. It announced it would distribute the government agricultural land to farmers as their private property. A good thing, I believe, for the future. The basis for rural democracy. But, that first democratic year, the announcement paralyzed the farmers. Who owned what land and who was to pay for seed and fertilizer? Nobody planned and nobody planted. There was no money. No seeds. No fertilizer. And come the winter, there was no food stored from the year's harvest.

Starvation resulted. The Italian army landed, bringing basic foodstuffs. It saved the country. This year, seed and fertilizer and cattle are handed out. Now it is time to build a government.

The Finance Ministry is in a decrepit office building from the old regime. A new Mercedes sits out front. Men stand on the steps, smoking. A concierge sits downstairs, knitting. The building is dim.

Still no power. I meet the Minister sitting in my overcoat. He is a nice lad twenty-eight years of age. Handsome and well-groomed in a fine, Italian suit. We might be in Rome. He was educated in the local state college. An engineer, like everyone else. That's all they taught back then. No need for thought.

He welcomes me and begins the speech of the nations, the speech I hear wherever I work. He insists his country is open to learning because this is the future and the future must be seized. As Minister, he is learning about commerce and finds it very interesting. Learning as he goes. And he is open to my recommendations. In the speech of the nations, one offers platitudes and clichés. A politician's speech. I listen and respond the programmed response. I am honored to be a part of the nation's future. I hope to contribute and that we, he and I, may have a free and open dialogue.

The problem of new governments. When new governments take over, be they in Eastern Europe or Africa, new leaders appoint their cronies, school chums, and families. Many are intelligent if uneducated, their learning coming solely from books, BBC or Voice of America and with an idealized vision of the world. In Africa, they are army Sergeants or the President's sons. In Albania, they are students from the technical university, trained to be mechanics or electricians. Each is given a Ministry to manage, and they must learn on the job. It is they who now determine the nation's future.

What is the capacity of a people, even the most intelligent, to adjust or to adapt, a people that has been subject to war and generations of a dictatorship bent on keeping out foreign influences? Young men and women, with ideals, ruling over a rusted hulk of a nation that lacks food, power, good water, industry, education and experience.

If the handicaps to a new leadership are obvious, the cancerous enticements from aid agencies are less so. What is needed is expertise, infrastructure, international guidance, and time to learn how to rule. What is provided Monsieur le Minister is a new Italian suit, a fancy Mercedes, and trips abroad, to Rome to improve food imports, to

Brussels to negotiate trade policy, to New York for the UN, to Vienna for bilateral relations, Athens for regional cooperation, Washington to the World Bank, meetings with businessmen in London, all paid for by ingratiating, seductive foreign governments, transportation, hotel and a large enough per diem to purchase souvenirs, suits, dresses, VCRs, and cameras, to bring home to a nation in need of intelligent rule, leaving nobody at home to rule. Then, the young Ministers realize they are important. They are at the highest levels of government. There must be protocol. There must be respect. No time to look in the mirror to realize who they are, to understand their crippling circumstance. These new states are like kids in the candy store, as foreign governments climb over each other to exert influence and develop markets for their goods.

This is but the beginning—the descent of donors, with assistance and programs for development, bringing hard currency, computers, high-paying jobs for the Ministers' cronies or family. Trade may be important, but exports take time. Donor money is coming in now and the Minister must travel to Geneva to organize a mission.

The Minister will be away for a while, he says, travelling abroad. In his absence, he has asked Nestor to be my guide and my partner. I am to work with him to improve trade policy. Of course. Yes, Minister. For the future of the country.

Nestor is not the only twentysomething in the upper echelons of the new government. The Undersecretary for State Enterprises is 24, the Bilateral Relations Department, 29. The Ministry is crammed with eager, young folk. I like Nestor, and he likes me. His face shines with hope of the new nation of the possibilities. He speaks English well, self-taught by listening to the shortwave. It was illegal back then. Had to keep the volume down. He joined a group to learn English, meeting in each other's basements, drifting in so as not to attract suspicion. They turned on VOA or BBC and listened to the lessons and practiced amongst themselves.

It is like a 1930s movie, I realize, people huddled in ragged clothes around a radio, listening for the truth. They resisted the dictator through language, he says; he speaks German, Italian, and English. And through books, smuggled from house to house. He has a book by Freud and one by Sartre. And music. He particularly likes John Bass, the American guitar player. Don't I know John Bass? No, I tell him. He is incredulous. Everybody knows John Bass. Do I like to run? Maybe we'll go running someday.

He leads me from meeting to meeting, to the Ministry of Finance to speak of trade flows, to the Ministry of Economy to speak of privatization strategies, to the state-run import-export firm that handles all the food imports. I shiver from the cold while officials explain how a new beginning was at hand, that the wealth of Albania will finally be manifest and the great nation will form a part of Europe. Cigarette smoke in rooms with closed windows.

They wish to privatize the state trading company to attract foreign investment. It will be a golden age. I do not ask the obvious: Who would buy the state trading firm? It is worthless. But protocol dictates that I say we must look into this and my interlocutor smiles. Indeed, a study might be commissioned using aid funds, a foreign expert recruited and brought over to write a study.

Between meetings, Nestor and I chat and drink coffee at kiosks, small prefab structures with enough room for an espresso machine, a gift of the Italians, a counter and a couple of tables inside. Most clients sit outside, despite the cold. The tiny huts dot downtown. More espresso than in Roma.

After the revolution, the government moved to privatize the state stores, distributing them to those who had worked in them under the dictatorship. The fastest way to create private enterprise was to jump-start, it was thought. For the ex-political prisoners, the move was an insult. After all, who ran the old shops but the old Communists? And were they to be rewarded for the years of oppression?

In the beginning, the ex-Communists monopolized commerce but then the human spirit arose. Someone laid a blanket in a public park to sell small imported items, smuggled goods, toothpaste, batteries, chewing gum, bananas, oranges, petit beurre bisquets, Snickers, chocolate or large bottles of "Joke"—a copied Coke. And then a small building was thrown up, a kiosk, really the remanufactured body of an old truck, on the grass next to the river. And then another kiosk appeared in the grassy knoll next to the presidential palace. After a while, wherever there was empty space, on sidewalks, in empty lots, espresso huts sprung up.

Around the kiosks are gangs of stern-faced, unshaven men, smoking, sipping coffee, talking and waiting, standing about and staring. What is there is do in a country without industry? Of what do they talk? Are they plotting a revolution? Are they dreaming romantic thoughts? Who knows? At first, I believe them unfriendly from their harsh stares, but they are as polite as can be when language divides. They stand and offer their seats. They offer cigarettes, America's gift to the world. They smile when their pidgin English is not understood. These gangs wander about, like geese in a field, smoking and smoking. Men without work, biding their time.

Tirana is dark, gloomy and cold, with a whiff of Eric Ambler, a center of Eastern European international espionage and intrigue. Men in trench coats wander in alleys while foreigners dribble in and out of office buildings, seeking allies. The Turks are here, negotiating political and military alliances. They plot, if you believe the Greeks, a political "crescent" from Istanbul through Bulgaria and Macedonia to Albania, isolating Greece with the goal of seizing Cyprus. The Iranians build mosques with community centers to teach their truth. French and German NATO-men inspect airstrips just in case the Serbs keep expanding. The Austrians seek building contracts. The Greeks come bearing gifts. Bananas. Coffee. Oranges. Joke Cola. Condoms.

I head to the currency market, where a horde of moneychangers stand in a small square with cash rolls exposed, much like medieval Florence. The birth of capitalism, buy-sell, buy-sell. A guy approaches, and we negotiate the exchange rate. The other men pull back. The rules of the local game. In Africa, a buyer is besieged by sellers, each shouting a different price. Here, it's one-on-one. I buy Lek and my moneychanger smiles at me. I am obviously nervous, stuffing the bills in my pocket.

"Be careful," he says. "Divide up your money. Button your pocket. Don't worry. It is safe here. We would kill anyone who tries to steal." He is not smiling. "But out on the streets, it is not so sure."

He leads me to a brazier and buys me a thick, juicy sausage plumped in a hunk of bread. A royal profit was earned, I fear. "The next time you need money, you come to me," he says. "I'll buy you another sandwich. You understand? To me. I'll give you a good deal."

My moneychanger is an Albanian from Sicily, who learned English from Italians back from America. Albanians have lived in Sicily for hundreds of years, he says. Speaking Albanian. Why did he come back? There is more money in Tirana then Italy. For now, anyway. This will not last, and he will not stay. But he will go home a little richer.

I meet a corpulent Greek businessman. "Where are you from?" he asks. The consultant must be wary but open to all encounters. I answer the query and so begins the litany. He speaks English well and is the representative of a shipping firm. Most of the emergency aid comes through his container ships and he facilitates operations. Yes, he knows New York well, and mentions a few landmarks. The conversation wears thin.

This is where I always get into trouble, in parties, meetings and casual talk. "Explain to me," I say, "what is going on between Macedonia and Greece." The Greeks have amassed an army on the border with their much smaller, northern neighbor because it calls itself Macedonia. The name Macedonia is Greek, he asserts. It cannot be stolen by another country. He is irritated. No, there is absolutely no compromise over the issue.

And so I say, "Frankly, we in the United States do not understand why you would fight over this."

"That is because," he says angrily, "in the United States you do not have history."

I back down. History, the refuge of nationalists and scoundrels. The Albanians are the original Illyrians, their history tells them. They speak an Illyrian language. They are ethnically pure. In the middle of Tirana stands Skanderbeg, the national hero who successfully fought the Turks five hundred years ago. The overthrown tyrant Hoxha saw himself as a modern-day Skanderbeg, defending Albania from outside infidels.

Albanians extol their racial purity. How they are the purest race in Europe with the purest language. Their books, teachers and myths tell them they must fight the outsider. Yet, this race is not pure. These Albanians are as mixed and mongreled as Americans. Blond and black hair, light, olive and dark skin, blue and brown eyes, they are a rainbow group. Most Albanians practice moderate Islam and live side-by-side with Albanian Orthodox and Catholics. Their culture, at least in Tirana, is a mélange of Italian television and Balkan tradition, beautiful women dressed like Italian soap operas stars, tight and sexy.

Nestor and I drive into the countryside. Once tree-lined roads are now bordered with stumps. "The government didn't move fast enough," Nestor says, "so the peasantry seized the olive groves and cut them down. Ten and twenty years of productivity wiped out on a few cold nights." Erosion is everywhere and the roads are flooded. An escarpment rises rapidly from the Adriatic into low, white hills. Rocky, Mediterranean soil. We might as well be in Spain or Greece.

We pass horse drawn carts crammed with hay. Sheep graze on the hills. Gray, decrepit structures rise on the horizon, light shining through their holes. As we approach, the tall rusting factories come into focus, with broken windows, crumbling walls, and twisted steel bars. Orange and blue chemicals leech from rusted tanks. Garbage is strewn along the fences. We turn and head into the mountains, coming upon cypress trees that blend into pines as the land rises. Nearby mosques and churches seem to protect them.

The countryside is dotted with white cement pill boxes, some large enough for a few men, others for a tank, all facing the sea to ward off the inevitable attack from foreigners, to fight the five hundred year old battles against invading Ottomans invaders or against the Italians and Germans in the next World War. Hoxha planned this defense, unmindful of modern warfare like the airplane or heavy artillery. 700,000 of these strange, obsolete but omnipresent bunkers spread all over the country. They will stay in the fields and the mountains for an eternity. How does one dispose of reinforced concrete buried deep into the soil?

We meet the city council of Lushnje, an agricultural community known for its jams and liqueurs. They are eight men with aged and weathered faces. An elderly woman brings mineral water and coffee. The room is small and dusty, the windows closed. The air fills with cigarette smoke.

I talk of my fact-finding mission to find out how America can help develop investment and trade. I would like to hear what the region needs to grow and enter the world economy.

Nestor translates. They wonder if it is possible to get American financing to develop their industries.

"It is possible," I say, "but we would have to bring out others to survey the situation." I cough and choke from the smoke.

"They say they can get credit now," Nestor says, "but it is very expensive and America could help if it would lend them money at lower rates since they now are a free country."

"You must explain to them that America provides some assistance for small companies but large investments must come from private sources."

The men do not smile. They seem aggravated as they speak. "Please, Nestor, I would like to know what they are saying."

"Yes," he replies. "Well, they don't understand why you can't finance them. They will pay it back. They always do. They say the banks don't do anything for them and the government is incompetent. In the old days, at least they could get some loans."

"Tell them I understand their frustration but the revolution is but two years old and it will take some time to develop financial institutions."

"They don't understand. I'm not quite sure I do either."

An elderly man stands. He points his finger at me and his voice rises. Nestor responds to him "What did he say?"

"It is not important," Nestor says.

"No. I need to know."

"What he said is you people came promising prosperity and freedom and all he has gotten is starvation and cold, that all the old values are gone, criminals are taking over and you won't do anything even though you come from a rich country. He says we know your capitalism is designed to steal our country and our resources. We don't need your help. That is what he said."

"Tell him this," I say. "Albania has lived in isolation for this entire century. You are just coming out of a terrible dictatorship. I cannot understand the suffering you went through but change will take time and patience. I am confident you will succeed and prosper. If you can get money from other sources, that is fine. That is what capitalism is all about."

"He wants to know how you can be so confident."

"Because this country is very rich and has been held back by bad government. You are a talented people."

The old man mutters, rises, and walks out.

"He is the former manager of the city bank, of the old guard," Nestor says. "He lost his job and is very bitter. But there is something else you should know. There are many, how do you say it, informal credit sources now."

"Informal credit?"

"We are a resourceful people. We have always survived despite the Nazis and the Communists and this Hoxha. Now that the Communists are gone, we are doing business, lots of business and so we are making money. I am invested in a fund that pays me 40 percent a month interest. It is good money."

"You get 40 percent a month interest? In dollars?"

"Yes."

"How is that possible?"

"It is possible. It is capitalism," he smiles.

"It is not possible," I say, "unless the risk is very high."

"No. No risk. Everybody is doing it, everybody with money."

"But who can pay these interest rates?"

"As I say, we are a resourceful people. We know how to make do. There are people who want to get to Europe, Turks, Kurds, Chinese, even Albanians. We have cigarette boats, these long thin boats that can carry eight people very fast to the shores of Italy. They pay $5,000 each for the trip."

"Smuggling people?"

"Yes."

"And the Italian Coast Guard?"

"Yes, once in a while a boat is captured. But more times than not arrangements are made for the return of the boat and if the boat is not returned, another is purchased. There is plenty of profit."

"That's illegal."

"Yes. So?"

"You are a member of the government, the head of the Ministry of Finance. You are putting your money into these funds?"

Nestor laughs. "Me? I put in a few dollars. Everybody does it. Did you see those guys standing on the square, outside your hotel? They're doing it, buying and selling people, cars, dollars, drugs. Whatever you want. The Minister himself is putting money into the funds. Everybody's doing it. It's capitalism."

"It's corruption. It makes Albania into an outlaw nation."

"I think you are being naïve. There are hardly any laws here anymore, except survival. The old ones are communist and the new ones are, let us say, obeyed rarely. We are a completely free market. After all, it is your capitalism." He throws up his hands.

"I am not naive," I say, irritation in my voice. "There are legal and illegal activities. And not only that, there's no way these funds can keep paying 40 percent interest."

"I'm not worried. Everybody's doing it. After all, look at Russia. They are stealing the country blind, getting money from you and putting it in banks. Selling gold and missiles and pocketing the money."

"I know that."

"What we do is so insignificant."

"Nestor," I put up my hands. "You win. I was wrong to have said that. I think countries work for goals like stability and justice. But it takes time."

We drive and arrive at a grassy knoll. He leads me to the top and a ruined archway. I stumble about mosaics hidden by grass and brush. Dolphins and lions and children stared out through the weeds.

"This is Apolonia," Nestor said. "A great Roman city. Julius Caesar rewarded Apolonia with the title of a "free city" for its support. His nephew Octavius, the future Emperor Augustus, studied here.

I look onto the valley beneath us. Cattle graze through empty scrubland. A mule stands beside an Eastern rite monastery. "It's wonderful," I say.

"Yes, it is," he said. "You know, we are the only pure race in Europe. Every other race is mixed, but not us. We remain pure." A return to that nationalistic impulse, sparked by a vestigial Roman town, a different time, a different civilization, and a different people.

The illness of the Balkans, the memory of the ages, the fear, the anger, and the hatred of the outside. Enemies seen all about. The Greek minority in the south. Will it secede? The Serbs in the north hate everyone, the Kosovans, the Bosnians and the Croats.

Hoxha, the paranoid dictator, insured that his people would never be threatened. He distributed television equipment capable of receiving only local programs and jammed radio signals from neighboring Italy and Yugoslavia. Music was played without words except for approved national hymns. He decided (as Mao had) that dogs kept workers awake at night and harmed productivity, so he ordered their extermination, creating an Anne Frank environment in which the canines were hidden in basements.

Albania should not rely on any country, Hoxha said. It had to be self-sufficient and manufacture everything. Electrical switches and fuse boxes, glass for housing and green houses, tires, fertilizer, cement, chemicals, clothing, pepper mills, and paper. And whatever Albania could not produce, it would not use.

To become self-sufficient, Hoxha created a nation of engineers and in this new age, the technicians devised methods to reach the outside world. They built televisions to receive foreign broadcasts and sold them on the black market. Foreign languages were learned from sitcoms and quiz shows. The result: teenage girls walked the streets of Tirana wearing homemade clothes copying Italian fashion.

Then the Communist tyranny collapsed. Ten percent of the nation was released from jails and work farms. Many had spent most of their lives under arrest. Burial sites were uncovered beneath soccer pitches. Lists were compiled of the disappeared.

The survivors' tales overwhelm me: A young woman was a university student eight years ago when her father was taken away. They sent her to a work farm where she remained until last year. She never saw him again. A doctor at the National Hospital tells me of how, in 1973, Hoxha liberalized the government and brought in a new, more trade-minded Prime Minister. Then the dictator changed his mind. After a state dinner, the Prime Minister supposedly committed suicide. The doctor found that this "suicide" came from two close-range bullets behind his ear lobe.

Back in Tirana, Nestor and I jog around the city's reservoir. He runs fast, pauses, returns, and jogs alongside me. The pavement is broken and I fear for a broken limb. Twice I broke legs, once in Morocco, playing soccer on the beach, and once in Uganda, playing tennis. I fear Tirana's hospitals far more than either of those. As we run, Nestor talks of his hopes, prancing from rock to rock, running with spirit. He says he applied for scholarships in the States, and I warn him not to be trapped by the American lure. He says there is no danger of that. He would never give up his family, friends and nation. I tell him the lure is irresistible. He says that he has a mission to work for his country.

We slow to a walk. "Will you come and meet my father," Nestor asks. "I told him about you."

"Of course."

"I also want to play John Bass for you."

"Oh yes, the famous John Bass."

"I'm sorry you have never heard of John Bass. I am very surprised."

"Well I haven't. Perhaps we can meet your father for dinner, in a restaurant. I will invite you."

"Thank you but my father cannot leave our house. He is in a wheelchair."

"Is he ill?"

"No, he is not." He falls silent.

"Nestor, what's wrong?"

We stop. "In 1953, Stalin died. The dictator Hoxha loved Stalin and he ordered all the men of Tirana to the central plaza. They put a portrait of Stalin on the wall and ordered everyone to prostrate themselves. For ten hours, they laid there. My father was young and a student at the University and he and his pals talked amongst themselves, making jokes and trying to endure the ordeal. It was like school the way they cheated and had fun. The next day, the police came and sent him and my mother to a work camp. For fifteen years."

"That's terrible."

"When he returned, he was a broken man. Physically, you know. He walked with a limp and had severe back pains. That's when they had me. For the last twenty years, he has been forced to do menial work, cleaning streets and picking up garbage. He's now crippled and spends most of his time in bed. He is always cold. Even with a brazier, he shivers."

"They were lucky," he continues. "They survived. Millions did not. Everybody has a story here, a torturer or a tortured and everyone is struggling to survive."

We walk to his home, down darkened alleys stinking of rot and feces to an apartment complex of four-story buildings wedged closely together. Garbage is strewn all about. Laundry hangs from above. Infant cries echo about. Water drips from pipes down the stairwells into the alleys. The hall and stair lights are out, the bulbs burnt or broken. It is late and cold is settling in.

Nestor's mother greets me. She is tiny, a peasant mother to this urban son. We communicate in smiles and nods. She offers tea and simple crackers. In the corner, Nestor's father looks at me wanly from his wheelchair.

"Go sit with him," Nestor motions. "You are the first American he has ever seen. It is important for him."

I put my hand on his and smile. He stares and smiles back.

"Most of his friends are dead or missing," said Nestor, "buried somewhere, under a football pitch, in the mines, or in some government basement. He needs hope, my father."

We sit and drink tea. I say how much I am happy to meet him. Nestor translates. His father replies in kind. I tell him what a wonderful son he has, that he will be the future of the country. The old man nods.

After tea, we enter Nestor's tiny room. It has a bed and a large poster of New York harbor with the sun shining brightly on the Statue of Liberty. A small bookshelf has books by Freud and the Indian poet, Tagore, both banned under the old regime.

What do you say to people whose doors and windows have been shuttered for a half-century? Whose ideas of the world were filtered through government propaganda and staticked radio signals? Whose consciousness is warped by memories of prisons, forced marches, labor camps, missing persons, harangues, paranoia, assassinations and xenophobia?

Every conversation is a sad one; every conversation, filled with pathos. Anger and fear will remain until the infants in their cribs grow and take over and look to soccer or music or social media to erase the memory of the horrors of the past.

Nestor reaches into the bookshelf and pulls out a cassette. He smiles. "John Bass," he says. "She kept me going through the darkest days."

And the voice rings out:

In the winter of 65
We were hungry just barely alive....
Now I don't mind chopping wood and I don't care if the money's
no good
Just take what you need and leave the rest
But they should never have taken the very best
The night they drove oh Dixie down
All the bells were ringing
All the people were singing
They went la la la li la la la li la

"That's Joan Baez," I say.

"That's what I said, John Bass."

I laugh. "Oh my! What confusion."

Nestor smiles. "I was wondering how you were so ignorant."

"You were right. She is a great musician," I say. The music carries throughout the apartment. I go to the old man; his eyes follow me as I approach. I touch his hands and wipe a tear from my cheek.

It is late and the sun has fallen. I feel my way down the steps, walk through the maze of buildings, past the omnipresent group of men standing and smoking and find the main road. I walk home happy, from the run and from Nestor. In this small apartment, with Tagore and Baez and Freud and the Statue of Liberty and the weak, old man in the next room. The flow of it all, the dictator, the tyranny, the revolution and the young man finding his way. A decrepit world. A hopeful world. It is a macabre happiness, born from the pain of the others, but it is this that exhilarates me, it is for this that I work, the storm of life.

❧

Who is clean and who isn't? Where does responsibility end? On the flight out of Tirana, I sat next to a friendly, gray-haired gentleman, a Member of Parliament for the opposition Socialist Party, the former Communists. He was once Minister of Health under the former government. He argued that what the new nation needed was experience. That much was certainly true. But what was this old man's role in the old regime? What compromises did he make to stay alive? But then I remembered that current President of Albania was Hoxha's heart surgeon.

By 1997, the Ponzi and Pyramid schemes that promised 40 percent a month profit collapsed as returns declined and lenders pulled out their money in panic. Anarchy followed, along with a desperate search for scapegoats and a call for government bailouts. Incensed crowds rioted and seized army barracks and its weaponry. Civil war erupted. Only with European intervention was serious conflict avoided. The President resigned and the old Communists bureaucrats returned to power, the only group able to maintain stability.

So what remains? Out in the farms, Albanians have their own land and are able to produce enough to sustain themselves. Since most urban dwellers have family in the countryside, food is plentiful. And when it is not, donors stand ready to import. In the cities, Mafiosi groups of businessmen, the Socialist government, and the groups loyal to the ex-President are in a constant stand-off. In the north, Kosovan Albanians still rebel against Serbian rule in a fight that threatens to enter Albania itself. NATO soldiers continue to patrol Tirana's streets.

It is an unhappy situation. Or is it? Compared with ten years before, the nation enjoys greater freedom. The horrors of Hoxha are no more. The economy is weak, but developing on a firmer base. It is open to the outside world, with all the pitfalls and possibilities. The nation is learning as it goes, not from radios and smuggled textbooks, but from experience.

This lesson is true here as elsewhere in Eastern Europe: capitalism cannot grow overnight. It needs its pyramid schemes and Mafiosi to take hold. Italy had its San Gimignano with families fighting from street to street and tower to tower for generations. Albania is at the beginning.

We in the West are spoiled. From a few aid dollars, we expect free markets, fair and legal dealings and rapid economic growth. This never works. What works is a slow evolution, in which a capitalist mentality and the rules of the game are constantly evolving. It is a perilous journey with thieves and fools throwing the world into mayhem.

It is what we call progress.

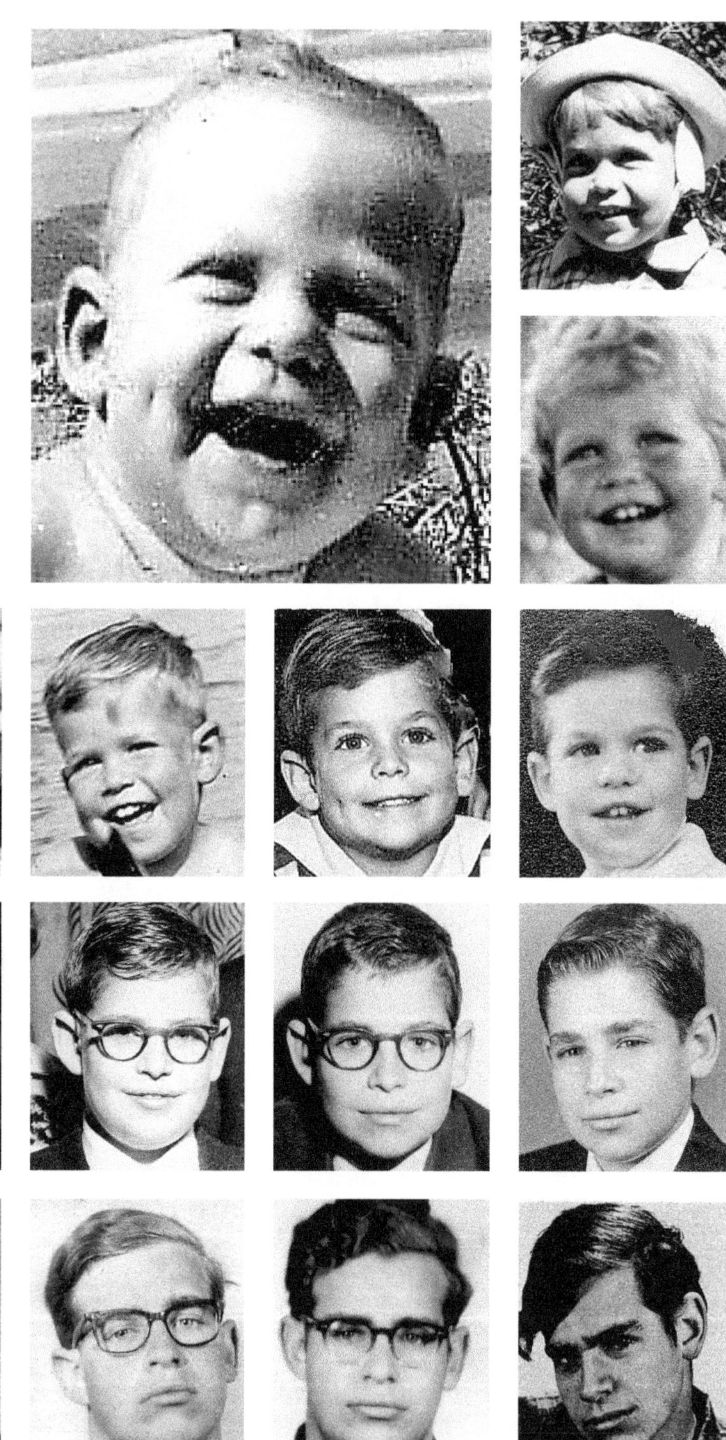

CLAY

(1995)

WHENEVER THE FAT INDIAN STROLLED IN, all the girls turned and waved happily, looking for his anointing cheer. His arrival after another long trip meant gifts and flowers, perhaps an invitation to dinner at the local hot spot. His presence was the most important thing, though.

Everyone at the firm loved the fat Indian, which is how he became known over the years although not to his face, of course. It was a sympathetic nickname with no animosity intended. He was certainly large, but not unattractively so. He dressed well, in double-breasted silk suits and Valentino ties. Not overdressed, mind you; just the right sort of style. And he was what the Spanish call *simpatico*. When the secretaries spoke with the fat Indian, they felt a friend, a confidante, someone who was legitimately concerned with their woes and cares.

Mihir Kumar was adored, especially compared with the other two partners. He was able to cajole long hours and intense work from the staff. Kevin, partner number two, once an Irish government paper-pusher, was gaunt and sprightly, with the angry zeal and pace of a man on the make, that ethnic character which compresses two thousand years of Irish repression into daily dealings. Unlike the fat Indian, his avaricious drive seemed desperate. His sexual needs overwhelmed the weaker elements of the young staff, but the secretaries still feared and obeyed him slavishly. David, partner number three, was sloppy, imprecise and lazy, an aged French hippie and Zen-Buddhist dreamer who walked about the office with his shirt out and hair flying all over the place. In moments of extreme tension, his outbursts were loud, but his French accent made them incomprehensible.

The fat Indian made it all work, stroking egos here, calming passions there, smoothing out the edges and presenting an image of a company of cool competence, very much like the image he had for himself. He worked hard for the firm, much more certainly than the other partners. Always traveling, it seemed, Vietnam, one day, Chad, the next and then Bolivia. Where didn't matter. His job was to build the business and the business was to provide assistance for the poor of the world. The clients, the donor agencies, demanded he go wherever they said at a moment's notice, and he always did.

He had a way about him, the fat Indian did. When he spoke in countless meetings, at the head of long tables, his audience paid attention, grabbed almost involuntarily by his aura. In Africa, Asia or Eastern European, they heard him as a guru, promoting private enterprise, efficiency and globalization. Perhaps it was the Indian in him, that faint Oxfordish English accent with slight exotic flare that gave the air of educated authority. No doubt he had a way with words, but his talent came from his ability to give the audience what it wanted, like a good performer. At meetings, he threw about words, "free market," "competition" "excellence in performance" without a hint of jargon, as might a lesser consultant, but also not ladened with significance or ornate substance that might confuse his listeners. No academic, he. Smartly designed handouts: *the goal, the purpose, the strategy, the result.* Simple but interesting slides on the wall: *GDP, industrial trends, scenarios for the future.* He walked about the room like a Las Vegas veteran, moving his arms about, seducing his audience and grabbing their love.

The line between banal and profound is as thin as thread but his logic always seemed impeccable, like a brief, well-written magazine article, say, *The Economist.* If you listened closely, however, and cut through the style and slides and soft Hindi tones, you would think that there was not that much there, other than the traditional party line of promoting growth. The mantra of the age, wasn't it? But they all listened and appreciated.

Mihir was Indian by birth and ethnicity but not upbringing. His father worked at the UN, one of those officials who was there at the beginning, in 1947, a stalwart member of the Congress Party rewarded for his loyalty. For Mihir, India was a faint idea, a place to visit from time to time to see distant relatives or attend marriages and funerals. Home was where the bed was. He grew up in New York and was educated at one of those Swiss private schools the international set use to care for their loved ones. He graduated to a beer-drinking, girl-swirling college experience at a Midwestern university. His friends and acquaintances and lovers and enemies were international. What was he but a citizen of the world, as are so many these days, with no grounding or history or nationalistic loyalty?

He was certainly not an Indian nationalist. Far from it. If someone asked about Rushdie, Pakistan, Bhopal or the Hindu revival, he would shrug slightly. You become removed as you fly from country to country, year after year. You read of revolutions and bombings and causes and conflicts, on and on with the hundreds of other political and social movements each country holds dear. But as an itinerant traveler with weak roots, they are just headlines, stories that flow downstream and out of consciousness. You ignore the horrors and do your job. That's what they pay you for.

Mihir was not without feeling, of course, but as he came to the next assignment, he left it behind. In the international world, emotion is fleeting, as it might be after reading a novel by Dickens. It is a vacuous feeling, one that develops after a constant onslaught of bad news. An avoidance. A numbness.

All he knew and all his concerns were for his clients. Like a good attorney or doctor, it was they he represented. For him, capitalism and free markets were the clear ideology to solve underdevelopment and create jobs. He did not care who owned the capital particularly or how they acquired it. Sons of ministers, old party officials, royalty,

Mafiosi or hard-working businessmen, the localities determined the legalities of it all. His work was to increase the wealth of underdeveloped nations and if that meant making the local wealthy wealthier, so be it. That was the way it worked in Albania, Russia, India, America, wherever.

There was always a hint of flirtation between the secretaries and the Fat Indian, a suggestion that he might get married again. Few knew his history, for office turnover was quite high thanks to Kevin's sexual predilections.

"Go ahead, grab one," Kevin would say, referring to one of the female staffers. "You need a family. You work too hard."

Truth be told, Mihir did socialize, dating women from the World Bank, the State Department, or a journalist from time to time. He was not bad looking, his personality clothed and camouflaged his size well, and he was available and smart and fun to be with. But he was off around the world too much and if he were home for a spell, the women were not. Too many crossed lines, too much distance, not enough time.

David, his French partner, urged Mihir to slow down and relax. "We don't need the business. We are rich." They were indeed. Kevin, with his inevitable sense of flare, went out and bought matching Land Cruisers for the partners, the company logo stylishly stamped on the side, a small square below the door handle. Consulting on suffering had its benefits.

Mihir's Cruiser had a defect from the beginning, a slight noise in the engine, a tick-tick-tick that the mechanic could not track down. Kevin urged him to return it, but Mihir demurred. Kevin thought laziness. But Mihir knew the familiar noise. It was like the slight chirp of a solitary cicada that nestled into the frame to live a happy and warm life.

Was he happy? Hard to tell. If you came to know him well, you knew him less. The initial meeting was always pleasurable, good fellow and cheer, great stories, promising friendship. You enjoyed meeting him and told your wife you should invite him for dinner, but you never got close. His world was his work, his smile, his charm, and beyond that, you were left to wonder.

Unbeknownst to most of the staff, Mihir was married once, to a pretty English girl with sweeping blond hair and a cultured manner that so complemented him. She was quiet, perhaps exceedingly so, and wore a slight smile that touched men and women as much as the largeness of her husband. They seemed so loving, once. The tragedy ended the marriage, or so everyone believed. The death of a child will do that, won't it?

But there had been other problems. He traveled almost constantly, months at a time. The client needed him in Ghana for a trade facility and then to Moscow to organize a bank for small enterprises. He wanted to be home, but this was work and it was to be for only a few years, to pull in a few dollars, for they were not wealthy back then. Trips mounted on trips on years beyond years and the work became more intense and the joyous homecomings, more routine, and then, when the lifeless, lame body of the child was laid out on the flat stone, cleansed of blood, she knew it was over. He didn't, of course. He put a hand on her shoulder and said they should have another, shouldn't they? Shouldn't they try again? She shuddered and broke down in heavy tears that, he thought, surely were for the dead child, the child that had run into the path of an oncoming scooter, wiping out their joy.

Soon after, she returned to Britain for a new start and that was that. For him, he returned to the road.

The fat Indian sat in the back of a black sedan that had seen too many miles on roads with too many cars. This road ran atop an ageless dike, separating rice paddies on the right from the new subdivisions on the left, houses for the new rich of this under-developed, Asian country whose hallmark had been, until recently, a devotion to the Socialist dream. The houses had balconies with brilliant views of pastoral bliss, of white dots of bent girls and women in glistening green rice fields with geese swimming serenely in their midst, like a Millet painting.

The car frame bent and jumped with every hole in the road. A sharp curve threw him down hard into the springless seat. The driver turned the wheel back and forth in a vain attempt to avoid potholes, weaving the car around bicyclists and scooters, wandering pedestrians and an occasional oxcart. The electric windows were shut tight and turned off, because the air conditioner was on, the driver said, even as the vents blasted Mihir's face with hot air.

Mihir was tired. He hated heat for he sweated profusely, ruining his elegant clothing. He had landed the night before, very late, from the last country, where the textile factory had been sold off to the brother-in-law of the Minister of Finance using a soft loan from the government bank. He had walked through the plant and through a crowd of workers standing idle, smoking and sipping coffee. He saw the rusting and silent looms that, perhaps, with some new investment and management could return to life, and with them, save jobs.

He had reviewed the numbers and was sure the cost of labor was misstated to please the donors. The accountants knew how much to show and how much to hide. But that was what was needed to compete against the Chinese and Indians who were not subject to the dictates of the World Bank, their labor force of untouchables, prisoners or plain unfortunates working to make cloth for boutique fashion houses and big-box stores, little League tots and two-for-nine-ninety-five discount shops.

He might report the plant was not following international standards, that there were labor issues to be addressed. But that would raise hackles and his objectivity would be questioned, he being Indian. After all, who asks the Indians about the age of girls who pull threads through Jaipur carpets sold on Madison Avenue?

So, for him, it was easy—no, it was required—to sign off on the sale of the plant. The labor issues were minor, he knew, as did the accountants, lawyers, environmentalists, economists and politicians in his team, the dirty little secret, that deception and little frauds are needed for development. It had happened first in Japan, then in Korea, and then in China. It was right, despite what do-gooders might say. It would lead to growth, health and a new world.

Afterwards, he had taken out his team of technicians and made sure to invite his clients, the donors who paid his fee. That was good marketing. He had picked up the check at the fine French restaurant, good wine and excellent foie gras, and later, at the flesh pots where women provided pleasure. No. To call them women would be an exaggeration because they were girls of questionable age although in Asia, age is always difficult to figure, isn't it? And as far as young, small-breasted women whose lives were already decided, age was not of much importance.

Mihir had gone along, thinking he wouldn't partake, for he had not found much joy amongst the bar girls. But that night, with his hirelings and his clients and the success of the day, the whiskey was good and flowing freely and the clients were having a really good time which meant Mihir was likely to get the follow-on contract. The karaoke was turned high and the bar rang with Germans and Japanese bankers and aid-workers slapping backs and buying booze and singing songs of good cheer and sorrow, *Auf Weidersien, My Way, Waterloo, Tipperary, We are the Champions of the World*. It all touched him so much—the camaraderie, the happiness, the well-being—and the girl who came to him was sweet, very sweet, and she giggled when he sang. She sat on his lap and nestled into his nape. He felt her warmth, the imagined sense of emotional unity with this child who led him upstairs for brief moments of bliss, bliss that was in any other circumstance impossible to reach now that his son was dead and wife gone. He, who is without sin? Only one life to live. He deserved it, he knew. He worked hard. Joy is so difficult to come by as the years pass.

‽

That was yesterday, another country and another industry. Now, he was in a half-wrecked limo heading towards a ceramics factory. Lord, it was hot, and he was hung over and exhausted as he stared through dust-crusted windows at hordes of snail-pickers and weeders in the rice fields, their backs bent to the world. Children in pressed, blue and white uniforms crowded the road. It was noon and school was out, supposedly to allow them time for their studies (the official government line), but really to head to the fields and weed thin strands of rice.

The car turned off the road into a small lot. He emerged into the hot wind. Cicadas erupted in the trees, the way they always did. They exploded wherever he traveled, always screaming as if to say to him "we're here and we know you're here and there's no hiding." His was a plague of loud, bothersome cicadas. If he took a walk along a country road, say to relieve himself, or to visit a farm project, the cicadas bombarded him. Not a gradual emergence of noise like an approaching storm, but an immediate onslaught that turned on and off as if some great deity threw a switch.

Of course, he was not insane and was not concerned at their omnipresence. The cicadas were, it seemed to him, one of those afflictions that struck certain men, like baldness, impotence or arthritis. He had mentioned it once or twice to his partners over whiskey and cigars but they all chuckled and rolled their eyes because the fat Indian always was interesting and telling a good joke. Then there were times when the cicadas didn't show up and that concerned him mightily. He lost sleep waiting for their arrival. He went for walks, searching for their loud greeting. He asked taxi drivers and hotel concierges. Frustrated, he turned to books, reading about the decline of the cicada in certain regions. He made sure to contribute to charities devoted to saving the cicadas' environment. He contributed a letter to a journal on cicadas that went unpublished. Over dinner, he would bring up the subject with clients, or on long flights to strangers sitting beside him. Everyone just nodded and agreed that the future of cicadas was a problem that should be looked into.

At the ceramics factory, a young woman opened the door for him. She wore a traditional, white and green pleated dress and a tri-cornered hat. She bowed deeply and raised her hands in a Buddhist greeting, hands together. He bowed in response. She had a glorious smile, a pure face, he thought, lovely and very sweet. She ushered him past a workshop with lines of tables of vague clay shapes into a small, enclosed corner office. Cold air struck him as he entered and greeted the manager. The aircon shocked the Indian into action, the coolness reviving his depressed and lagging spirit, eliminating the hangover and returning him to his happy, outgoing persona.

They exchanged business cards. The manager was not a large man—few in this country were—but he had strong arms and a firm handshake. "We Asians know how to make things work, don't we," he said with a conspiratorial air. "But you live in Washington. Are you American?"

"No sir," Mihir replied. "Not at all. I live amongst them but I surely understand our values, our Asian values. I spend most of my time in this part of the world."

"That's good," the manager said. "Because we must do things the Asian way. Not the American way. We need to make profits."

"I have worked all over the world. I understand the need of small businessmen, the problems they face and how best to help them. I will try to do my best for you."

"The Asian way," the Manager said.

"Yes, of course," the Indian responded. "Tell me about your business."

"Clay is what we do," the manager said. "For generations we have taken clay from the rivers of our country, mixed, shaped and kilned it. We make many things, dishes and teapots, little clay dogs and Buddhist shrines. We make replicas of Hindu gods for the tourists at Angkor Wat and miniature peasant houses for little girls. We've been doing this forever."

He continued. "We were owned by the state until we bought it back. Yes, it had been ours before the coup d'état, and then we managed it. Now we own it again. It was hard under the Socialists. If the electricity didn't flow and the right clay wasn't provided, there would be no dishes or vases or shrines. So we persuaded the government to give us our own electrical generators and clay deposits and we earned enough for our daily rice. In those days, that was more than anyone could hope."

"Clay is in my skin," the manager said. "It's all I know. But now I need to modernize and bring in new machines and develop new products for export. The world is changing and I have to adjust."

They left the coolness of the office box and passed large droning and churning drums, propelled by worn leather belts attached to grinding motors. The manager had a limp, the fat Indian noticed. Was it the American war? Imprisonment? An industrial accident? One knows not to ask in Asia.

Two workmen stood to the side, looking quizzically and nodding as they passed. "What I require," the manager said, "is modern mixing equipment, Japanese or German. New drums can mix far more clay than these smaller machines and use much less electricity. I can control the mixture better, and produce a better quality product. Control is everything in clay. If you have control, you can make anything the world wants."

The manager led him to a table where young girls worked on tiny figurines. "This is our new product," he said, handing it to the Indian. "For the European market." It was the cartoon character Goofy—a white, clay, Goofy—smiling happily. "We've been experimenting for the last year. Trying to get it just right. I brought in an expert. Cost me quite a lot," he said.

"Very interesting," the Indian said. "These are quite small. They must require close work."

"Oh yes," the manager said, "but here in Asia our girls have tiny fingers. But that is not the problem. The problem is we need the right density, tensile strength, moisture and clay content. European requirements are quite stiff, very exact. It has taken much work. These figures will be covered in lucite in Germany and heated to extreme temperatures. They must be able to absorb the heat without shattering. It won't do to have this little man explode in plastic, would it?"

Mihir noticed a boy down the table carefully painting the ears of Goofy a bright red, offsetting the blue on the body. Next to him were hundreds of Goofys and Mickeys and Dumbos, beautifully painted, lined up one after the other.

"Aren't they beautiful," the manager said, picking up a fully-painted Goofy. "They will please so many children this Christmas. Imagine, these lovely clay figures, floating about in clear plastic. I would love to see the smiles of the boys and girls in jolly England when they open these presents. It would be a glorious sight, don't you think?"

Mihir peered over the work floor, seeing a clean, open operation. He noticed how white everything was, the clay, the ground, and the workers' uniforms. Everything except the cheerful little figurines. No environmental issues to speak of, he thought. A well laid-out enterprise, the manager clearly understood his clay. He felt his clothes droop and straightened himself smartly. Presentation is everything.

"Business is doing very well," the manager continued. "Our salary structure is quite competitive with China and Burma. We're talking to the Mexicans to produce Aztec gods for their tourist market. Our prices are that good. The Europeans like working with us. With the loan we can bring in modern drums, increase production ten-fold and hire not 300 but 3,000 young workers. And that is what we want. Make jobs and grow. That is what it's all about."

Mihir described the formalities. A financial expert was required as well as a social inspector. There would be a review of the proposed collateral. Perhaps they would provide training to develop better accounting. He would have to file a report and the international agency would get back to him.

They emerged from the shadows of the factory floor into the bright, glaring sun. Mihir walked tentatively, suddenly dizzy. Cicadas erupted as he approached the car. He looked down, noticing the light white clay dust coating his shoes and cuffs. A chore for the hotel, he thought.

The young girl in traditional dress emerged from the little shop. She opened the car door and smiled at him. She put her hands together in the Buddhist parting. She was 12, maybe 14. It is so hard to tell, Mihir thought. But in Asia, it doesn't matter. He smiled back and bent low and she smiled even more. He paused and wiped the sweat from the back of his neck and looked into the hot, decrepit car that awaited him. He looked at the girl and moved towards her. He touched her cheek, just a brief caress with the back of his thumb. She jumped back, startled.

"Oh I'm sorry," he said, raising the palm of his hand because he knew she did not understand, "I'm so very sorry."

He needed a bathroom but was determined to await the hotel. Rural latrines in Asia are putrid, frequently little more then fly-infested spots on the soil behind the factory where workers and managers mix their feces. With the heat and the large workforce at the factory, Mihir preferred to move on. He may be Asian but he preferred the comfort of a Hilton bathroom.

At the hotel, he rushed to his room. He threw his jacket on the king-sized bed and turned on the TV to CNN. He took a bottle of whiskey from his satchel, poured a drink, and carried it into the bathroom, where he relieved himself. He showered, washing the dust, dirt, and depression from his head. He looked into the mirror, thinking he might have to diet someday.

Mihir poured another drink, called room service for ice and checked his messages. An evening meeting with a donor client was confirmed. The client wanted to try the new Italian place in town.

⁓❧⁓

You may scoff at the luxurious needs of this profession. Poverty and plenty seem paradoxical, but not if you understand the context. You awake in a foreign hotel, inevitably depressed, with a vacuous feeling.

No one to talk with. Alone. You shower and shake yourself back into the real world but it isn't until breakfast that you come alive, breakfast buffets with steamed dim sum or scrambled, fried or poached eggs and bacon or sausage, pancakes or croissants, fresh rolls, toast and banana bread, salmon slices, juicy mangoes, oranges, melons, bananas and papaya, imported strawberries, and yogurts and granola. The feeling of emptiness is gone and you are ready for a day's work.

The luxuries are part of it all—the first class airplane seats with warm face towels, champagne and caviar and cognacs, the evenings in lavish restaurants with Indonesian shrimp, American rock lobsters, Japanese sushi, Argentine beef, Chinese suckling pigs, and good wine to wash it down. Conditions in Eastern Europe and Africa are not quite as comfortable as Asia or South America, but one suffers what one must.

Does this seem too flippant? International consultants are professionals in this global economy and, like all professionals, enjoy the good things of life in those moments when they can. They soothe the soul during assignments mired in urban muck, angry workers, poverty and suffering. Perhaps that's why Mihir became so fat. Too many croissants. Too many flights.

Mihir no longer made the annual pilgrimage to mother India to see his distant relatives. He was too busy with his travels, he wrote them. They appreciated that. A man who has his own business, moreover the president of his own firm, in America and in Washington no less, he must be very important.

He never considered returning to his ancestral home. He must surely have understood why, even if he never spoke of it. He could not be in complete denial. Or did he really forget? Did he suppress that last, fateful trip, eight years ago? When his dear son of suburban American pedigree, so happy amongst his adoring, hugging distant relatives in this strange land, spotted the elephant amble by across the street and ran toward it, as he might have in the peaceful, tree-lined cul-de-sac of his home, to collide with the oncoming scooter. It must have been the noise of the collision that made the elephant turn and look at the boy lying in the street. A crowd gathered and pulled the scooter driver from beneath his vehicle, him with a broken leg, and pummeled him with sticks and kicks and punches for driving so fast. The blows came down harder and harder as the crowd realized that the little child with pale skin and blue eyes was without life.

They put the child on a pyre, surrounded him with garlands and set it afire. Later, in the airport, with an extra ticket in his pocket, Mihir wandered numbly by a souvenir shop and glanced at a large, sandstone Ganesh with a caring, sweet smile. He was struck by the smile that seemed so much like the joy that once beamed from his son's face. He heard a cicada from somewhere down the aisle. Was it then that he first heard the cicadas? He thought it strange, a cicada in an airport but they do get in everywhere, don't they?

As he sipped his whiskey in that Hilton, his mind was restored, Mihir's thoughts turned to the design of the report. There would be a neat summary on the first page, with boilerplate language on the global trade in ceramics filling out the introduction. A second chapter would offer background with macroeconomic trends, GDP, trade, and inflation. Then the analysis of the ceramics business, the possibilities for increasing production, the new types of technology involved. There were perhaps five or ten pages worth of relevant information, but some of the young lads in the office would fill it all in and make it look substantial. The thud factor is very important in Washington. If it doesn't thud, it's no good. He knew the whole report might have been written in five or ten pages but the client won't like it. You don't spend 100G for a pamphlet, do you?

David would make the document all pretty. He would draw maroon lines on the border of each page, with blue or green boxes highlighting critical issues. He had a perfect, French sense of design and, more and more, the clients preferred color. Color printing was expensive but they budgeted enough to cover the cost. Likewise, the report would be bound not in cheap plastic but in a silk cover that had become all the rage. The Asian influence, no doubt. It would be presented at a formal dinner in Washington with good wines and a little present for each attendee. There was enough profit built into the project for that. Kevin would argue about the cost; he always did. But, Mihir argued, today's expenditure is tomorrow's profit. Presentation is everything.

It had been an exhausting trip but now it was time to prepare for dinner with the next client. A hotel project on a beach in the Andaman Sea with environmental issues. He rose and put on a clean suit, looked in the mirror and straightened his tie, combed his hair straight and sprayed it. He looked closely and there, on top, were the first hints of gray, not a problem because in this world more gray hairs means experience, and experience means more money.

He prepared to leave. Then he heard them. The cicadas. They seemed to come in a swarm. Out of nowhere. He looked about the room, under the bed and in the closet. He turned off the television. They didn't stop. The buzz grew louder. He sat and took another drink. He opened the window to a wall of humidity and ripped off his clothes. He took a cold shower, gulped down more whiskey and jumped into bed.

He closed his eyes. But they wouldn't go away.

SMILES

(1996)

Chechnya War — Bill Clinton reelected — Taliban capture Kabul — Hutu slaughters — Tupac Amaru seize Lima embassy — Nuclear Test Ban Treaty — Coups in Sierra Leone, Niger, Burundi — Dolly the Sheep cloned

When they asked Kirk Chase his origins, he would say, quietly, "cattle shit and scrub dirt." Simple as that. Quiet, taciturn, matter of fact. He might have added booze and snowdrifts, spuds and desolation. Or a father, never at home, off riding in cheap rodeos. Or driving cattle into sheds as westerly snows descended. Or a half-crazed mother taking solace in a bottle. Or decrepit schools with semi-literate teachers. Or mending fences. Or sweeping butts. Or sitting alone watching crows. Or hours and hours of cowboy and storekeeper rantings about the ways of the world. Or women desperate for love, grasping for fulfillment from a tough, adolescent manchild.

Kirk knew how to ride but didn't like it much. He never took to rodeo. "Any fool who'd get on a bronkin 'orse probably doesn't have the brains to get off, or if he did, they've been all been knocked out." That's what Kirk said.

In Kirk's case, it was a slight, quiet smile that opened the way out of the snowy northern plains of his youth, a talent to judge and then abandon rottenness and, ironically, keeping a solid optimism in the face of it all. A quiet, positive irony, he was, that knew how to accept and plug on, adjust with no complaints. The tough and angry cowhands he scrubbed stalls with took to the waif and made him a mascot, throwing him dimes and quarters that he carefully squirreled away.

Another talent: to choose amongst the cigarette-dripping, beer-swilling and tobacco-spitting homilies. "Ya' gotta' getcha self a girl, boy, get someone who'll cook for you, that's wha' cha need" "Get outta here. There ain't nothing here for you boy. You too good for all this, get out and leave yo' momma, if you gonna survive. You want to end up like me? Like her?"

He left it all behind fleeing to Laramie, the metropolis that had enough night cattle work to keep him fed while he day-schooled, then onto the state university, and from there to business school, and from there to work.

The Kirk Chase who got his first job at Eastman Chemical was a quiet, studied young man, with a slight sense of humor. The older managers, the guys who worked their own way up from loading crates to filling vats of ethers, polymers, acetates, and polyesters through the factory pits to the supervisory jobs working for the VP, they caught sight of him right away. He worked hard, didn't complain and knew when to shut up. Everyone wanted to help the kid who knew how to spill a back-home-in-cattle-shit yarn.

He seemed to do everything right. When in distribution, he cut costs. When in sales, he increased volume. He was a natural. No enemies, plenty of friends. He married his secretary, a pert blond named Annie, bought a house, and had four kids.

He was a good man, this Kirk Chase, with his slight smile and his good judgment. When the company was sold and they gave him a bonus to retire, he accepted, thinking if they were so foolhardy to pay him not to work, he might as well take it and move on. They never knew what they lost in buying out Kirk Chase for although the numbers made sense, the talent was gone.

The fat Indian put Kirk Chase and me together to work out a Thai company called Kwai Bangkok Petrochemical. "Work out" means to develop a strategy to save companies that once relied on government handouts. The fat Indian owns Cricket, a consulting firm in Washington; he gets the contract, takes a sizeable cut, and then hires consultants like Kirk and me to do the work.

Kirk knew chemicals, backwards and forwards. He understood markets and labor issues, the cost to ship a canister of polyester to San Diego, the insurance rules, the angles you play to get in ahead of the Koreans or Indians or French. He knew how to negotiate the price of feedstock.

Me, I'm the guy who knows the consulting business. I know what reports are required, their tone and purpose. This is a political business; you make your money not just from the facts but from massaging the clients. The people who pay our bills, usually international agencies, want good, strong reports that recommend programs of action. Not too negative. Not too positive. Too negative suggests the whole program should not have been done in the first place. It could lose our client his job, or, in this case, our job. Too positive is just too Pollyanna, making the client think you're just telling them what they want to hear. The right tone requires experience.

For consultants, who you work with on teams is critical. You spend a month or two living with a guy you never met and will never see again. If the mixture isn't right, well, it's like ethylene and water, the project doesn't jell. Once, I went on a mission to Ouagadougou in Burkina Faso with a guy name Ken. Ouagadougou is a desert town, bordering the Sahara. Our job was to improve the operations of a string bean cooperative. Burkina string beans are small and tiny and are used in the best French restaurants that call them *haricots verts*. They have a delicate taste, much finer than the usual American fat string bean. Burkina farmers are given loans to plant beans and paid a percentage of the sale by the co-op. If the crop fails or is of poor quality, the farmers fall into debt. Once in debt, there is no escape.

It's no surprise that today, Burkina farmers work off the debts of their fathers and grandfathers, in debt peonage.

The quality of the string beans is what's important. They should be served fresh and as crisp as when they were picked. Every day, an Air Afrique plane hauls them to a Paris wholesaler. He inspects the beans for quality and offers a price. Usually, the price is below the original agreed amount; the Frenchman finds spots on the beans, says they are too soft, or invents some other reason that they aren't up to the standards of a five-star restaurant. The Burkina cooperative has the option of taking the proposed price or dumping the beans, since there is no other market. They could fly the beans to another country but the only airline that serves Burkina is Air Afrique, and it only goes to Paris. With a low price, the cooperative receives less money, and the farmers fall deeper in debt. I hope the Bordeaux at the five-star restaurant measures up to these *haricots*.

Anyway, back then I worked for a firm call Aidtechs Inc. (These consulting names are really creative.) Aidtechs gave me Ken to work with. He seemed all right at first. He had traded grains out of the Chicago pits and knew the ins and outs of international markets. But after the first couple of days in Ouagadougou, Ken began to turn in early. Usually, consultants work at night, comparing notes and developing questions for the next day's interviews. After a couple of days, I realized Ken wasn't turning in at all but going out on the town. Ouagadougou is not the largest of towns, so I asked him if he knew someone there.

"No, I don't. But that's no problem. It's easy to meet people. Nice bars. Friendly people. You hole up too much in your hotel. I find if you get out, you learn a lot more."

Ken got out, but without me. He clearly thought I crimped his style, another violation of the consultants' pact. When you travel in a small country as a team, you try to socialize together, to make the work bearable, even if your partner is a wallflower, which I guess I am. At first, I let it pass even after I got word that Ken was whoring about in some of the low, ecstasy discos in Ouagadougou. What was important was getting the work done.

But then the US embassy called and told me that Ken was shopping a deal to import soap. Soap may not seem to be a big thing to trade in, like cars or guns, but everybody uses soap, and if you can get the country's president as your partner and you can get a contract with Ivory Soap at the other end, there's good money in soap. You take the president's brother out for drinks with companions, you convince him that you know the head of Ivory Soap (and since you are an American you must know the head of Ivory Soap) and you offer him 20% of the profits, deposited in some Singapore bank.

There are two choices when you're out in the wild: grin and bear the other consultant and do the work yourself, or turn the guy in. I turned the guy in. I confronted Ken and asked him if it all was true. He admitted it. I told him that there was an intrinsic conflict of interest in his deal making, and his little drinking/whoring problem was getting in the way. I fired him and finished the mission myself although there wasn't that much to do. I suggested more modern refrigeration techniques and tried to propose a plan for new bean markets in London and Rome. This didn't work in the end. Burkina is French territory, in fact if not in name, and politics rules everything which in practical terms meant that the monopoly remained in place. *Les haricots* verts kept flowing to *les restaurants de cinq etoiles* in Paris and the farmers kept falling deeper in debt. But my recommendation was neither too positive nor too negative and everyone was happy.

When I returned to Washington, the contracting company, Aidtechs, hauled me on the carpet for undermining the mission and giving this guy Ken a bad name. Turns out, Kenboy was a cousin of the wife of some US representative who sat on the House Ways and Means Committee. I got a bad rep, at least at Aidtechs, and that was the end of me at that firm. As a consultant, you don't let these things bother you too much. There are hundreds of consulting firms doing this business, maybe thousands, so I moved on and found work elsewhere.

Kirk and I, however, made a good team in Thailand. He was the technician and I was the project manager. We got along. I was attracted to his modest smile. He told me how to save cattle from snowdrifts, the difference between Guernsey and Brahma, and the best way to castrate a young bull, all manna for a city dweller whose talent peaked at hailing taxis in rush hour. He was what they used to call a down-home type of guy, all laid back and easy.

He was very serious, though, perhaps too much. He understood the rules of the game: if the business could not be put on a profitable basis, it would have to close, not only throwing all the workers into unemployment, but affecting the town, restaurants, local suppliers and shippers. Everyone. He didn't mince his words, and that, in the end, was to be his downfall.

These jobs are not easy. You pore over books and records knowing that some information is incomplete and some not there, vanished behind file cabinets, so to say. Company managers are suspicious of your questions. Who are these foreigners coming in and tearing down everything they built? You talk to the bankers holding the bankrupt companies' debt and persuade them to take 20 cents on the dollar because that is all that's left. You have to talk to politicians who face angry mobs, rioters or worse, revolution.

The unemployment, the cut in salaries, the suspension of supplier contracts, none of this is your fault. Left on its own, the company would go under and everyone would be out of work. But you try to explain this to the fierce 250-pound, muscle-bound stevedore in the corner, the guy who earned his living like this for the last twenty years, with eight kids and a car to pay off, who doesn't speak any English but who stares and spits when he sees these Americans come by with their white shirts and ties, going from office to office doing who knows what with magical machines. Tell him he's too old, that he's got to work for half of what he used to earn or twice as hard. And if he doesn't want to follow orders, that's alright too because the company will hire a younger, stronger man who will do a better job for half the price. Go ahead. You tell him. You tell that angry, muscle-bound guy.

In this case, Kwai Bangkok Chemicals was in terrible shape. Chemicals are commodities, like wheat or copper. You buy feedstock at prices on the open market, process it through costly machinery paid for with borrowed money, and you ship it to your customer. It's all spreadsheets and accounting. If the numbers add up, you win. If not, you're out of luck. If another firm buys feedstock cheaper or gets cheaper interest rates for the machinery or keeps its salaries down or gets a subsidy from its government then that company will sell chemicals at a cheaper price. It is a simple equation but, as I say, try to explain it to the tough stevedore.

Kwai had too many employees over the years and the owner, Mr. Prakob, a sweet old man, never felt right about layoffs. The machinery still functioned but was not the most modern, the old man having spent the profits more on salaries than upgrades. Necessary repairs and overhauls were put off and the introduction of computers was delayed.

The paternalistic tradition kept the business going; Thai plastic and auto part companies were also imbued with the obligations of the Asian way of doing business. They bought Mr. Ho's ethylene at high prices. But over time, the firms' plastics became more expensive and they had little choice but look elsewhere. The Koreans were exporting cheaper chemicals to Thailand. True, the Korean government is subsidizing the feedstock, but customers didn't care because Prakob's price was higher than the Koreans. Slowly orders dried up and Prakob fell behind on payments. The Thai banks cut off his credit. In the past, Prakob went running to friends in government to make things right, to put the squeeze on the banks or his old customers, or give him a subsidy, but this is the new world order. Poor old Prakob faced disaster. So he turned to us to try to rationalize his operations, become more efficient and meet the competition, all those words that grease the capitalist world.

Mr. Nopadol was the plant manager, Prakob's assistant, a small man with a kindly face, neatly pressed pants, and carefully polished shoes. He answered every question with a smile and a "yes," even if the answer should have been "no." He was unable to say "no," an Asian characteristic that breeds initial admiration and, eventually, contempt. Every question produced a smile and a "yes," even though the answer was "no."

He showed us around the chemical facility, loading docks, refining equipment, and storage areas. Kirk carefully noted the types and age of the equipment, the number of workers in each area, the type of feedstock, the level of output, the backlog in orders, the work hours, and the transport costs. He was a marvel, Kirk was. He worked with one of those small, handheld computers, typing in his notes on a small keyboard. Even if Kirk knew nothing about chemicals, his manner produced strong confidence, typing in these little notes.

But he did know. His questions were informed; he detected contradictions in his information. "Why do you pay more per liter for petroleum than does the local market?" he asked Nopadol.

"Yes," Nopadol said, "I will have to look into that."

"You cannot make a profit if you pay too much for your supplies," Kirk said.

"Yes," Nopadol responded, smiling. "You are absolutely right."

"And your transport costs, this company you are using, they seem very expensive."

"Yes," Nopadol agreed again, smiling. "You are absolutely right. We must look into this."

Kirk was a matter-of-fact type of guy. "If the steer is old and barren and limping and foam spits from its mouth, you shoot it," he said. "If you can give it some medicine to keep it going long enough, then you do that." A simple life choice. It's all in the diagnosis and the possibilities. But try telling that to the 250-pound stevedore.

Kirk knew chemicals, which was why he was on the team. I knew the process, which was why I was there. I knew the Asian way. It didn't surprise me that Prakob paid too much for transport or fuel.

Kirk and I discussed it over dinner in one of those five-star hotels that specialize in flaming dishes and musicians in folk costume.

"The high prices may be a favor to the brother of the banker or to a local politician or maybe Prakob owns the transport company and is siphoning off profits," I said. "It may be any of these, or all of them."

"Yeah," Kirk said. "But it doesn't matter in the end does it? If the company can't sell the manure because it's too expensive, you got to get cheaper feed."

"But there are too many secret relationships. It's a political question. Prakob may be getting lower interest rates so he can pay higher freight costs to the banker's cousin. That's the way things are done."

"Don't matter," Kirk said. "Simple numbers. They can cut some workers and maybe get a better contract from the suppliers of feedstock but if they're siphoning off money to a cousin or a Mafiosi, they're still gonna stay in bankruptcy."

"Let's ask Nopadol," I suggested. "Let's see what he says."

"Yeah, we can ask him," Kirk said. "But it don't matter."

So the next day, we asked Nopadol about whether it would be possible to reduce costs in transport and for fuel. He smiled, "Yes, yes, of course it is possible. If we have to do it." And what about the workforce? Salaries were too high, it was either cut the workforce or cut the salaries, which would be more appropriate? "Yes, yes, of course, whatever you recommend," he said.

We spent a month looking at Kwai, from early morning to late in the evening, no time for the famous Thai diversions, the drugs and prostitutes and tours of silk factories and temples and boat trips and exotic music, not that Kirk would ever have been interested. Kirk was devoted to his Annie whom he called regularly at 8 PM local time, 6 AM Laramie time, before she had a chance to get out of bed. Meanwhile, I turned on the TV and got the latest stock quotes, trading a few options here and there, making some adjustments in the portfolio and calling my broker about possible new sales.

We developed a business plan: how much the company was in debt, the operational deficit of the company, that is, how much the company was losing every day, what was needed to reduce costs and increase prices to put the company in the black, to save the company and the jobs. Pretty black and white. I've done hundreds of them, cement factories in Turkey, footwear shops in Brazil, steel refineries in Mexico.

Subtlety was required. We couldn't just come out and say "Mr. Prakob, you are running the company into the ground." No, you have to say, "Mr. Prakob, you have a wonderful company but times are changing and new models of business are growing. Now, firms use computers to understand their costs, they get the cheapest feedstock possible and try to reduce costs and this is how we propose you do it . . ." Always praise the client.

Kirk didn't quite agree with this approach, which is why I was on the team. You have to stroke clients, appeal to their egos. Kirk said that if two and two doesn't equal four then you've got to tell them it doesn't add up.

We developed a presentation that showed how much the competition spends on the same production. This is called competitive analysis. We showed Prakob how the competition pays $5,000 a month for its workforce while he pays $15,000. In every category, feedstock, transport, interest rates, Kwai Chemical did poorly. Then we presented our suggestions: a reduction of management to be replaced with computers, cut the workforce by 20% and bring in larger containers and loading equipment and end purchasing arrangements with Thai companies that just charged too much.

We put all this on PowerPoint presentations with colorful charts and graphs and different scenarios for Mr. Ho to approve. We met with Prakob and, after he agreed in principle, we turned to the bankers. Then we met with the union representatives.

There was to be a formal meeting with the Board of Directors the following Tuesday. Most of the work was finished. It had been a tough month, and I needed to get away. I booked a weekend tour to Angkor Wat.

Angkor Wat is like Macchu Picchu or the Egyptian Pyramids, a vast area of palace and temple ruins in Cambodia filled with Hindu and Buddhist sculptures unlike anything in the world, 1,000-year-old bas-relief carvings that stretch for a mile along walls describing the Mahabarata and Ramayana Hindu myths, remarkable carvings detailing areas of hell or heaven, quotidian life, slave labor and war.

I flew to Cambodia on Saturday morning, expecting to return the next day. My guide, Hak, was a pretty young woman, 21, with a soft smile and slight, accented English. She was diminutive, like all Khmers, even tinier than the Vietnamese, with a sweet, soft face. Her shape, like her countrywomen, was enticing. I watched her soft movements closely as we walked in forests and over fallen temples, careful to avoid the mined fields, vestiges of the recent wars.

Hak spoke phonetically, "The hiss-torrr-ee of Ang-kor Wat is ver-ee in-ter-ess-ting. It was found-ded in the nin-th cen-tu-ree." But when her complex English sentences became too difficult, she broke into an attractive giggle. Her lectures were serious but, during rain breaks, she would smile and ask questions about America. Her giggle was very attractive. Did I mention that already?

Yes, I was smitten. But only for two days and it was all quite proper. Nothing to offend Kirk or my wife, for that matter. I was smitten as I might at a screen actress.

"What does "oo-la-la" mean?" she asked me.

"It is an expression only women use, mostly French women," I said. "Americans mostly say 'Oh my god,' or 'Oh my.'"

After that, every time we saw a ruin, a beautiful statue, or a lovely river, she exclaimed "oo-la-lah," and looked at me seductively. She conquered me.

Hak spoke of her future. She had wanted to attend law school but the family sent her younger brother instead. She will save her money and follow him, but it costs a lot of money and even then, after you get out of law school, there are no jobs. I suggested that law school might not be right for her, but maybe she should expand her father's business, a motorcycle shop. She was surprised and looked seriously. "But to be a lawyer is very important," she said. "You can get a job with the government."

When we travel, we dream. We think of paradise, of Shangri-La or Tahiti. Of course, this was Cambodia, where the Khmer Rouge ran its killing fields, but there were no sign of the killing fields in Hak's face, her smile, her soft voice and easy movement. It was if the landmines still maiming her countrymen did not exist. I was in Shangri-La.

Afternoon rains would come and we sought shelter in the ancient temples, standing very close, she smiling at me as we spoke. Children besieged us, selling trinkets, postcards, and flutes, yelling prices and when I smiled, they smiled back and they told a little joke or made fun of English and laughed and giggled. Lovely children who showed no signs of the past troubles of their country, happy and winning.

It was early afternoon, a few hours before my plane departed. As always, she sat in the front of the car and I in the back. She turned to me to explain about Khmer culture and became tongue-tied with the word "anthropology." "Oh my god," she said, using her new expression and then giggling and smiling joyfully at me. She turned to the front of the car. I was enthralled, ready to abandon my life to this beautiful, intelligent young woman. Then, by chance, I caught a glimpse of Hak's face reflected in the side-view mirror, a direct view from the rear. It was a harsh, stern face, angry and tough, the face of countless pictures of Khmer soldiers at war. The scowl scared me. I tested her, asking her something or other and she turned back with her sweet face restored. We spoke some more and she returned to the front and I saw her glance down at her watch with that angry face.

What a delicious actress! Was there anything she told me that was true? Did this story develop over the years? She was like those kids turning on the charm and sweetness to sell postcards. What a remarkable ability to shift personality, back and forth, at a moment's notice! Is this a nation of actors, what with French colonial rule and the Khmer Rouge and the Communists and the Chinese and the Vietnamese and the Americans and the current government and the insecurity of who is your friend and who isn't? Is this what has been learned from years of government oppression and surveillance? Africans are renowned for listening closely to what is said to them by the foreigners who dominate them, be they colonialists, businessmen or the World Bank, and parroting it back in a manner that persuades the foreigner that this fellow is smart, he gets the point. I certainly have fallen for it too many times. But this smile, this attractive face. Oh my poor Hak!

We like to believe our own stories and those who service us, those who rely on our pay and goodwill. Our butlers and taxi drivers, entertainers and guides, teachers and politicians further reinforce our beliefs. The world smiles at us and then turns back to the reality of survival. How that side view mirror haunts me.

I returned to Bangkok. What happened while I was gone is not clear. Kirk had not wanted to go to Angkor, preferring the here and now, he had said. He just wanted to review the material. He had returned to the plant over the weekend, the security guards said. He had met with Prakob and Nopadol on Saturday and did other work on Sunday. His notes show changes in the business plan, increased spending on retraining, reduced payments to suppliers. He had written: "N agrees with everything I recommend. P seems on board. But lunch did not go well."

Then, apparently, Kirk returned to the plant. As the car approached the gates, three men jumped out and opened fire. He was killed immediately.

The aftermath was difficult. I moved to another hotel and was given police protection. The international news reports suggested a labor issue, that there were to be layoffs and, clearly, we had touched a raw nerve. One report commented, "Life is cheap in Asia."

I made one last visit to Kwai Chemicals. I looked at the man at the factory gate. He saw nothing, he had told the police. I looked at the security guards. They all stared ahead. I suspected everyone. Both Prakob and Nopadol were overwhelmed with grief and sorrow. They were so sorry and ashamed and they couldn't believe that such a thing could happen in their country that was so civilized. Wherever I went in the factory, the workers stared. I wrote a note that I asked to be translated and distributed to everyone in the company. It said:

Kirk came to Kwai Bangkok Chemical to try to save this business. In order to do that some difficult steps were needed including the loss of jobs. For that both Kirk and I are very sorry, but the loss of jobs is not our fault. It is the reality of the situation. Kirk was a foreigner. The people who killed him have done nothing other than destroy an innocent victim. They are criminals.

In the months that followed, I was called by the US government, reporters, groups protesting world capitalism, groups protesting the Thai government, charities looking for donations, people who felt oh so sorry and just wanted me to know how bad they felt. I became a celebrity for a while. Calls came from old, lost girlfriends and old consultants, all of whom I wanted to remain lost. I even got a call from Ken from Ouagadougou. After a while, I just stopped answering and spent my time playing the stock market, reading mysteries and walking the streets, trying to restore my equilibrium. I turned down dinner invitations and put off calling business associates.

Whenever consultants return from assignments, it always takes time to reenter, to learn to appreciate the little dramas of American day-to-day events after the larger than life dramas enjoyed overseas. There's jet-lag to adjust from. There's lying down with the wife and getting used to her body beside you, rather than having CNN on all night long. There's common conversation about the weather or politics or sports all of which vanishes in the consulting battles overseas. Of course this time was different. I was wandering a bit too much, my head off in the clouds, enough for those who loved me to recommend a shrink.

But then came the call from a TV news magazine, one of those shows that sells detergent by washing other people's dirty laundry. The call wasn't direct, at first. It came from Crickets, the consulting firm that was directed by the government to cooperate with the investigation. Investigation? What investigation? The investigation as to what Kirk and I were doing out there in Thailand.

I sat for the interview. The young woman asking the questions had her script in front and a director standing on the side. She smiled at me, a sweet California smile. She was quite gaunt, perhaps anorexic, her face overly made up against the bright glare of the lights. She adjusted her seat, nodded her head at the cameraman and began talking. She just wanted to know exactly what went on out there, before Kirk's death. I told her, matter of fact. We were helping a company get its house in order and become more efficient to survive.

"You mean," she said, "to compete against American firms?"

"No, not quite. To compete against Korean firms."

"What right do we have to tell other people how to run their companies?" she asked. "Isn't this a bit of American intrusion into other people's affairs?"

"Well, actually, they invited us to help. Their firm was going bankrupt."

"So they had no other choice," she said. "It was sort of blackmail. Either they lay off people and follow your instructions or they go out of business."

"We were there trying to save jobs," I said.

"I see. And it cost your partner his life."

"Yes, it was a terrible, terrible thing. He was one of the best men I've ever met."

She paused a second. "Would it surprise you to learn that the company did not follow your advice?"

"No," I said. "It would not surprise me at all. Kirk's murder must have sent a chilling message to the company management."

"The company did not lay off any workers and they say they are making a profit," she said.

"I don't know the details," I said. "I'd have to look into it."

"In fact, there was no reason to lay off any workers or to put in any of the advice you suggested, we have been told."

I caught the drift. It was out to sea. "There were reasons," I said. "There were excellent reasons…."

"In fact," she cut me off, "your partner was killed for no reason."

"You don't know what you are talking about. It is possible, in the aftermath of the murder, the government came in and bailed out the company, but I don't know the details."

"Did you look into that possibility while you were working at Kwai Bangkok Chemical?"

"No," I said. "That was not an option under the terms of our employment. We were supposed to help the company become profitable, all by itself."

"The company says it is profitable, that your recommendations were too harsh."

"I would have to review all of their books, but it is not likely."

"I guess not," she said. "Isn't this an indication that we in the United States do not know what is going on overseas, that we are offering advice to places where we don't really have any business being?

"No. We are the leaders of the world. We understand business. If other countries are going to compete, then we have to help them."

"Obviously, this time, you did not help them and now a man lies dead."

"You have no idea what you're talking about."

My last comment did not make the final cut. Hers did. In the days before the showing, I became tense. I lost sleep. I withdrew further into longer walks and late night reading. I drank more. I knew this TV program would have no effect on my career. News shows are dramatic for an instant but in a week, all but forgotten.

But it still had its effect on me. I was being blamed for bad judgment, imperialism, and ultimately for Kirk's death. I was being blamed not by my bosses or those who understood the situation but by media, looking for a quick buck. And Kirk was rotting in the ground. I wondered what Annie thought?

When the show aired, it did not produce the Watergate-type response its producers sought. For a few days, I was assaulted again by phone calls from journalists and well-wishers, cranks and family. But within a week, the interview disappeared into TV reruns. The truth of the matter is America is not interested in events overseas. It turns off shows with factories and foreign faces.

Self-doubt is the great destroyer. In this industry, where we give advice that affects hundreds and sometimes millions of people, self-doubt eliminates confidence, and without confidence, all business is lost. Our reports do not say, "If A is done, a thousand people lose their jobs. If B is done, taxes increase. If C is done, corruption increases. Take your pick." Our reports provide definitive opinions, based upon experience and knowledge. Even where there is doubt, definitive phrasing covers it up. No man is a prophet in his own land, but in this industry, the reverse is true. You arrive as a prophet to fix problems. Without self-confidence, you are useless.

I needed to convince myself. I made calls to Bangkok and did some research. It turned out that Kwai Chemical was awarded two major contracts by the Thailand Government so they might return to full operations. Their loans were renegotiated at favorable rates with the state bank. More inquiries suggested that someone high in the Ministry of Defense had an interest in the import-export firm that handled the export of plastics and those exports were being used to launder money. Bangkok Chemicals played an intricate role in the scheme.

The sweet, smiling TV anchor was wrong in her accusations, but where she was right she had no idea. It is a problem that I have struggled with in each of my assignments. You see, usually we write our reports recommending "rationalizations," "divestitures," "readjustments," and all those bland words that imply layoffs, unemployment, and reduced incomes. Suffering, in other words. We know the need for these actions are not our fault. We are working to save companies and preserve jobs, but we consciously ignore the 250-pound stevedore in the room.

But the problem lies in whether a singular economic system can be placed on top of many cultures. Cultures think differently. Can the system that began with Kirk sweeping cow dung in some god-awful lost plains town be the same as in Bangkok or Cambodia?

We go out, we consultants, by the thousands every week, around the world, moving and adjusting economic and social policies in birth control and hygiene, business and engineering. Like imperial tribunes, we work with those who smile at us, like Hak, accept our money and then move on. They willingly accept our advice but then bend it to their local conditions, hoping against hope that the square peg fits in the round hole.

After Kirk's death, I went to Laramie for the funeral. His widow, Annie, was surprised to see me. She appeared older than I imagined. She greeted me at the door of a modest suburban house. I introduced myself. She was flustered, not knowing what to say and invited me in. She was short and plump, an All-American woman, soft-spoken or so it seemed. We sat for a few minutes and exchanged pleasantries. Truth be told, there was little for me to say. What could I say about a man I only knew for a month in a far-off land? I told her how much I admired him and that was why I wanted to come, that I had thought I lost a friend despite the brief time I knew him.

In Bangkok, I had asked Kirk why he took the job. He clearly did not need the money, with a lifetime of savings and a buyout from the corporation. He said it really wasn't his idea. It was Annie's. When the offer came through she urged him to take it. He was puttering around the house, he told me, and getting in her way and clearly unhappy. She was too busy with the grandchildren and he was making a nuisance of himself. It would be an adventure, she had said. He had worked his entire life and did not know how not to work.

I wanted to tell Annie that it wasn't her fault, but I didn't have the courage. Did she think it was her fault? Did she think it was my fault, not to be there by his side that weekend? Maybe something was said to Kirk, a hint or a threat. Knowing Kirk, he would have ignored it. Could I have warned him off? More likely there was no threat, and I too would have died if not for Angkor Wat.

I wanted to tell Annie that she did not put him into danger. That in all my years working overseas nothing like this has ever happened. You hear about these attacks every now and then, but they are rare. I've never experienced anything like it. It was in many ways an accident of fate. But I held back. No one wants to hear about fate at a time like that.

Kirk's funeral was a small affair, with only their children, some old friends from the corporation, and a few neighbors. I saw Kirk lowered into the ground. I was invited back to the house for the wake and stood about for an hour before slipping out and returning to my hotel. Then I bought a bottle of whiskey and drank myself to sleep.

TIES

(1996)

I GOT A CALL that Dad was in the hospital. A delivery bicycle struck him as he stepped into the bike lane without looking. Dad was not used to bike lanes. He didn't drive anymore and his eyes were always wandering, looking at dogs and babies and pretty women. He used to rant about delivery men riding on sidewalks, but he ranted about lots of things—people walking their dogs on long leashes, people looking down at their phones bumping into him, electric wheelchairs whose drivers always thought they had the right of way. There was a bit of irony that he would be brought down by a bicycle.

The collision itself wasn't all that serious but as he fell backwards, he tripped on the curb and hit his head. The deliveryman stopped, clearly shaken, but everyone told him that it wasn't his fault. They urged him to be on his way, thinking that lawyers or immigration officials might cause trouble, good liberals that we are in this part of the world.

I left work and went to his side. He had a concussion and subdural hematoma, the doctors said, bleeding in the brain. They put him into an involuntary coma and drained his head. They needed to wait to determine brain damage.

I called my wife and told her I would spend the night at his apartment. It was my home once, close to parks and public schools, a typical New York upbringing. I left for college, married, raised two children who had themselves left and had their own families and now I was approaching my own senior years. I certainly recognized the old place but it was as in a dream, a vestige from my life eons ago, books and vinyl records jammed haphazardly on shelves in every room with knick-knacks from worldly travels pushed in between. Old posters filled the walls, Van Gogh, Pissarro, and Hudson River landscapes. The sofas were torn and leaked cotton, the Indian rugs stained with wine and coffee, bare and with scratch marks from a long lineage of cats, all dead. Dust everywhere. Dust all about. Windows soiled with urban grime and bird droppings.

I wandered the rooms, recalling the past, tired and in something of a daze. My mother had died six years earlier. Once a grade school teacher, retirement did not suit her well. She withered and faded. We disposed of all of her things at the time, leaving gaping holes all about, empty drawers, empty hangers, empty jewelry boxes and an emptiness in our lives.

The kitchen was bare. Dad threw out her old implements, the blender, a rotisserie, and the pressure cooker in which she made thick and succulent soups. Shelves once filled with dishes and glasses were empty aside from a few plates and cups for his immediate needs. He cooked, mostly pasta and canned sauces or eggs, and from time to time he bought a rotisserie chicken at the local Dominican place. No salads, aside from when he visited us. He always came wearing a suit and tie, as if attending a formal dinner. He ate our greens sparingly and politely.

After Mom died, we all moved on, as it happens, the memory of her fading. We survive by forgetting or ignoring our losses, someone once said. I wondered how my Father remembered her. I had wanted him to move to a safer place, an assisted living facility, but he wouldn't hear of it. Waste of money, he said. He was getting along fine. Perhaps he just wanted to keep her memory alive in these walls.

My parents were good people, I guess, as most teachers are. They rarely showed emotion between themselves or with us, me and my brother. Precious few kisses or hugs, just nods and words of encouragement. But who remembers the early years? Perhaps there was love then. Perhaps not. This was my recall. Was this why my brother fled? Was this why I felt so alien in this apartment?

In the den was the old desk, from my father's father, with stuck drawers and handles missing, refinished once but now marred with coffee rings. An easy chair for reading sat in the corner. The room was once shared by my brother and me, but nothing remained of ours, aside from a view out the rear window of other rear windows above an alley where pigeons found refuge. I went through the desk, disposing of rotten rubber bands, dried ballpoint pens, broken pencils, and unused postcards.

I rummaged through the shelves. Old linens, white with roses running around their trim, ironed and piled neatly, unused for so many years. Formal dishware with porcelain serving dishes and a walnut box of silverware, tarnished by time. An old Royal typewriter, a pocket transistor radio, and a few of my old games. A half-dozen overcoats, a bunch of sweaters, and a pile of umbrellas.

And then, at the back of a closet, I found his ties. There were hundreds of them, all stored neatly on racks and hangers, a collection for the ages. He always wore a tie to work, always perfectly dressed. And through the years when I needed a present for him—for a birthday, Christmas, Father's Day—it was always a tie, expensive and silk from France or Italy.

But I had no idea of this, this collection, for lack of a better word. There were rows and rows of them, some narrow, some wide, knitted, cotton and silk, bland and colorful. Ties with stripes, polka dots, and solids. Most were conservative, dark purple, blue, or grey. Some were sedate yet colorful, pale yellow, lime green, rose, and saffron. Others shone bright, stark reds and sunny yellows for celebrations. To one side was a collection of Liberty ties each with bright tiny and joyful fruits and flowers, blueberries, strawberries and oranges, corn flowers, roses and daffodils, bunnies and kittens and curlicues.

I edged through them as one does a field of tall grass, hoping to find a surprise in the next row. Some he inherited from his father, others were mine from when school required formality. College ties of our alma maters with crests and symbols, peace ties, museum ties with starry nights and water lilies. Funny ties, one with Marilyn Monroe and a deep décolletage, another with Groucho Marx and a cigar, and one with lights that used to blink, its batteries exhausted.

Old ties always come back in fashion, my father said, like suits with wide lapels, then narrow, and then wide again. Styles always change with time, he said. They did, I thought, until they didn't. Like men's business hats, some styles simply fade with the ages, left for lawyers, bankers, politicians and mourners.

To be a success in life, you have to be well-dressed or no one will take you seriously. That was his adage. Every morning I watched as he donned a suit and white shirt, pressed by my mother. He shined his shoes and selected a tie and then determined how to use it. Sometimes he made a Windsor knot, and others, a half-Windsor or a Grantchester. It was like a game for us, to guess the shape of the day.

He taught me as well, standing behind and throwing the tie about my collar and going through the motions, guiding my hands and then having me repeat the process two or three times. The knot has to be neat and tight, almost to a strangle, that way it lasts through the day. That was what he said. I learned quickly and was always the best dressed at parties and celebrations although in those days best-dressed was not an advantage. I can still do them all today, eyes closed, although I haven't worn a tie in years.

The next day I returned to the hospital. Dad was awake but semi-conscious. Yes, he remembered the accident and the crowd that gathered around and the rush to the hospital in the ambulance. He recognized me but was confused. I told him about my discovery of his ties, but he didn't react. He kept repeating he was ninety-six when, in fact, he was eighty-nine. He had long declared that he would die at ninety-six, it being the best time. I didn't contradict his error and sat by him talking about the ties to no response. He fell asleep and I crept away.

The doctor said it was still too early to determine the damage, but he was optimistic. On the way home, I bought a bottle of wine and Chinese food. I called my wife again and told her that I thought I would be away for some time. She offered to come, but I thought it made no sense. In my head I thought a solitary communion was in order.

Dad had a useless television, an old large Sony attached to rabbit-ear antennas. He never used it except when weather or tragedies struck, and now I realized it didn't work at all. He listened to the radio and read his morning newspaper perfunctorily, having given up politics after Reagan and Clinton. "Nothing to be done," he declared, strange for a man who devoted his studies to politics.

I pulled out shoe boxes filled with photographs, plunked them on the floor, and spread them out. There were black-and-white pictures from the nineteenth century, of anonymous ancestors staring straight into the lens, of my grandparents at a beach in funny bathing suits, of my parent's wedding, of vacations at the Falls and the Cape. Faded color pictures were of me and my brother as infants, as smiling children, and then as sneering teens. And there I was, a joyful groom standing next to my bride and there were my children through their ceremonies, schoolings, and maturation. There were pictures of the cats that crawled through our lives, and of my parents' travels, the Taj, the Eiffel Tower, the Grand Canyon, cruises and balloon rides.

There were no pictures of my brother as an adult, he who fled the nest and never looked back. My brother and I kept in contact at a long distance, both in geography and emotion. He lived alone in Florida in one of those adult communities. Divorced three times, he played golf and drank, or that's what he said and that's all that I knew. I called him after the accident and said I thought it was serious. He said he thought Dad was always clumsy. He thanked me for letting him know and that was that. I wasn't surprised. I had called him after our mother died and he thanked me then as well. He didn't come to the funeral. Didn't see the purpose, he said. She was dead and that's that.

I had seen all these photographs before, of course, but their images faded in my mind and, as the last drop of wine was finished, I determined to save them. Pictures of my two kids reminded me that I should call them as well, the son in Silicon Valley, making his millions, and the daughter somewhere in Asia, saving the world. But I decided not to bother them and wait to see how Dad would do.

The next day on the way to the hospital, I dropped the photos off to be scanned. Dad was awake when I arrived and I related to him my joy at going through the pictures. He nodded and mumbled that those were good times. I asked him the identity of the nineteenth century pictures. He couldn't remember. I read him the newspaper. He stared straight ahead, uninterested. Or was he just confused? The doctors still could not say.

I sat and chatted about the family and my kids and their hopes. He nodded off but I stayed, staring into space. Then he awoke and I spoke, not knowing if he understood what I was saying. From time to time, nurses and doctors came by. It was exhausting, sitting and waiting and not knowing what would come next. The next day, I told myself, I'd bring a book and perhaps a radio.

That night, I looked through the shelves. Dad had taught government at a community college. He was one of those progressive liberals typical of academia, a scholar but not of the first rank, as they say. His small works and articles were largely forgotten, but his library remained, hundreds of books lining the walls many unopened since my youth and protected against my "why do you hang on to them?" with his snarlish reply "you don't burn books." Works of Raymond Aron, George Orwell, Amitai Etzioni, Thomas Merton, Daniel Bell and the like. Classics by Marx, Engels, and Mill. All of Shakespeare, of course. What was he doing with three copies of Hamlet? Dictionaries, a thesaurus, an encyclopedia and outdated tourist guides of far-off lands.

His vinyl recordings were in similar shape, scratched and dusty and for the most part not used for decades, a mixture of philharmonic, jazz, and musicals. There was Toscanini and Nat King Cole, the Five Spots and Vladimir Horowitz, *My Fair Lady* and Brubeck. And the 78s, inherited from his parents and grandparents, Caruso, early Armstrong, and all the big bands, Goodman, Krupa and the Dorseys. He was not much for Rock and Roll, didn't like Dylan and thought the Rolling Stones were all noise and "derivative." Looking through them, I realized that I was seeing works from ages gone by, sixty or eighty years. Different times and tastes. Relics.

Early the next morning the hospital called, my father's blood pressure was dropping rapidly. I rushed to his bedside. He was in a coma and breathing deeply. It was only a matter of time, the doctor said.

I asked why the sudden decline and he responded, "These things happen." I asked the doctor if my father had chosen to die and he replied he didn't know, he wasn't on duty the night before. Was it on the charts? He looked and saw nothing. I asked the attending nurse and she replied, "I can't really say."

I wondered what went through his head as he lay there, confused but semi-conscious. What were his thoughts as life drained away? Did he have thoughts? Did he remember his life, the ninety-odd years, his own childhood, his pleasures, his tensions and all that he accomplished? Did he remember his wife, his children? Me? What does it mean to give it all up? To face the fate that we all must?

And that was that. I held a small funeral. I told my children not to bother since they were so far away, and of course my brother didn't come. My wife and a few mourners showed up, mostly friends of ours, in a small chapel. A minister who did not know him said a few words of no consequence. Then he was cremated, as he wished.

I returned to the apartment and wandered about the artifacts of life. I didn't want to haul them to my house where they would end up stored away, leaving my children to face the same dilemma. Anyway, my wife would kill me. We already had piles of mementos in the attic and basement, old electronics that I just never got around to throwing out, VCRs, cameras, phones. Our own pictures. No, they were his things, not mine.

No one wanted his things. A friend suggested a yard sale for charity, but yard sales always remind me of that scene in *Zorba the Greek*, where black-clothed hags descend like crows after his death, fighting and grabbing over his things. To see strangers haul away Dad's would be the same. I took the vinyl records to the local charity store but they refused them. They had too many already and not enough space. I called libraries and schools about his scholarly books, some 75 years old and surely worth something. No one wanted those either. Even the guys selling stuff on the street wouldn't take them. They couldn't give them away.

I spoke with the building manager. My parents paid a low rent thanks to the rent-control laws, and their apartment was quite valuable now. He was eager to help me vacate and told me to leave everything. No need to clean or paint; the place needed a complete renovation with new wiring, plumbing and fixtures. It had to be modernized, he said. As far as my Father's things, he would get a dumpster. I just had to sign a few papers.

I found an old suitcase and opened it. It was worn inside but had no odor. I took large plastic bags and lined the interior and carefully packed the ties. I walked about his home, once my home, and looked out on the street below as I had as a child. Nothing had changed, the buildings across the street, people walking dogs, children running and laughing, an ambulance siren, a honking horn and cars lined up, awaiting the light to change to cross to the other side of town.

I took the bag and caught the train up the Hudson River, towards home.

THE MAN WHO WOULD BE KING

(1997)

Arafat returns to the West Bank — Sri Lanka Civil War — Tony Blair elected PM — Computer beats chess champion — Coups in Sierra Leone, Zaire, Cambodia — Harry Potter — Princess Diana dies — Kyoto Protocol — First Hybrid Car

I REALIZED WHO I HAD BECOME. What Wally made me. Wherever there was a revolution, change in government or change in alliance from the Commies to the Capitalists, I was the man to be sent, the "agent of change." I helped guide Romania to privatization; Slovakia to debt resolution; Tunisia, South Africa, and Vietnam to regime change. After a few years, you get to understand the required lingo, the clichés, and you learn how to write the reports that the customer wants. You become an organ of an organ. Was I now Wally's puppet? Was he using me? Running me, as they say in spy parlance?

It was two weeks after my father had died. He was a vital man, interested in the world about him. He had spent almost a decade taking care of my mother who had Alzheimer's. All was well but then he slipped, hit his head and lay half-alive for three months in a solitary bed, mumbling and confused as to his whereabouts. And then he died. Life is like that, here today and then gone.

Dad and Mom lived the twentieth century, from horse carts and candles to the radio, movies, the automobile and the airplane. And then the computer and internet! They did the Charleston, survived the depression and war and thrived in the material fifties and then jetted all about the world. Amazing the life and the progress when you think about it.

The struggle to survive and earn a living, the wars and turmoil, took their toll. My parents were not the most emotional people, cold and withdrawn for reasons long since faded in the past. Who remembers old horrors? Or worse, the absence of feeling? Perhaps this, the reason for my bachelor life and drink. But they paved my way, as they say. I was their fruit, I realized too late, the product of their lives. But, as the Buddha says, one does not need to understand origins to gain knowledge.

I was exhausted from the wait beside my father's bed and then the mourning. After that, drifting, drinking and depression. Work was hard to come by. Consulting contracts had dried up and competition was growing from large firms. I wondered if I was too old. Or too drunk.

Wally arranged a job for me in Mongolia, of all places. In the heart of winter I packed my bags and booked flights from New York to Portland to Japan to Beijing to cold and isolated Ulaanbaatar. The Beijing flight was delayed and I radioed ahead. I arrived in China wrapped in a heavy winter coat, carrying a garment bag crammed with xeroxes and a computer case. A large Chinese female police official grabbed me by my collar and pushed me through crowds awaiting flights and to the customs exit. Then, she rushed me to the tarmac and onto the last bus to the plane. I was hurried on and taken to the rear, past impatient passengers and seated next to a large sleeping Mongol. Behind me jiggled cardboard half-torn crates, piled floor to ceiling, held together by ten-cent twine. If the plane stopped short, the crates would fly forward and decapitate me.

We flew over the Gobi Desert and landed at Ulaanbaatar. Again, I was rushed into a VIP car and driven down rough, narrow country roads, past a horse cart and a following sheepdog heading across a tawny hill. We descended into the smoke-filled, Soviet-style city, the small Mongol capital with abandoned factories beside coal furnaces spewing black smoke and large white cement apartment blocks. It was a scene I'd become quite familiar with, nearly identical to the crumpled, empty factories in Romania and Bulgaria. After the end of the Cold War, thousands of consultants like myself were continually sent to reclaim and repair the ruins of these decrepit cities and farms. I recalled the starved Romanian peasants trampling to the fields in search of scarce food, carrying huge scythes in their arms, as in a medieval painting.

At the hotel in Ulaanbaatar, I collapsed onto my bed and turned on CNN. There were riots in Albania as pyramid investment schemes collapsed. Mobs attacked the army barracks and seized its weapons. Civil war had begun. Tirana, the capital, was the CNN city-of-the-week, with reporters replacing consultants in high-priced hotels, watching mobs in the street burn down offices and loot stores. Correspondents clutching their earpieces yelled into cameras about the failure of expensive consultants to turn Albania into a functioning liberal democracy. Experts in the studio concurred, bemoaning the legions of aid workers. I closed my eyes. No matter what the consultants advised, the Albanians did what they liked. After all, they were an independent, sovereign nation, not to be dictated. There was no telling those Albanians that capitalism did not work the way it seemed, with easy profits and quick wealth, that there were rules, some natural like that invisible hand and common sense like you can't print money if you don't have money. But for CNN experts that day, there were "too many foreign consultants" who did not "recognize the Albanian reality" That's what I heard this first night amidst the Mongols, trying to sleep against jet-lag and cries of street-walkers in front of the only suitable hotel in town.

The next day, I headed to the main government building, passing through the central plaza. Genghis Khan stood mightily in the center, a symbol of how power comes and go. It was frigid and the wind blew hard. Photographers paced back and forth around the Emperor with toy cars and stuffed animals, waiting for parents to bring their proud progeny for a birthday snapshot. I wondered what he would have thought.

The Minister was short and stocky. He shook my hand firmly and spoke directly, looking eye to eye with great confidence. He was middle-aged in contrast to the young revolutionaries in other "new" countries. He spoke English well and laid out his case right away: "We have a small window of opportunity. We were ruled for 600 years by the Chinese and the Russians. We have two months to put an economic program together for the parliament. After, there are elections. So, we have no time. We need to move fast, very fast, bring in private enterprise, break the back of the old government bureaucracy, privatize, admit foreign investors, and exploit the mines. The people are restless. There's rising unemployment. We have a window of opportunity to develop capitalism and reform the government. A window of opportunity, my friend."

There is a Kipling tale called "The Man Who Would be King," later made into a fine movie, in which two minor British soldiers happen upon a Buddhist kingdom in the Himalayas and are welcomed as gods and saviors, only to lose the people's trust and be driven away. And so here I was, The Man, who would enable Mongolia's immediate transformation to capitalism with quick fixes, new institutions, and integration into the global economy in this window of opportunity. The Minister demanded two months of action after 600 years of oppression in Mongolia, during which time capitalism in the West evolved from Florentine city-states to slave plantations, robber barons, Mafiosi, complex financial markets, and all the rest that ingrained markets in our souls. How do mentalities evolve and accept structures? Can Mongolia really change overnight?

The Man Who Would Be King was chosen to recommend the laws, establish a new Central Bank, privatize valuable mines, allow free trade, open investment and create liberal business policies. I knew what Wally would say, the process must begin somewhere;

my role was to introduce the logic of the western economy even if the laws didn't make sense. Eventually the ideas would take hold, institutions would form and adjust to local conditions and cultures. Yes, I knew what Wally would say.

But speed kills.

Despite my misgivings, I sat down for what turned into two weeks of interviews in smoke-filled rooms with long greetings and Soviet-style formalities with a translator who may or may not have understood the conversation.

"Can a foreign businessman open a shop in Ulaanbaatar?"

Translator pauses and translates.

Pause, for thought. "What type of shop?"

Translator pauses and translates.

"A shop to sell clothing."

Translator pauses and translates.

"Yes, it is possible."

(For a true sense of how this went, read the above conversation aloud, over and over again, very slowly, in a small, cigarette-smoke filled room for the next thirty minutes.)

How accurate was this translation? How much did they understand? How much did *I* understand? I met with an official in charge of overseeing small business. He was twenty-five, as they always are. A new computer sat on the desk. Papers all about. A copy of *The Economist* laid bare for the foreign visitor to see. He struggled to say the right words, like a college student who hadn't read last night's assignment. He opened his notebook and, in response to my questions, read his answers directly from the words written before him. Long answers. Detailed answers. The translator scribbled quickly, did not understand the response, asked the respondent to repeat, and then translated awkward answers, somewhat off the mark. Rinse and repeat.

The interviews go on and on, laws translated and old reports offered. Meetings after meetings with officials who spout the party line as they had under the Russians. Yes, by now I had enough experience in dozens of countries with smoke-filled interviews and documents to diagnose situations, but with little knowledge of country, less its history, even less its culture.

"We have to move fast," they said. "The legislature meets in April and we only have two months to reorganize the country. We do not have much time."

I was not the first there. World Bank and IMF consultants had already swept through with the message of free markets, competition and global forces, a message reinforced not with guns or political threats but with the greatest power: money, lots of money, money to allow the new government to take control.

It was, by then, an old story, eight years since the Berlin Wall fell and gaggles of consultants went forth to conquer this new world. They, me included, stayed in fancy hotels and flew first class. We negotiated new regimes in hotel bars as the profession's anthem, *The Girl from Ipanema*, played in the background. Familiarity bred our reality, sustained and reinforced through promotions, new contracts, and the victorious ideologues back home.

Am I being too harsh on us consultants? Do not doctors have the same mores, styles, and language reinforcing their internal logic, values, and myths? Engineers? Accountants? Professors? Lawyers? They all have their lingos and those who don't know the phrasing, syntax, or beliefs lay outside their orbs.

The Ministers wanted rapid reforms, but in Mongolia half the population is nomadic, roaming the plains with sheep and goats and yaks and camels in constant search for fresh grasslands. The land belongs to the country and the vast plains are open for all to roam. No fencing allowed. No land registration. No ownership. How does this jibe with the mantra of private property?

A Western ideology created in academic cubicles demands foreign investment, open and liberal, to attract capital. But Mongolia fears China moving in and buying up the country. A billion of them versus two million weak Mongols. How does national defense jibe with a free exchange of capital?

Will the "window of opportunity" open up to a cold, Mongolian winter?

A member of Parliament, a quiet, polite former economics professor, met with me and described the forces for and against change. Four times a year, he met his nomadic constituency that wandered about the countryside with their herds, erecting their *geres* as they went and putting out an antenna to watch solar-power TV. When he visited, the herdsmen came from miles around, crowding into a tent to listen to his words of wisdom.

The last time he went, he spoke of the fluctuation in meat prices and relations with China. He described new government initiatives. Then, the hands went up. The first question: *Is OJ Simpson guilty?*

After the meeting, I wandered the streets enjoying the clear blue February sky, the type that fools you into walking without a coat in sub-zero temperature until stinging pains attack your limbs. I came upon the central Buddhist temple, a structure wedged between apartment buildings. Hundreds of people filed quietly through the temples, many appear ill and aged. They spun prayer wheels, kneeling before the altars.

I entered a temple. Soft chimes rang amidst quiet voices of prayer. Mantras and incense smoke filled the structure. The walls were lined with small statues of Buddha, one after another, up and down, the same face. In the middle was a huge replica of a golden Buddha, standing 70 feet high.

A monk approached, motioning for me to follow. We circled the Buddha three times. I grew dizzy from the smoke and dropped to the floor and watched the endless parade of cloaked monks. I closed my eyes and slept.

❧

That weekend, the government organized a festival for the forthcoming total eclipse of the sun in a large field under the epicenter. It was going to be a big show, to celebrate the nation's independence and the bright future ahead of it. On the plane north I met Janet, who worked for an American NGO on a mission to audit an aid program. Projects like these keep donor agencies going, in food, education, infrastructure, railroads and roads. Implement, review, revise and re-implement. And then audit. Lots of work and lots of money.

She was on her last trip and searching for a new job. She was sad and downtrodden, looking here and there without focus. Why not become an independent consultant, I suggested? No, she needed security, she said. In a job. As much security as a consultant then as in a job, perhaps more, I argued. No, she said with a hint of irritation, she needed a real job. I stayed quiet.

The plane landed on a small airstrip with sheep grazing on its edge. A shepherd served as ground control. A guide met me in a decrepit Russian jeep lacking doors and we headed over rolling and empty, snow covered hills and past herds of goats, my face frozen from the biting wind. I held tight to a worn leather strap, thinking how a wrong turn would lead to instant ejection.

The landscape was barren with no trees to be seen. This was the Mongolian grasslands, eaten bare. Even in the Moroccan desert there are faint attempts at sprouts. Here, nothing. A world without shade.

We arrived at the encampment. The field was spotted with *geres*, bright, white mushroom-shaped tents. It was frightfully cold. Short, broad-shouldered people in heavy fur-lined coats walked about, arranging the housing as in an unfinished hotel. A scratchy loudspeaker blared out a feminine voice *"Welcome dear visitor to our country. We wish you a good time and welcome you to come to the welcome tent"* in five different languages, over and over, destroying the bucolic, country setting.

My *ger*, like all the others, was leather, painted white on the outside. A small flap opened to a circular space held up by bright orange wood supports. An aluminum stove stood in the center on an earthen floor. Five beds ringed the tent. Wood was piled in the corner.

Food was brought and two young women entered in traditional costume. They knelt to start a fire but the cold remained cold.

Fortunately, I brought a bottle of Mongolian vodka. What's an eclipse without vodka? In the distance a band started tuning their instruments, running up and down the scales. Janet, the American aid worker, placed her bag across the tent. Then, a young Swedish man pushed through the flaps and grabbed a cot followed by a young blonde American woman and a Mongolian friend, dragging bags of camera equipment. A Japanese couple arrived and nodded.

We shared lunch and vodka. It remained cold but, huddled in our coats, we felt we were at the center of the world. Eric, the Swede, looked every bit Swedish. Blonde, clean faced, and scarcely a smile. He'd just turned thirty. "I always go looking for eclipses. That is what I do," he said. "There are hundreds of us. It is very rare, these eclipses and when they happen, they must be celebrated. Very mystical, don't you think?"

"I agree with you completely," the Mongolian woman said. "Don't you think so?" She looked around.

"We are a tribe of eclipse seekers," Eric continued, "travelling around the world each year to see the moon come between the earth and the sun, the way people scuba dive or spelunk. We are students, salesmen, photographers, scientists. I came for the eclipse, but I am also searching for truth. To find real meaning."

"Yes, yes," the Mongolian woman nodded. "You are absolutely right."

"I would also like to get laid, you know," Eric added with a sly smile.

"What do you do in Sweden?" I asked, steering the conversation back to safer ground.

"I don't have a regular job. Jobs are hard to come by. I work a little here and there, so I saved to fly here. You have to do it. It is important." Thirty years of age and without a job, I thought. Money to roam, searching for a mystical truth but nothing to do. The new world order.

The Mongolian woman handed out her business cards. Her name was Chinua. She was small and slightly plump, but certainly less so than most Mongolian women. The cards read professional guide and translator. "Last year I had a job with a mining company. We went all over the country exploring but they left. They weren't interested."

"Why?" I asked her.

"I don't know," she said. "I guess they didn't find anything. So I am looking for work now. But it is very hard.

Meanwhile, Heather, her blonde American friend, assembled her camera equipment, large, expensive lenses, rented to get a good picture of the eclipse. Perhaps to sell to *National Geographic*. The Swede moved to sit with her and pulled out his own camera. She was not interested.

"I take good pictures," he said to no one in particular. "Last year, I spent a lot of money enlarging a wonderful picture of an eclipse. I framed it and gave it to my sister. The next day, I found it in her basement."

"How sad," I said.

"You see, I am the head of the Swedish Losers' Club. We specialize in failing at whatever we do. Pictures. Jobs. Whatever. As their representative, I come here to see how I can fail." Heather was not impressed. Obviously, I thought, the Swede will not get laid tonight.

"So you are a photographer?" I asked Heather.

"No, I am an actress but I decided to come here because I feel close to Mongolia. I am a Buddhist. You know, I was here in my previous life. I was a Mongolian."

It was going to be a long night, I thought.

"She really was," Chinua agreed. "I know it to be true."

"And where are you from in the States?" I asked.

"New York, I live in the Village. And Paris. I have a boyfriend in Paris."

"But you are not from New York, originally?" I could always smell a liar. Especially a liar who was once a Mongolian.

"No, I'm from Virginia. But I'm from New York now."

"And you are taking pictures for yourself?"

"Oh, no, I'll sell these pictures. I am a professional photographer. I spent a lot of money renting these lenses. "

Silence. I noticed Janet staring straight ahead. "Janet here is about to become a consultant, although she doesn't know it."

"That's not funny," she scowled.

"Was it supposed to be funny?" I asked.

"I don't think my problems should be mocked."

"What's the problem?" I asked.

"Never mind," she said.

I understood. Consulting was not considered by many "real work." A banker friend once remarked to me "you're just a part-time worker," but a long time had passed since I felt like a part-timer. Most consultants were in the field one of every three days. The high-pressure types 50% of the time. This gives the impression of "part-time," but in reality, the rest of the time is involved in marketing and trying to maintain a normal family life. I felt sorry for Janet. She didn't understand.

In the field, a Mongolian orchestra dressed in traditional white Mongol hats and long white leather coats started up "Alexander's Ragtime Band." This song, written at the beginning of the century about a New Orleans jazz group by a New York Russian-Jewish émigré was now being played in the middle of the Asian tundra! Then, dancers emerged in folkloric costumes, jumping and yelling in close coordination or as close as one can dance in zero degrees on frozen land. A horseman arrived with a hooded falcon on his shoulder. He removed the cover and the bird soared up and around in a widening spire. The master whistled and the bird dropped quickly to his shoulder. The center held.

Once, years later, I was on a road outside Palmyra, the ancient Roman city in Syria, A Jeep passed by, a falcon fluttering on the driver's arm. I motioned to him to stop. He was friendly and stood posing with his bird. We shook hands and he drove on. I wonder where that poor falcon is with his Arab master today, caught in the Syrian cauldron.

Through the day, performance after performance: singers, with high guttural voices chanted Mongolian folk songs, their high sound lost in the open air. A narrator provided long introductions in English explaining their significance. Then a contortionist turned her body into a pretzel on top of a chair balancing on a table on a snow-covered field surrounded by lots of foreigners jumping up and down to stay warm.

I wandered to the top of a small knoll and came upon a group preparing for the great event: a New Jersey salesman who must be at every eclipse, he said; a guy from NASA sent to observe; bearded, Slovakian scientists here to measure with a spectrograph; cross-country skiers from Cincinnati, disappointed that the snow was so uneven; and young men filming the eclipse on spec for IMAX. The head of Nestle/China flew up just to take a peek. An American couple from the embassy stood with two little adopted Mongolian girls on their shoulders, as pretty as can be.

A young boy approached with a sweet smile. He pulled a sachet out of his pocket and offered it to me. I pulled back instinctively. He insisted and ran to get help. No, he was not selling anything. He wished to give it to me, a medallion with fur attached. As a gift for coming to his town. I was embarrassed at my rudeness.

Night descended, and with it the harsh cold. I swigged some vodka and then some more. An army truck brought thin sticks of wood with which soldiers built a bonfire. Kerosene was thrown on the pile and the fire started with a brilliant burst. The crowd roared. Then the fire went out. Then more kerosene. Same result. The wood was too green.

I drank and wandered about, tripping into an encampment of reindeer people, nomads who wander the far north with their herds, a tribe whose closest relatives are Finnish Laplanders on the other side of the world. The reindeer were small and mangy, their shoulders slumped. Their horses were small as well, the horses that conquered half the world, it is said. Hard to imagine them overwhelming China, Central Europe, Russia and Tibet.

The band played on. Couples danced in their heavy clothing. I wandered about happily, the cold wind sobering my drunken face. I sipped and observed. Out of nowhere a hand grabbed my shoulder and pulled me into a ring of singing soldiers. One arm on one shoulder, another on the other, we circled and circled, round faster and faster. I shrieked in joy, huffing and puffing under the weight of my coat and big boots, unable to stop the force of the Mongolian armed forces moving me round and round in ecstatic exuberance. Me, dancing with the descendants of the Khan under a brilliant star-lit night with a bonfire that just wouldn't take! Yes, there is joy in the world, Wally was right. A glimmer of light on the night before the grand eclipse.

It was glorious. The stars shined bright over the plains, the music was endless. Exhausted, I tripped and weaved my way back to the *ger*, pushed through the flap and saw a mob. A handsome German boy sniffed after Heather, while Sven sat staring.

"See, I always lose," Sven muttered.

The Japanese sat silent in the corner, smiling and inebriated. Janet, unhappy, stared angrily at the American blonde. Three guys stood about, one sitting on my cot.

"We need a bouncer," Heather pronounced.

"Right-oh," I responded and stood.

"What do you want?" the interlopers said. They were young and strong. I was big and wearing a very heavy coat, masking my frailty.

"Time to leave."

"I don't think so," another came at me.

"Then I will leave," I said. The guys smirked. "To fetch the soldiers. I hear the Mongolian jails are quite modern."

They left and I returned to my cot.

"It is much too touristy here," Heather announced. "I only like real life. The real scene."

"You *are* a tourist," I reminded her, "and this *ger* is the real scene, unless you want to sleep with a yak."

"But she is right," the horny German said, pushing close to her. "One would expect something more basic."

"You want basic? There are herders on the hill. Why not go and join them?"

"*Pleeeze*," the German scoffed with his deep accent, leaning more and more against the fair Heather. The Japanese laughed and nodded.

"Tourists never want to be tourists," I said to Janet, she sitting quietly on her cot, me trying to cheer her up. "They want the other tourists to leave so they can be authentic. 'Nobody goes there anymore, there's too many people…'"

"You're drunk," Janet said.

"Drunk but sober," I said. "The title of my life story."

Silence. "So how is the acting profession?" I asked Heather, trying to make trouble.

"It is hard," Heather said. "You know, if you are Matt or Brad or Gwyneth you can call your shots, but for most of us, it's not easy. I had a big break last year. A Ford commercial. But that was it. The New York scene isn't easy. The casting couch is still a reality."

"What is a casting couch?" Sven asked.

"You don't want to know."

"But you must be a *gut* actress," the German chimed in.

The Japanese nodded, yes, yes.

Heather was clearly not impressed. The studs were circling but the woman was a Buddhist goddess, not to be moved.

Janet was not a goddess. She was morose and disdainful of the pretty young blonde attracting so much attention. I didn't like Heather either but one gains amusement where one can, an alcoholic's mantra.

"Don't worry about your job," I said quietly to Janet, thinking to change the subject. "Something always comes up. You are obviously talented and, if you don't get a job right away, you can always consult."

"No, I don't want to consult. I'm not the type."

"What is the type?" I asked, maybe too drunkenly.

"You don't understand. I need security. And I am losing my job."

"It is not the end of the world."

"You don't understand," she said.

No, perhaps not. Being a consultant, footloose and fancy free, I didn't understand others searching for jobs in the name of a security that didn't exist. But I did not say this.

"No, you don't understand," she repeated. "I am losing my job because I don't want to travel. I travel. So does my husband. We scarcely see each other anymore. We are strangers. They want me to keep coming out here, to China. Thailand. Nepal. Two days on a plane, a few days in the town and then two days flying back. By the time I return, he's off to Paris or London. I can't keep doing it. I will lose my family and my life. I need a regular job. At a desk."

"I see," I said, feeling embarrassed at my lack of sympathy. The profession's curse: always on call; and always on a plane.

I asked Heather for lens paper for my camera but she didn't bring any. This is not a photographer, I thought. A poor little rich girl, actress, photographer, and Buddhist. She was not stupid, this girl. Just young, foolish, and too full of herself. Which is why Janet disliked her. But then I considered Chinua, her Mongolian friend, looking for jobs, here to make contacts with foreigners. She was like Heather, except she did not have the world as a playground and a rich daddy. And the Swede, wandering and searching. And the German looking to get laid. And the Japanese, smiling. Here, waiting for the experience of an eclipse. On the edge of the world.

We sipped vodka. The German and Sven ogled Heather. Chinua stared at me, hopeful for a job. Janet stared ahead. The German was bored and announced he was leaving. Heather said nothing. We were now alone, on our cots. Sounds of laughter in the distance.

"Tomorrow morning," the Swede said quietly, "a fire will shoot from the edges of the sun as the moon covers it. The gasp of the powerful, losing its power, at least for a moment. Then, from the hill, we will see a shadow race across the ground, covering the valley.

And then rapid dusk. Birds will sing loudly as if night has fallen. We'll look for the beads, the little spots as sunspots that shoot out. We'll probably see the glimmer that will be the Hale-Bopp comet. Then, with the sun's absence, a cold wind will blow through. The thrill of darkness for just a moment, and then the aurora, the necklace about the sun. Peaceful beauty. Silence. And then the sun will appear on the side and the shadow disappears from one end of the valley to the other, the birds will resume their flight and day resumes. It is something like you've never seen, never experienced. It is a miracle."

It was late. I curled up on the small cot. The tent was cold. Voices sang outside, the night's celebrations, the conversations, and the drink and dance all led me to toss and turn under a thin, small blanket.

We might be anywhere, the nomadic tribe in this tent, a hundred miles from nowhere, waited on by servants, financed by a government that seeks western approbation, western attention. Focusing the world on a unique event that places Mongolia in the center of the world.

Early morning. Voices outside. I rose to go to the bathroom and pushed open the flaps. I felt cold moisture on my head. The sky was filled with clouds. I blinked and then realized and turned back into the *ger* and said, "I have bad news. It is snowing." Silence.

"What?" Heather said, sleepily.

"It is snowing," the Swede yelled. He sounded like a child. "Don't you understand? Clouds. We will see nothing!" He threw himself on his cot. In the distance, the squeaky loudspeaker blared morning music.

We ate our breakfast quietly.

"Perhaps it will clear," Janet said. "There is still a chance."

We climbed to the crowded hilltop in hope. Young women gave out cardboard dark glasses to protect our eyes. Hundreds of cameras on tripods pointed to the east. A faint glow came over the horizon and then, for just a moment, the clouds broke, allowing just a glimmer of the moon moving across the sun. It was a wonderful sight, a tantalizing view, but no brilliant sun flares, no running shadows, no beads, and no aurora. Just a glance, a moment's view. The clouds returned.

I returned to the *ger* to pack my bags. Sven sat on his cot, staring ahead. "You see, I am President of the Loser's Club, and once again. . . "

"But we had a very nice evening," I said.

"Yes. A nice evening." A smile came over his face. "But next year there will be a better chance in the Leeward Islands." He nodded his head. "Yes, I'm sure I will go."

I hitched a ride to Ulaanbaatar with Chinua and Heather. We drove past roaming herds of goats and sheep, horsemen guiding their path. I thought of the stories of the great American grasslands where the deer and the antelope played. This, the history I wrote about once, a vain academic attempt to imagine life a century before. Here and now, I was seeing it, cattle men wandering on plains that spread for a thousand miles, pushing their herds from pasture to pasture, cutting hay, moving to lower winter lands and higher summer lands, back and forth across eternity, living as they always lived.

We stopped at the home of Chinua's parents, a small wooden house in what had been an industrial town. Their tiny yard held a cow, a scurry of chickens, a goat and a dog. Over dumplings and yogurt and vodka and bread, the father spoke of how wondrous it was to have his daughter out in the world, speaking English, and with foreigners. The mother sat silently, hands folded. A Buddha sat on the mantel next to a black and white photo of the couple, then young, staring into a camera, unsmiling.

❧

Back in the capital, the Prime Minister ordered me to prepare a document to outline steps needed for reform while my Washington bosses demanded that I file directly with them and not with the locals. Procedure, they said. But the Mongolian was insistent.

"We cannot delay," he said, irritated. "By the time your bosses go through everything there will be a new government. This is a window of opportunity. We must act now. Think of yourself as the King of Mongolia. The future of the nation is in your hands."

The consultant has three bosses: the donor, the government, and himself. The consultant must protect his or her own livelihood, ensuring everyone is happy enough to gain the next contract. So I wrote my report and sent it to DC. And then I wrote another report with a list of reforms together with the issues each presented and gave it to the Minister. I asked him to keep it confidential, perhaps rewrite it in his own words.

On my final night, I returned to the frigid hotel room. I turned off CNN. I packed my bags and drank. I wrote to Wally. It was time for another assignment. Did he have anything for me?

TOGO

(2002)

**The Euro is introduced– Civil Wars end in Sierra Leone and Angola —
East Timor independence — Ivory Coast Civil War — Arms Reduction
Treaty — US Dept. of Homeland Security — Moscow Theater siege**

CONSIDER THIS: You are in a sparsely appointed hotel room in the small West African republic of Togo. You look out onto a dark green ocean and an empty beach. The windows are sealed. There is no electricity, no elevator, no air-conditioning, no television or computer. It is sweltering. You might go for a walk but it is dangerous. The locals are desperate, without work, and you, a white guy, are a perfect target for a quick grab.

In the last twenty years of your work, the world has seen more progress than all of history. Except in Africa. There, a million Rwandans were slaughtered in ethnic violence. Millions of Sudanese were starved by their government. Warlords terrorized Liberia and Sierra Leone with child soldiers. Wave upon wave of bloody conflict struck Kenya, the Congo, and the Sahel. Putsches, coups, and dictatorships permeated the continent. Poached elephant ivory, conflict diamonds, and refugees desperate to find a land of peace are the main exports. A visiting President Clinton proclaimed a "New Africa," although refusing to send help to besieged Rwanda and failing to condemn an African leader who denied the cause of HIV, leading to the death of hundreds of thousands, and perhaps millions of South Africans.

"The New Africa." The new version of The Emperor's New Clothes.

You are exhausted. You pace unclothed to survive the tropical heat in that malodourous room. You are unshaven, your headache lingers, a hangover or a migraine. It makes no difference. There is no water, of course, with the pumps out. For days on end, you gaze out over the steaming and empty white sands of the Atlantic beach below. From time to time, a young man brings you sustenance, eggs, sandwiches, fruits, water and Bourbon.

You are one of tens of thousands of professionals wandering the African continent, promising development and technology, good health and environment, trade and investment, and equality in a place where the rules are bent against it. You are Americans and Europeans, financed by governments and the United Nations, but all functioning under a banner of philanthropy. You all do well financially. You ride upfront in jetliners, you enjoy good international food and drink in the best hotels in the outer world and you will return to your homes and your families and the good life.

You are imprisoned, like Cervantes in his last days. You no longer wish to tilt at windmills. You are unable to function, too weak, tired and exhausted. You are Graham Greene's "Burnt-Out Case," Joseph Conrad's Kurtz and Paul Theroux on "The Lower River." You are at the end of the road. You know your time is passed.

Sometime around the turn of the century, the biggies got involved in our business—the Gates, Clintons, and a hundred other billionaires who decided they knew best. They would try their best with their data and dollars, flooding Africa with more experts and more theories all stirred and blended so you couldn't tell the righteous from the villains. Egomania disguised as charitable endeavors.

Then came media personalities—Bono, Affleck, Madonna, and the rest who got into the game. Then corporations advertised their self-worth by donating shoes and clothing for every item purchased in their stores. Fair trade became popular; corporations determined which producers met their standards.

The outer world became an aggregate of business, corrupt bureaucrats, self-important billionaires, greedy politicians, and academics all champing at the bit to get into the action, overpowering defenseless governments with money and personnel.

There were more consultants than mosquitos to swat. Some did good work, others got in the way. My pal Linda Polman, the journalist, told how in Rwanda, NGOs competed with one another to give help, unwittingly encouraging Hutus to continue their war of extermination against their Tutsis countrymen. Warlords sold licenses to charities to work in warzones, providing them with funds to purchase more arms. In the Sudan, Christian groups purchased Sudanese slaves to emancipate them, increasing the incentive for more slaving activities.

Then the Chinese arrived casting to the wind weak Western attempts to promote honesty and transparency. They bribed corrupt regimes, and built roads and ports using Chinese laborers.

The time of the indie consultant had passed.

I came to Togo in 2002 from Zambia, where I had worked on a privatization project with the smartest man I've ever met. Paul was a good friend and workmate. He rose rapidly in the Zambian bureaucracy because of his talent and extraordinary ability to tell Westerners what they wanted to hear.

Paul was a joy to watch as he worked the embassy cocktail parties. Humorous, serious, good-looking and affable, he'd listen seriously to a German businessman urging the use of German technology in the Zambian copper mines and would respond of how interesting that his own analysis had eliminated other methods and wondered why the Germans had been so good at it. The foreigner would wander away marveling at how smart Paul was.

He had served in a socialist government, rising to the top. But now, the government had moved on to the prevailing Thatcher/Reagan theories, promoting foreign investment. He became head of privatization, reporting directly to the Minister of Finance, who, in turn, negotiated agreements with international agencies. Paul understood the internal logic of the current dominant thought and gave it to the conqueror, the international banks, and the consultant, me.

He was rumored to be in line for a ministerial position, specializing in proposals that led to immense amounts of foreign aid. Together, Paul and I developed privatization legislation that would lead to the sale of bankrupt state institutions. We had honest disagreements, back and forth arguing over whether native Zambians should maintain controlling interest. His position was that there was no political will to give the industries to foreigners. I reminded him that foreigners would not invest without control.

It was true that Zambia was a special case, with skilled management and wealthy copper mines. As a former British colony, it maintained a good educational system and, unlike other African states, integrated its East Indian population into government and commerce.

This was the most successful consult I had done in Africa. Consultants always seek a sign, a glimmer of a new generation without the baggage from the colonies and the post-independence struggles. Paul restored my spirits. I stopped drinking and came to view what might be the future of Africa. We spent weeks together working and travelling about the country, to the mines, the game park, and south to Victoria Falls. He was frank and direct with a gift for being funny in a way that was perhaps on its face cynical, but allowed you to catch warmth and good-natured humor.

As my work with Paul drew to a close, he stopped coming to the office, every once in a while and without warning. He called in sick, taking off a day, and returned appearing quite healthy. Then, without any warning, he quit. He didn't say goodbye. Paul returned to his village and tribal group and rested until succumbing to AIDS.

Paul's death was for me, the death of hope. And now, here I was in Togo, the death knell.

⚬↝

It was Wally's doing, this Togo thing. One more mission to assess an African economy, its "competitive edge," and the environment for business. One more mission to an impoverished and desperate country that survived from subsistence agriculture and French aid, where few spoke openly against a petty, stupid, military dictatorship. One more round of meetings with entrenched, small interest groups, businessmen protecting their meager incomes, and workers fearful of dismissal and its disastrous consequences.

He asked me for "a favor" for the French. They needed to disperse funds remaining in their annual budget and required someone who spoke the language and could make a show of providing advice on international business. But here was the rub: the contract demanded sixty days, all work to be done in-country. I was to review all previous studies. And I needed to work with an in-country consultant, named by the French whose fee I would pay directly, in cash.

His name was Kofifi, young, mid-twenties, nervous, and poorly educated. He stammered. He wore the same suit every day, drooping over his slight frame. This "local expert" chosen by the French was employed by a Togolese consulting firm, a small operation in a second-floor walk-up. Why the French chose them, I could hardly guess.

Kofifi was supposed to meet me in two days, but I decided not to wait. I sought out the USAID office and was told that the agency had closed and left. I called the local World Bank office. The director was hesitant. He spoke in a low and despairing voice. "Things are bad, very bad," he said. He was sick. Might I call back in a week?

So I called the US Embassy. Yes, a political officer would see me if I came by. Her name was Sally Winters. Tired and clearly at career's end, she laughed as I told her my mission.

"But what are you doing here?" she asked. "I get a hundred consultants a year and they all ask the same questions. Nothing has changed. "

"I know, I know," I said. "I'm only following orders."

"Well, good luck to that. Look, the reason USAID pulled out is this is a military tyranny. President Eyadema is stupid. Uneducated. He was a Sergeant with the French militia. And after independence, he shot his way to power. We can't work with him."

"Can the French?"

"The French have to. Togo owns the lifeline inland to Burkina Faso, the road and train service. They do their best and, you know, the French being French, they don't want any outside interference."

"Can you suggest any businessmen I might see?"

She sighed. "They don't want to speak with you."

"I'm a professional."

"I know," she cut me off. "Look, the few foreign investors here are at Eyadema's mercy. They say the wrong thing and they get kicked out. The local guys, they say the wrong thing, the next morning they're in the desert."

"What would you suggest?"

"I'd suggest you go home."

She was right, of course, but I had signed a contract. I was stuck here.

Kofifi finally showed up. "Not to worry," he said. "Everything is under control. We go see the Papazians."

We drove along the broad and picturesque beachfront, palms blowing all about. It was scorching hot and the sea breeze provided no relief. At the port, vendors hawked radios and bananas. We turned onto a rough path and parked at a flour mill. The entrance was lined with pickup trucks waiting to purchase wheat for the country's bakeries and to be smuggled into Ghana just ten kilometers down the road. Tall, bare-chested men groaned as they heaved the heavy sacks onto their vehicles, white dust covering their blackness.

"Tote that barge," I muttered.

A small, aged white couple welcomed me. They were the Papazians, owners of the mill. They poured coffee and sat behind old wooden desks, facing each other. The woman scowled as I asked about business in Togo. She said, more than annoyed, "We've done this already. A hundred times. How many times must we say the same things over and over?"

Of course, I'd heard the same complaint a hundred times myself, I told her. In a hundred countries. That's the way things are. She sneered.

They were not happy. They lived at the flour mill for thirty years, refugees from Lebanon. I remarked there were quite a few Lebanese in West Africa. The old woman interrupted me saying, "We are *not* Lebanese. We are Armenian. We do not deal with these Lebanese."

I heard wrong. I apologized.

"We are from many countries, but we are Armenians," the old man said more gently.

During the First World War, the Turks murdered more than a million Armenians, driving them out of their homeland to refuge in Lebanon. Two generations later, they were forced to move again, scattered to the winds. The Armenians set up flour mills up and down the African cost, fairly immune from government outrages. If anything happened, the wheat would cease to come and the nation would starve.

The Turks deny the horrors they perpetuated. And these old, angry folks were evidence against them. Many years later, I ran into a retired military commander in Syria who came from the east, near the Turkish border. He was strong and direct, this soldier. He stared at me as he spoke of how his father took in Armenians fleeing from the rampage and married one who was his mother. Today, I often wonder what happened to that soldier and his family, descendants of Armenians escaping horrors and now living amidst their own horror in ethnic and political strife.

Back in Togo, a young African entered the mill house sporting a white suit and dark glasses, carrying a parcel of papers. "You see that boy," the old man said. "I educated him since he was a little child. I've made him into a good technician. I don't need European technicians. And that way I don't have to pay so much."

"You must be quite wealthy."

"Wealthy? What is wealth? I work seven days a week, ten hours a day. I make this place run. Me and my wife. Our workers, they live well. This is my life."

"Anyway, I'm here to find out the views of business people towards the government. How can regulations be changed to promote more investment?

He shook his head. "We don't talk politics here. We just run this business. People want to eat bread, we give them flour. We make sure the right people get jobs and get a good deal on our flour, and everything goes well."

Over the next week, Kofifi led me about, past small shops with tattered rag doors, cheap clothes hanging from rails, radios piled beside canned drinks, aluminum pots and plastic balls, car batteries displayed on wooden tables, wrenches, tires, and *whateveryouwantforyourcar*. Tall, strong, black women strolled about the streets balancing brightly-colored garments on their heads. Roadside food vendors squatted beside small wooden fires. Men hawked lottery tickets. Near the hotel, tourist kiosks offered cheap wooden statues.

One day we drove out of town, passing small Protestant temples and charity clinics, Evangelists, Adventists, and Baptists, UNESCO and Save the Children. The car was not air-conditioned. My clothes wilted. I wilted. The land was brown. Emaciated young calves wandered the road and gaunt chickens picked and pecked wherever they might. A farmer scythed a meager sugar crop.

In business after business, Togolese businessmen repeated the same complaints: foreigners own all the commerce with the outside world. This is their empire, their private domain that controls the sale of canned soup or soap or cheese or cheap Chinese toys. Once, European colonists profited, now it is Arabs, Indians, Chinese, Armenians and all the other earth wanderers, trading up and down the coast, bringing razor blades and cheap perfume from Europe, smuggling currency, buying, selling, buying selling.

"Somehow," a Togolese trader complained, "these foreigners avoid taxes and they import goods cheaper than I can. It is not fair. And I thought we were independent!"

He was right. It was not fair. Up and down Africa for twenty years I heard the same refrain: "The foreigners control everything. They subsidize goods, set prices, or give charity where and when they want, protected by the tyrant. It was better under the colony." It was all true.

Kofifi and I worked together for a week. And then he came less and less often, stopping in once in a while for lunch or a small interview or to ask for his salary. The litany had run its course: a foreign consultant descends and is taken to the usual firms, those willing to speak generalities and avoid saying anything that would raise the rancor of the President.

So I was left alone in that damned hotel room. I survived by drinking and dozing, munching on Ritz crackers and cheese, talking to myself, and pacing the room. I complained to my journal about life's condition and this and that and the stupidity of this work that paid oh so well but was bound to fail. I reviewed the few interviews with embassy and government officials who spoke in homilies and reading old reports that covered the same issues: fear, closed economy, no investment, fear (again), and stagnation.

And then, late into the night and deep into my cups, I wrote my pal Wally of a new concept, the Togo Syndrome, a condition created when governments order missions for political purposes that are transformed into projects by country officers, at their cubicles, and then reviewed by committees, rewritten, and transformed into a semblance of rational thought for an irrational project, in conformance with the correct political slants and current terminology, then sent out for bid and, finally, contracted to a consulting firm whose principal mission is profit and which, in turn, digs into its rolodex for one who would carry out the imperfect project without causing problems in a land with a petty, stupid, military dictatorship, with entrenched, small interest groups, businessmen protecting their meager incomes, and workers fearful of dismissal and its disastrous consequences.

The Togo Syndrome: Missions created not to succeed but to solve a political or bureaucratic problem. Projects meant to "show the flag," make a loan, or to spend the excess budget, but bound to fail. I thought the theory brilliant and said so.

Of course, the idea of the Togo Syndrome was insane. It would go nowhere, whatever its merits. There are hundreds of thousands anonymous consultants, working in health, infrastructure, finance, environment, agriculture, and all the others, away from home for weeks and months at a time working in lands alien to them, struggling with translations and cultural differences. Each of these men and women examine conditions, issues, and possible solutions to the problems they face. They each write long reports with deep analyses and send them to offices in Washington, New York, Paris, Rome, Geneva, Manila and all the other HQs where they are read, considered and put away, millions of words of varying merit lost in file cabinets, hard drives, the Cloud to wherever lost words go, to the Bardo and beyond.

In the meantime, "experts" in academia, think tanks and bureaucracies develop theories that are published and become part of what is called "the literature," some of which are lauded because of their literary style and complex analyses and then copied over and over to become the clichés of our time to be cited by others, contributing to "the literature."

The Togo Syndrome will not become a cliché of our time because it is already confined to the dust of our time.

My ideas lost their brilliant sheen in the sobering light of dawn with an empty bottle and trucks and buses droning along the coastal road. I downed aspirin and ate an orange. Sweat poured from my body. I tried the shower but there was still no water. The room smelled of whiskey, old cheese, orange peel, and sweat. I stood at the window, hungover, an aging and naked body peering out at the empty beach in the dangerous town. A burnt-out case.

Three days later, came a knock on the door. It was Wally, my boss, in his suit and tie, impervious to the wilting heat.

"Get dressed," he said. "And pack a few clothes. We're going on a vacation."

I said nothing. It was like being arrested. We descended to a waiting car, a large SUV, air-conditioned with a refrigerator in the rear that held whiskey and ice. "So, I'm back in America," I said sardonically.

"You're a mess."

"Think so?"

"I arranged for a hotel in Ghana where we can have some time to consult."

"That's what they pay me for, I'm told."

We reached the border. The cool air refreshed my body and soothed my anger. We flashed our passports and sped onward into Ghana.

WALLY

(2 0 0 2 / 2 0 1 5)

But he attained to honor, and honor, he used to say, is the natural goal towards which every considerable talent presses with whip and spur. Yes, one might put it that his whole career had been one conscious and overweening ascent to honor, which left in the rear all the misgivings or self-derogation which might have hampered him.

—Thomas Mann

OVER THE YEARS, we met countless times in top-shelf DC steak joints and sordid African bars and would talk for hours on end. I remained a recovering academic, always searching to understand the guy, his ideas, his logic, his politics. But no one is consistent in life. Certainly not Walt Whitman Stein, who could take both sides of any dispute and argue them in ten different languages. At times, he was an idealist. Others, a skeptic. He knew what could be done to help others and what could not. He was a realist and would not try to save a drowning man if he could not be saved.

Wally was of a rare breed in Washington. He didn't care about rank; his ambition linked to a vision, not a position. He could be on mission digging ditches in Djibouti out in the "outer world," as he called it, and be as content as overseeing office operations. As for the rest, those bureaucrats sitting in cubicles about him, he paid them little mind. If they were bothersome, though, he treated them with disdain and mockery.

We would drink and he would spout homilies: "I hate zealots and ideologues, the true believers who will not bend, their hardened views narrow and inflexible." Or "Rigidity is our enemy. People change. Conditions change."

Together, we ran projects in the poorest parts of the globe: Mumbai ghettoes, Cambodian factories, and Sahel deserts. Wally loved these places. They were challenges that frustrated me and energized him. I never understood it.

We were in Ghana at a seaside resort. He had just pulled me out of a failed mission in Togo.

"You feeling better?" he asked.

"Physically, yeah, but I'm exhausted. There's no run left in this horse."

"Bah, it's not that bad."

"Not that bad. You know what I've just been through?"

"I've seen worse."

"You really are sympathetic."

"You'll get over it and move on." Wally was always deaf to problems that might disrupt his own narrative, so much so he didn't hear the message, from me or others.

"I'm finished, Wally. I'm done with this life."

"Trust me, it'll pass."

The whiskey took hold. "Look, if we add it up, what have we accomplished?"

He shrugged. "You don't add it up. You're stuck in the American myth again. Trying to solve what are conundrums and quagmires."

"What's wrong with that?"

"The world is filled with fake success stories. You have these guys like Bill Gates who say data is everything. They try to measure things like health and life expectancy. They make human dots into data to dehumanize us all. Engineers, they are, who think they can stress-test lives and then proclaim their so-called successes to the world. 'Look at me. Look what I've done! I've raised the economy of Africa by 2%!'"

"So?"

"How can you test the quality of life? Happiness? Who is better off, a woman slaving in a polluted urban slum who gets health care and a measurable salary, or one who lives in the countryside living the way her ancestors did but maybe dies younger?"

"So, you don't measure?"

"You know Oliver Sacks, the neurologist?"

"Yes. And no."

"He goes off on his own and ignores data. Drives his colleagues mad. He observes. You should read his books. He observes, not measures, and then has breakthroughs that others couldn't see because they didn't look. Gates and his friends are like the old Commies who built engineering schools all over the place, made automatons of their citizens. They're so enthralled with science, math, and data, they forget to look around. I wonder if Gates has ever read Twain or Steinbeck. I bet not."

"You fighting with Gates now?"

"Washington wants measurements. They want success stories. They set goals, higher national wealth or life expectancy, but what does that mean? It means pushing peasants off their land where measurement is limited to a meager meal into urban slums where they work in sweatshops for pennies and increase the 'national wealth.' They want to know 'what works,' then they give it a name it and declare it a 'measurable strategy.' It becomes a cliché as if that strategy can be used for all conditions and places."

I was drunk and he was drunk with anger.

"What was it that Orwell said? 'The cliché is a way for governments to cover up atrocities, ideas papering over reality, hiding the essence of things.' Meanwhile, the people we serve lack voices and the power to influence policies. Measurement hides manipulation by those who work for their own self-interest. Muck in the swamps with peasants and laborers, not a computer keyboard or a calculation and you see the world as it is."

I thought he had come to save me from the Togo horror, but here I was listening to his rants. I tried to change the subject. "Yeah, but that's not the issue, is it? For me at least. The issue is we go in, work for years to create conditions for growth, and then some war breaks out or there's drought or the government steals the funds or markets change and we're back to square one."

"So?" He seemed bemused.

"I can't be satisfied with two steps forward, four steps back."

"Two steps forward are forward. Even if for a while. It is worth it if just for a few years, as children laugh and play and people enjoy life without fear or suffering. It may be brief and end in horror but that's life."

"You have patience. I don't."

"Do you know why Christian missionaries do better than all the bureaucracies, the NGOs, the United Nations and the rest? Because they value lives, even small, brief and tenuous lives. That is why they are against abortion. Because they believe any life is better than none."

I was shocked. "You getting religious?" I asked. "I wouldn't have believed it."

"I don't wear my beliefs on a T-shirt."

"But you are. . ."

He waved his hands. "My beliefs are irrelevant. But you, you are upset by all this because you see things that most people only glimpse at, if at all. You see and touch it and sense all that is so exasperating."

"Yes, that's right."

"And you want out?"

"Yes."

"But you know, just because you don't see it anymore, doesn't mean that it doesn't go on. Leaving is an excuse."

"I'm burnt out."

He shrugged. "Look at you. Do you think Chinese workers in sweatshops ponder the evils of the world the way you do? Do they get 'burnt-out?'" His face softened a bit. "You are a spoiled generation, just because you read a lot, are wealthy and live in the most successful nation ever, you can bemoan the starving in Bolivia and the end to icebergs and suffer intensely and then feel good about it. But there's no feeling good. There's only effort."

I changed the subject. "I met these Armenians who run the grain factory, refugees, stuck in Togo forever."

"The Papazians?"

"You know them?"

"Sure, I've met them a number of times. She was a real looker back in the day. Fun to be with back then."

"No longer. Old and bitter. I don't want to end up like her, like them, milling for the rest of my life in countries in despair."

He nodded. "You are a good man. Someone once said the crime against life is not to feel. There has never been a civilization in which the crime of torpor, of lethargy, of apathy was as common as it is now. And you feel. Perhaps too much. But that is a fine quality."

I fell quiet. Wally ordered lunch. Fried fish, fries, and more drinks. I dove into the pool and swam laps. When I came out, he was on his computer.

"Let me tell you something. What we do is try to create a basis for growth, the right of private property, a little honesty, and good laws for investment."

"I know that."

"But you know who our enemy is? All those do-gooders who flock in, giving food and destroying local production, those billionaires needing good PR who amass their fortunes from the rest of us, or those charities featuring Black babies or cute animals gaining donations from people whose lives are unfulfilled. They donate tons of money to locals, who then fall into cycles of dependency, expecting more and more handouts. Corrupt officials are corrupted through salaries and locals are seduced into working for charity rather than production."

The thing about Wally was he was neither sinner nor saint. His works, those he managed and those he carried out himself, tried to make the world just a little better place for a short time before the demons returned. He was like a medical researcher, perhaps like Oliver Sacks, looking to alleviate suffering with unpopular methods that might or might not have consequences. He saw the world as neither good nor evil but nuanced. He tried to balance greed, religious and ethnic zealotry, politics and bureaucratic infighting with the needs of people struggling to survive.

His personality was aggressive. He didn't brook fools or manipulators. He rankled old-timers, pushing his agenda and violating procedures to get his projects funded. And he didn't listen, that was enraging, as if he alone *knew* what needed to be done.

His enemies were countless; he was blamed for riots in Egypt, corruption in Uganda, and for decades of failed projects. We like to cast blame for the state of the affairs. Consultants always come first in the litany for their advice, and then the locals for their laziness, ineptitude or corruption, then the old colonizers for the legacies they left, then businessmen with their monopolies and oppression of workers, and then the do-gooders who don't realize the horrible consequences of their acts. People believe what they need to believe, what is in their own interests or biases. But they are rarely right.

Wally ignored the accusations and the hostility, constantly pushing for what he thought might be done to assist in food relief, financial crises and small business. Unstoppable. A madman. I never knew what drove him, why he kept going on and on, until it was much too late.

In 2015, Wally was celebrating his 70th birthday and his retirement somewhere on the horn of Africa. After the party he returned to his small apartment. Then he vanished. The thugs who took him demanded ransom but Washington's policy is never to pay, to do so would be to encourage others. Then, it was said, the thugs sold him to Al-Qaeda.

All this was public, in the newspapers, on TV and the internet. At least he was still alive, I thought. But I laughed, thinking that Al-Qaeda didn't know what they bought. Wally was a polyglot. He spoke Arabic along with ten other languages. He loved to argue and debate, and despite his being Jewish they kept him alive. I kept thinking of O'Henry's *The Ransom of Red Chief* in which a child's hyperactive behavior leads the kidnappers to pay the boy's father to take him back.

Six months later, Emir Ahmed Abdi Godane, the Al-Qaeda terrorist, was tracked down from a signal in his jeep, picked up in a Kenyan listening post and sent to Washington. The Pentagon announced the successful killing. Then, a week later, President Obama announced that my friend Wally happened to be in the same vehicle. Newspapers reported it for a couple of days. Word was that an internal investigation was to be launched. After the usual sorrow and the pity, his death vanished, just like he did. News these days has a short shelf life.

There was no responsibility taken or given. There rarely is in Washington. If a Chicago cop shoots an unarmed civilian while firing on a hoodlum, all hell breaks loose. But with Wally, it was a grievous error, a bad oversight, a slip-up, a lack of adequate information, and a dozen other implied excuses. Time to move on and forget the death of a man who devoted his life to helping others for almost half a century, a public servant and unsung hero who disappeared from existence, our sight and our memory in the sands of Somalia. What is it they say? No good deed goes unpunished.

The DC rule is and has always been to deflect accountability. When a drone kills a bunch of foreign civilians or hits our own troops in "friendly fire," no one is blamed. Once we wanted to bring Henry K. and Tricky Dick Nixon to justice for firebombing innocents in Cambodia. This time it was Obama, Mr. "Hope," who was in charge.

The man where the buck stops, as Truman once said. Truman, the man who gave the order for Hiroshima and Nagasaki.

Yes, I am bitter. There are no statues for Walt Whitman Stein, who was just a poor unlucky bastard in the wrong place at the wrong time. I mourned him with tears and not a little bit of anger and had a few drinks in his memory. He was a mentor and friend. Together, we worked the humanitarian hovels in what he used to call the "outer world," with all the frustrations, losses, and petty corruptions, weeks on end living out of suitcases, assessing charities, determining "felt-needs," and developing relationships with those seeking to do-good in lands where doing good is a chimera. When things went awry, when bureaucratic bumbling or civil wars stymied our efforts, we commiserated over booze and sybaritic fare, strengthening our resolve to keep pushing forward.

The thing is, a year before the kidnapping, Wally was on home leave when he asked to see me. He told me of his work in the horn of Africa, promoting the private sector in Ethiopia and Kenya and of the incredible opportunities. He suggested I come and work with him. He could arrange it. It was perfectly safe, he said.

I turned him down. The idea of returning to the frustrations and failures in the African continent gave me shivers. He insisted and pushed and argued as he always did.

I may well have been in that same Jeep with Wally and the terrorist if I obeyed his plea as I always had. But this time I said no.

TOM & JERRY

(2 0 1 5)

Boko Haram in Nigeria — Charlie Hebdo massacre — Civil War in Yemen and Ukraine — ISIS in Iraq and takes Palmyra, Syria — Conservatives win in the UK — FIFA scandal — Greek debt crisis — Iran nuclear deal — Cuba — US diplomatic relations — German diesel fraud — Climate Change Treaty

"IT'S REALLY SO NICE to see you, Tom. After all these years."

"I didn't know if I should come."

"Of course you should have."

"You're very busy. The young woman at the front desk was quite resistant."

Sonia Bishop waved her hands. "No, no, she's my gatekeeper. In this barrio, everyone has a need and everyone just *needs* to talk to me."

"Yes, of course." She was not the slender six-foot beauty of his youth, he thought, now big and wide showing the breadth of years. Her charcoal black face and piercing eyes were the same, though. She wore a business suit, like a banker. No, this was not the woman of memory, she who played with them when the earth was young. She was different.

"When I heard about Jerry, you were the only one who I might turn to."

"Yes, I read the news. Terrible, terrible accident."

"A tragedy," he said. "Some fool in a government office tracks a Jeep on a screen halfway around the world, pushes a button and poof! Jerry is gone."

Sonia nodded. "I'm sorry. He was a nice man."

"It was murder."

"I'm sorry," she repeated. "

"At least he died doing what he loved. He probably didn't even hear the incoming."

"I don't know."

"No, of course not. Nobody knew, Jerry or the one with the button. Remember when we used to fear the man with the button in the White House? Pretty ironic, no?"

Her mind scrambled to get hold of the situation. Tom had come out of nowhere, without warning. No call, no appointment. She'd have to push back her meetings. Father Rojas, the TEFL conference—no, she could miss that—and the auditors. Yes, the auditors. That was important. Out of memory he wandered in. She saw the resemblance but that was all. Because of poor Jerry. She'd have to deal with this.

"You kept up with him?" she said.

He smiled. "We were quite close. For years we wrote back and forth while he traveled."

"What did he do?"

"You didn't know?"

"No, I'm afraid not. It's been a long time, Tom." She sat back and glanced at the clock on the wall.

"I thought maybe you two…"

"No," she smiled. "We didn't. What went on is buried in the past, like most things."

"Jerry was a good man, dedicated, like you. He went from job to job, consulting on health, infrastructure, other things. He knew Africa and Latin America better than anyone around."

"Doing good work."

"Like you."

She accepted the compliment.

"He was always glad to be away from the tensions of home, saving lives. What did Marti say? 'With the poor people of the earth I want to cast my lot.' Nobody much quotes Marti anymore. Jerry loved those leftie mottos, the teachings of Chairman Mao and all that."

She smiled. She was losing interest. "And you?"

"No, I left good works long ago. Went into business. Boring stuff. Now past my prime."

"You married?"

"Yes, two boys, long gone. Wife's into yoga and saving the earth. Not my thing, saving the earth."

"Which one?

"Either. Both."

"Did Jerry ever get married?"

"Yes. A sad story. To a shrew."

"That's not very nice."

"Saving the world isn't the most lucrative job. She kept on him to move to a 'better neighborhood' with 'good schools.' New cars and all that. He couldn't care less, of course, always an ascetic. But he had to keep working to pay the bills. Even at his age. And so he ended up on a stupid assignment in the desert." He shrugged. "Under a bomb. Now she'll get the blood money."

"That's not fair. Surely you don't blame her?"

"I don't blame anyone. For anything. Too old for that. But you, what you've accomplished here in the barrio, it's quite wonderful."

"You know about my work?"

"I keep up. Curious about old friends, what they are doing."

"It's hard. As you say, we're past our prime."

"Doing all this for forty years."

"At first it was just making due, feeding the poor, fighting the slumlords, then riots and pushers. The city didn't give a damn. The school building was a mess, not worth saving they said. Back then, nobody wanted to live here, so we got it back into shape, the community, churches, schools and volunteers."

"Community development, huh?"

"Whatever you want to call it."

"No wonder Jerry was so proud of you."

"What do you mean?" She looked at him strangely. "Anyway, now it's prime real estate."

"But you survived, a voice at the table and all that."

"Yes, but listen. I have a couple of people I have to speak to."

"I'll go."

"No, no. Sit here. I'll be back in fifteen minutes, maybe a half hour. Read this. You might be interested." She handed him a bound document, rose slowly and walked out, a large elderly woman with a slight limp.

He looked about at the tired bureaucratic office so unlike the gleaming freshness of his hygienic corporate world. Worn furniture, a musky odor and dust all about. Loud laughter from the reception area. Dark skins. Multilingual notices of regulations and meetings on the walls without order: Neighborhood watch. Food co-op. English lessons. Another country, he thought. Certainly not his.

He turned to the document, a proposal for a new neighborhood center with offices for daycare, a health unit, counseling and meeting rooms. A play area on the roof. Three stories.

They came together in the Peace Corps. Tom, Jerry, and Sonia, a weird clique. Two Gringos and the Haitian-American beauty working in isolated and desperate towns in the Dominican Republic. American volunteers sprinkled all about the island as a faint bulwark against the bearded Cuban across the water.

Every few months they played together, "ugly Americans" roaming the streets of Santo Domingo. They would drink rotgut through the night, arguing, barging loudly into restaurants. Men hit on Sonia constantly. Tall and statuesque, domineering in her way and with the bloom of youth, she played and flirted and returned to her playmates, Tom and Jerry. They consumed life, he thought, swimming naked in secluded coves, riding on horseback through cane fields, bagasse whipping at their faces under the intense Caribbean sun. Flirting and loving.

"OK," she said, falling into her chair. "I've taking care of that. Auditors. Again. Each time a city official needs a headline, they hit on a poor agency, looking for evil. All they find is pennies spent for the wrong program. Now, where were we?"

He pointed to the proposal. "This new headquarters. Quite impressive."

"Yes. Well, it's not going to happen. The neighborhood is changing, gentrifying with different people, wealthier, not colored. The old folks are dying out. Our board says we're not really needed anymore, we should move to Newark or merge with a larger organization. But we're staying put and hang on and keep doing what we're doing to the remaining wretched refuse until the wrecking ball swings in."

"Who pays for all this?"

"Who? The city, foundations, the church, do-gooders. I spend my time on proposals, grant applications and then preparing reports, assessments and audits, not to mention the constant tours of the 'hood I give to potential donors. In between, we do our job, me and the staff. People walk in the door desperate for help, child support, food or sanctuary from drunks and druggies." She shook her head. "Now they say the city is better. We're not needed. But what do they know?"

"Sad, very sad. That's why I went into business. I couldn't take the constant disappointments and failures. One step forward, two steps… but you know all this."

"It's not like that, Tom. You work day to day, providing a little bit of assistance to those in need."

"I know that, Sonia. We both know that. But the situation is so desperate, so depressing. Look at my old town in the DR, then a few huts on a hot and barren beach, with bad water, a few milk cows, no school, and every tropical disease. We dug wells and built outhouses and what's there now? Golf courses, tennis courts and hi-rises. Krauts,

Limies and Gringoes replaced the people we loved and they, they were pushed into the urban hovels. Nothing has changed."

"Tell me about it. The Dominicans are deporting Haitians, their neighbors for generations. It's truly upsetting."

"Absolutely. The politics remain the same. Corruption, as always. So I saw the future back then and came home with a bad hangover and not just from rotgut. I couldn't move on."

The luxury of the middle class, she thought. To avoid pain. "But why business? It was so not you."

"It was something to do, earn a living, raise a family."

"You regret your life?"

"No, not at all. We make choices and live with them. By them."

"I guess everyone lives in their own way," she said. "You lived for yourself."

He bristled. "You live the best life you can, with human dignity and peace of conscience. I'm OK with that. And I always cherished those old days. I really admired how you and Jerry have hung on."

She shrugged. "What choice did we have?"

"You sound like a priest."

"No. This for me is the right way to live. We have success all over the place—housing, full bellies, detoxed druggies, the young ones off to college. A community that worked together to survive. Sure, every once in a while an infant gets tossed out a window, a guy ODs or an innocent is killed by a stray bullet. There's still tragedy around here, but that's the way of the world. In between is struggle and joy. Jerry must have known." At least, she thought, he died a painless death. But no, she wouldn't say it.

He smiled, relentless as always. "Of course. Is there any way I can help with the new building? Organize a benefit or two? I do have connections."

"No, it won't work. The board is against it and so is the city. It's the land they want and we're in the way. No amount of money will help."

They fell silent. She glanced at the clock again.

"We three had a good time back then," he said. "It was authentic. You know what I mean? A life that will never happen again."

"Yeah, I guess. Too long ago."

"The vacuum of time. Seems like yesterday. Remember the night we spent with Graham Greene?"

Sonia smiled. "That was fun, wasn't it?"

"An amazing evening. He drank us under the table."

"I guess I had forgotten about it."

"Did you sleep with him?"

"What?" She said loudly and angrily.

"Jerry and I often spoke about it."

"That's really none of your business. And what is this Jerry and I stuff?" She was irritated. This conversation was getting weird. She had work to do.

"Oh, nothing. As Jerry went from job to job to conflict zones and refugee camps or on famine relief, I was sort of a brother confessor. We wrote long letters, especially once the computer came into being and a lot of words recalled the past, the good times together. He needed support, Sonia, he really did. A bad marriage and a world of want. It wasn't easy for him. The promise of youthful love became a swamp of misery. But he kept going. Never gave up." Tom shook his head. "I don't know how he did it."

"You do what you can for the moment, for each individual person."

"You were always positive like that."

She nodded and they fell silent. "Well, it was good to see you, Tom. I'm sorry about Jerry."

"Thanks. I came here to tell you something, though."

"Yes?" She wondered where this was going.

"You know Jerry was in love with you."

She laughed. "It was not for very long."

"Oh, it was. It was. Not that you stayed lovers. You kept in contact for quite a few years and for what he told me once in a while you came back together briefly."

Sonia shook her head. "We were kids. He was very needy. I fell for that too many times."

"Yes, well… after you guys drifted apart, he kept on."

"What do you mean, 'kept on'?"

"He sort of watched you from afar. He'd send me clippings. You and the Mayor. You on a march for something or other. News stories about the community center."

"He stalked me?"

"In a way. Yes."

She stared at him "'In a way'? How close?"

"Not close at all. He never approached you or even came near you. And, after the Internet, he just searched you."

"But why? It was so long ago."

"One time he came back from the Philippines, tired and exhausted. We went for drinks. He told me about the civil war over there, the incredible urban poverty and then a long flight back with reports to write and troubles at home, how his wife just didn't understand. He was a mess. We got very drunk."

"You guys always got very drunk," she laughed.

Tom looked at her smile. Sonia always forgave, he thought. If you were a friend, the greatest outrage was laughed off and the friendship continued. Is that why she is so successful? A sense of forgiveness?

"He knew he was half-nuts, keeping you in his head. But he also knew why. We sat on the floor, pouring whiskey, slobbering about the good old days and he let on about his craziness. He blamed his parents. They were survivors from Hitler. I knew that but it didn't seem very important. Came out of Austria very late, made it to Brazil and finally to America. His mother was quite beautiful and he suspected that she used her charms to save their lives. His father, an academic of some note in Vienna, philosophy, I think, but here, an unknown, his English never very good. He ended up working as a dry cleaner."

She stared into his eyes, making him nervous. He paused. Her expression asked why this tale? "Anyway, there was no love in his house. No touching. No hugging. No warmth. Just anger and bitterness. Shouting and recriminations. We never think of the lasting effects, the consequences of past horrors, passing from generation to generation. In college, Jerry was a loner. A nerd, afraid and enclosed. What we would call a nerd today."

"He certainly didn't seem like a nerd to me."

"And that was the thing. He said you were the first to touch him, to stir his emotions, to show him there was something outside a fearful existence."

"And so he stalked me."

Tom sighed. "Not to harm you, Sonia. In any way. After all, you didn't know."

"I know now." She was angry. "So, he stalked me because of the Nazis?"

"It's over," he said forcefully. "He's gone."

"So why are you telling me this now?"

"I think he wanted you to know. You gave him life. Because of you, he worked the world, trying, like you, to end the world's horrors."

She stared away. "It's been almost half a century, Tom. This is nuts."

"I know. Unrequited love's a bore."

"What?"

"A line from a song."

"You have no idea how crazy this is. To think that someone might carry a torch for that long. It's fucking insane."

"No, Sonia, you're wrong. What I'm saying is you changed his life. It is as much because of you that he ended up smashed to smithereens."

"Now you're blaming me for that?"

"No! You gave him purpose, you lighted his candle, you were the… what do you guys say? 'Agent for change'? You have no idea how many people he helped. Because of you."

"Well, if that's what you think. I'm happy for him."

Hates, joys and cruel disappointments all jumbled together. He looked at her, hoping that the camaraderie from years before would reignite. He knew that there are those who hold their memories tight, searching for joy in a slideshow of distorted memories to overcome the constant drone of life's problems, and others who live for the day but for whom the past is blocked, lobotomized and best forgotten.

"I can see it's the wrong time," he said.

"There's never a right time, Tom."

"I just thought you should know. Thanks for seeing me." He stood to leave.

She rose awkwardly and walked him out, hanging slightly on his arm. "I'm sorry if I disappointed you but I think your friend is…"

"Was."

"…was a little loony."

"Like the world."

She smiled and touched his hand and turned back into the office. The receptionist looked up, "Who was that?"

"Oh, nobody of consequence. Really. Nobody. Did Father Rojas call?"

Tom wandered along the narrow side street past boarded brownstones with "For Sale" signs. Cars were double-parked and trucks were blocked. Horns blared in frustration. He turned onto the avenue. Bodegas and pawn shops mingled with espresso bars and bright restaurants offering vegan food, soul food and tapas. He entered a tavern, Sancho's, a sign in the window announced evening jazz.

He ordered a whiskey and looked at a corner table with young women, white, Asian and Black talking loudly. They laughed and drank, tapped on their phones and shared pictures, seemingly without any care in the world.

The bartender was young and Black. "Everything OK with you, guy?"

"Sure, fine. Pretty girls, huh?"

"Yeah, local professionals. But you. What's up with you?"

He shrugged, "Why do you ask?"

"Not very often an old white guy comes in at midday for a drink."

Tom stared into the mirror and saw an aged face with ruffled hair, wrinkled skin and tired eyes. He noted the time, a quarter to three. "Just troubles with love," he said.

The barkeep nodded and laughed. "Even at your age."

"Guess so."

"It never ends, does it?"

The bartender poured him another drink. "Here guy, one for the road."

Tom smiled, slapped a twenty on the bar and left.

AYE AYE

(2 0 1 8)

Excerpted from the novel, The Shadows

MY NEIGHBORS ARE FRIENDLY. Not close, mind you, but close enough. New York pleasant, you might say. Brief chats in the lobby or elevator, with a joke, some gossip or a weather report. I've walked their dogs and watered their plants. I don't get involved in family squabbles. I ignore crying babies or those embarrassing husband and wife fights that echo down the hall. No, not close but polite and friendly.

The brief interactions are good for me. I've never had many real friends and of those, most have moved away or worse. I've withdrawn, to be truthful, what with the situation as it is.

All this changed some six months ago with a faint knock.

"Someone is at the door," I said to Ellie. My wife stared. The buzzer didn't work and hadn't for decades. Ellie scoffs at my failed masculinity, leaving broken things broken as I do. Why exert energy to fix a useless thing? The knock grew louder.

I answered still in my nighttime garb, shorts and a smelly T-shirt with Gandhi on the front, faded and worn by years of washing but oh so comfortable. I was unshaven and had not "prendre ma toilette," as the Frenchies say. Clothes and linens were tossed about the room. They were all clean, but I had not got around to putting them away. For a month or so. One forgets, working alone at home, caring for a loved one and not separating day from night.

I opened the door. It was Amy of 3C. Standing next to her was Liz from 11B.

Amy wore a folksy, gypsy skirt. "We just came by to see Ellie," she said. "You remember Liz?" I nod. Liz Currey. Pretty and blond. A newscaster, once on a prime network but now a local affiliate as age reduced her appeal. "And we brought cookies! From that new store down the street. They're very good."

I was speechless. No, shocked. 3C Amy. She, like us, aging. She, like us, got in early, bought her apartment with thousands when the place went co-op and before prices soared to millions. We are the impoverished, so to speak, in a world of new wealth. Our view on the ninth floor is better than hers. Ours looks out across the river and deep into the west that was once the American landscape and now, new-age developments. Amy is stuck with neighboring roofs, smokestacks, and hung laundry.

"I'm really busy and as you see. Not open for visitors."

"No worry. We're here for Ellie, not you," she said, smiling and pushing gently into our home.

Amy is a class-warrior. Bravely, she fights for world peace, the homeless, and the working poor, civil and women's rights, Gay rights and the rights of animals. All the rights. Anti-war, anti-guns, and anti-nuclear. Once quite attractive but now, like all of us, weathered by life. She has done well in her fights, living on a city pension, enough to cover the growing monthly maintenance bill. There is profit in virtue.

They approached my poor, defenseless wife. "Hi Ellie. It's me, Amy." Ellie smiled. "I think she recognizes me," she said confidently.

"She don't recognize no one."

"Don't speak for her, Virgil. Men!" she laughed and turned back to Ellie. "This is Liz. You remember Liz?" Amy was speaking to my wife as one does to a child.

Ellie smiled and stared at them, or rather through them. Her latest style.

"You don't mind if we sit and chat a little, do you?"

"Be my guest." I was resigned.

"You don't have any tea? I don't wish to be a bother, just show me where it is and . . . "

I went to the kitchen. Our cabinets are old, and wooden, their paint scarred. The frig groans and makes no ice, the oven spotted by years of spilled sauces. Our kitchen bears all the marks of usage and age, a monument to Ellie's cooking. My neighbors' are spotless and unused, a place to store snacks and drinks.

I dutifully switched on the kettle. We don't use fire to avoid accidents. "I actually lied a little," she shouted from the living room. I sighed.

"We're really here for both of you."

I said nothing, pouring the water.

"You don't have herbal, by any chance?"

"Today, we only offer caffeine."

"I guess that will have to do."

"You have a charming apartment," Liz Currey commented, being polite. Our apartment is filled with relics from our past lives, our prized sandstone Dancing Ganesh in the foyer, a bronze Sukhothai Buddha by the window, African masks in the hallway and shelves filled with Ellie's books, badly needing dusting. Austin and Trollope. Murdoch and Lessing. Faulkner and Baldwin. A certain charm, I guess.

I was polite, quiet in this new world where the wrong word stains forever. I smiled and inquired as to the purpose of their visit.

Amy spoke to Ellie as if she understood. Amy is a liberated feminist, dyed in the wool, convinced that all men are complicit in her failed campaigns and so she involved Ellie, poor mindless but now oh-so-liberated Ellie. Liz chimed in as well but I paid no attention.

"What do you think?" Amy looked at me.

"I'm sorry," I apologized. "I have work on my mind."

Liz smiled. She was attractive, with a solid, fortyish maturity that attracts men of my age, a direct look that caught me although I wondered if this was her TV presence.

I perked up. Liz shrugged. "The thing is when Amy told me about your wife. I just *knew* this would be perfect for you."

I looked back and forth. "This? What is this?"

"Don't you listen?" Amy gruffed. "What is it with you?"

"Again?" I pleaded.

Liz continued. "I go to this spa. It's Ayurvedic. A very special place. Very well known. The French and Germans go there."

"The French and Germans," I muttered.

"Yes. The spa works wonders with people with your wife's disorder."

"Wonders? My wife's disorder? What disorder might that be?"

"You know," Liz said, a hint of desperation in her voice.

"Virgil!" Amy's voice rose to a faint *sforzando* crescendo.

"Oh, that disorder." I turned to my Ellie, "They're here about your disorder, honey."

Ellie stared down, picking at her hand. "Why don't you shut up," I heard her say. "Why must you be like this?" After all these years being as tight as any couple ever has, we finish each other's thoughts. I say a few words and she completes the phrase. Corrects it, rather. She is my moral guide, which everyone says I badly need. I speak and she corrects. In my mind, that is, because Ellie no longer speaks but I know what she would say if she were all here.

We, Ellie and me, are a tribe of assumed knowledge, language, custom, and body movements, as I guess most close marriages are. Shrinks call it dependency, but I never understood why two bonded organs with different sensibilities are not stronger together than apart. I x I = I squared. Anyway, I still hear her. She never left and still remains my censor, my alter-ego and partner.

Liz continued as if she was relating the news. "Yes. There are incredible stories about the spa. You just won't believe how people have regained their memories and personalities. It's all using ancient medicines, massages, and aromas."

Perplexed, I kept my eyes glued on this cheerful angel, showing nothing, a trick one learns in endless and pointless business meetings.

But how to react? How many times do "they" suggest organic, holistic, or miracle remedies for depression and cancer? Or Vitamin X or Y or that new over-the-counter remedy that cures flu, virus, rheumatism, arthritis, and the evil of all evils, impotence? How many times do "they" claim eternal salvation if only their advice is followed? You know who "they" are. You've heard what "they" saw on television or read in nutrition blogs or health columns or heard in church or what so-and-so told them or what "they" truly believe. And ultimately, what would not have happened if only you had listened to "their" advice.

"Shut up," Ellie said, interrupting my stream of internal, irascible consciousness. I want to be polite. I really do. And despite what some might say, I do try.

"Does sound incredible," I mumbled.

"Doesn't it?" Liz became more enthusiastic, not catching my sarcasm.

"You've tried everything with traditional medicine," Amy said, "and you certainly must know about the wonders of Eastern medical treatments."

"And," Liz continued, "we contacted the spa. They're willing to pay for all the treatments!" She was so enthusiastic I wanted to kiss her. There hasn't been so much optimism in this place since Goldie, the neighbor's puppy, invaded and ran about joyously, yapping and yapping before peeing on our seventeenth century Harami rug.

"Pay for everything?"

"Yes!" she screamed. Very *fortissimo*. "They know who I am so they made the offer."

"Would you be coming too?" I exclaimed.

"No, no," she laughed.

"Too bad." I feigned disappointment.

"Let's get serious," Amy said. "I am really trying to be a good neighbor here and when Liz told me…"

"OK, Amy. What's the catch? Why the generosity?"

Amy smiled. "You're always so much the cynic, Virgil. It's so painful."

"So?"

"They need real-life case histories," Liz said. "To get the message out. Nobody believes these days. Everyone is so much a skeptic. They need case-studies to publicize."

"Ellie as a guinea pig? Honey," I turned towards my poor wife. "Would you like to be a guinea pig?" She slept.

"No," Liz protested. "Their method actually works!"

I rose and went to Ellie. I touched her hair lightly. Her eyes opened and stared into mine. "Here she is, my sweetness, my whole life, the balance to my imbalance, she, the poster child for the ravages of extended age, the crippling, debasing, and agonizing rot the fates produce. And you propose a silly and absurd solution."

"You're being obtuse," Amy said.

I love the word obtuse. Says so much about the speaker, says "you don't agree with me and so you are stupid while I am right."

"You have nothing to lose. You can even gain some benefit while you're there, take a few treatments for yourself…."

"Oh, they have Bourbon there?"

"If you want." Amy, condescending again.

"Why are you doing this?" I asked Liz.

She smiled. "I want to help. You know we go through life self-absorbed and we're all so successful and wealthy and have everything we need and we're so lucky and we get so few chances to help our fellow men and women and here is my chance to contribute, to make other lives better and so I leapt at the chance. Two years ago, I was so depressed. We divorced, my husband and me, and I couldn't see myself going on. You know what I mean?" Tears swelled. She paused a minute. I wanted to go and hug her, but Ellie screamed in my head.

Liz continued. "Then a friend suggested this spa. I hesitated, just like you, and I understand that, but still what choice did I have? So I went and it was so miraculous. I was rejuvenated, my life restored, and then I realized I can give back. I am ready to devote my life to it."

"It?"

"Saving others."

"I get it."

"What do you get?" Amy pushed.

"It, Amy. It. I get it."

She sighed, "I don't think you're taking this seriously."

I may be a retrograde, a conservative and insensitive white man, but I do have a few good qualities. "Let me think *it* over. Ellie and I have to talk." Amy gave me *that* stare. "No, seriously, I'll let you know."

I showed them the door, threw the tea down the drain and poured a stiff Bourbon.

I took Ellie by the hand and led her to the bathroom, removed her smock and undid her diaper. We entered the shower together. I turned on the water, making sure it was lukewarm. I sponged her body, her long legs, now so sinewy, her slim waist, her shrunken breasts, and then slowly dipped her hair under the spray. She smiled, shaking the water off. She likes showers, the best time of day for her, or at least I think it is. I toweled her and restored her clothing.

To be sure, most of the horrors are gone. Those years when slowly, day-by-day and month-by-month, her memory slipped and she was so aware. Nothing worse than knowing that something you knew yesterday is gone. That a childhood experience, a close friend or a joyful taste, are fading, a day to day terror that she bore stoically as if the same biological process that ended her humanity protected her from that knowledge.

Even through the worst of it, she seemed to accept her fate, while I sat by her side wondering who are we without our memories, personality or identity. Does anything remain of us without consciousness? Is she with us, or is she just a memory, a breathing specimen that bears no resemblance to the laughing child, the playful teen, the lustful woman, the literate and verbal being that shared life's pressures with me?

We went to the kitchen and I served soft ice cream, mixing in three pills, three pills that "may do something." Experimental, they say. Or maybe not. A placebo? A 50-50 chance, they say, they being doctors with Rolexes and modern, expensive labs with the newest, high-end equipment, government finance going to corporate coffers. There's no guarantee that the medication will be effective, they say. Newspapers report that researchers say they may be "barking up the wrong tree."

If you know statistics you wouldn't bet on this horse or dog. Or life. Lesser men weep.

You go a little crazy living by yourself. Yes, I live with Ellie but our conversations are a little one-sided. We of the aging class live in a fantasy of our own making, thinking we understand the new worlds about us but are really stuck petrified from years before. This, a world of which we think we are a part.

Others may have folks all about, friends and family. They attend church. They hire shrinks. But most of us of our "condition"—that is, Ellie's and mine—we live by ourselves, day to day. Not without hope, because hope isn't in our vocabulary, but what they used say as "making do." And making do for me means cynicism with a little bitterness and anger on the side. Friends come by, then they call, then write, and then are no longer there, carried downstream avoiding the fate that someday will come their way.

I'm OK, mind you. I get along and we get along, but we don't mix easily with others. I mean, I don't mix well. Ellie? She gets along with everyone. Or used to.

I sighed, and looked out the window. "So what do you think, Ellie? Should we give it a try?

She stared blankly at me.

❧

The spa was one of those walled estates on the North Shore of Long Island with a large Georgian mansion at its center. I expected Gatsby with martinis, but instead there was Dr. Swaraj, a middle-aged Indian gentleman garbed in white, his office bare aside from a plain cotton rug. We kneeled to the floor. Two young women, Aye Aye and Shakti, sat on each side of us.

Dr. Swaraj spoke with an Oxbridge accent. He was so, so happy to meet Ellie. It was his supreme desire to spread the word on how the spa repairs the ravages she suffers. Miss Liz Currey recommended us, and she is a dear, dear friend and supporter, he said. No payment. None whatsoever. An offering for Ellie, as a favor to Liz. And for this, all we needed to do was sign a raft of papers, non-disclosure, non-liability, security and confidentiality agreements.

Perhaps I was ignorant of Ayurveda, he asked. I admitted that I was. He smiled. Ayurveda descends from the Gods themselves. The name combines the concept of *Ayur*, or life, with *Veda*, or Science. He devoted his entire life studying and praying, but his knowledge was nothing, miniscule, compared to the centuries of learning that his predecessors amassed. He was nothing, a mere insect, compared to the ancients. Old remedies are often the best, don't you think?

I grew impatient, thinking of leaving. "You're being too harsh," I heard Ellie say. "Why can't you just accept? You might learn something." Yes dear, I argued, but you are not here. You are off in another world.

Swaraj guaranteed Ellie an amazing improvement over the following two weeks. I am not sure I am repeating this correctly because, frankly, my mind wandered as his speech droned on. But what I remember now was that Ellie's treatment involved a change in diet, breathing exercises, and medicated liquids poured on her head to increase blood supply to the brain. In addition, a daily prayer meeting was to be held each morning at five to celebrate the sun's arrival. He expected me to accompany my wife.

Ellie stared and I went along. One tries anything out of desperation. I was skeptical, but with nothing to lose I was open to believing that Dr. Swaraj had a remedy, any remedy. Like those poor people who buy multivitamins to cure cancer, I would try anything.

Through the days, while Aye Aye and Shakti guided her from room to room and God knows what torture, I escaped for walks along Long Island Sound, past Gilded-Age mansions, a golf course, and marinas crammed with gleaming white sails.

Late one afternoon, on the fourth day, Ellie and I strolled by the water, watching the sun fade and yacht lights sparkling against the grey dusk. We sat on a piece of driftwood, a long rotted tree trunk. I took her hand and squeezed. She stared ahead. I put my arm around her, seeking that feel that always responded to my touch, but her body was limp. It was her natural state now, as natural as the decaying wood beneath us.

"Hello," a voice said from the shadows.

I turned and looked at a child-like figure in the dim light.

"I am Aye Aye, your wife's helper."

"I'm sorry, I couldn't make you out."

"I didn't mean to frighten you."

"No, you didn't." I invited her to join us and she sat at a distance. "How do you think it is going?" I asked.

She nodded a little. What a tiny figure I thought at the time, hardly four feet tall, with fine features, a sweet, almost angelic face, a tiny waist, and delicate fingers, miniscule but so strong. How old might she be? 15? 30? Older? It is amazing how existence and consciousness owes nothing to height and weight.

"I mean, do you see any progress?"

She spoke haltingly, sounding out every syllable. "Your wife is very ill and it has only been a short while."

"So you don't see any change?"

"It takes time. But I give Ellie three massages a day with different oils. Her skin is very soft and malleable. She doesn't seem to be in any discomfort."

"I guess that is good."

"Yes, very good. I have known many people whose skin is rough and aged. Their joints ache. They suffer spasms and all sorts of conditions."

Looking back, I understand she was trying to tell me that the treatments would not solve anything. This was no shock and I certainly was not disappointed. I have lived my life protected from disappointment by deep cynicism, no less than here.

We stared at the water, the three of us. Aye Aye turned to me. I could not see her face. "You are a very good man, I think."

"No, not really."

"I think so. Many people drop off their mates and go off to do all sorts of things. You stayed. You are a good man."

I whispered, "We have lived our life together and this is no different." I felt Ellie shiver. "I think it is time to return. She is cold."

"Yes, of course."

It was dark and I stumbled as we made our way home. Aye Aye took my hand and led the way. Her hand was as soft as a cat's paw, her grip strong and controlling. When we reached the residence, she nodded and said quietly, "Have a good night."

Thereafter and every day at dusk, the three of us met on the beach. As she gained more confidence, Aye Aye sat closer. I related to her the joyful years Ellie and I spent together, playing and travelling, how we shared books, movies and plays, arguing over this and that but united in our journey. Ellie was so beautiful, so smart and personable. Me, I was withdrawn, not comfortable with others. Symbiosis, I thought. An idyllic couple as much as there's ever been.

"And you," I asked. "Where are you from?"

"I am from Burma."

"You've come a long way."

"One goes where one must."

"Do you have family here?"

"No. No family."

I felt I was prying. "This is a beautiful place to work."

"Yes, very beautiful."

We fell silent. "Are you happy you came?" I asked.

"Yes, I suppose so."

I always have found conversation difficult with South Asians, filled with politeness, offering words they believe others wish to hear. I suppose it is the same in America, but they do it with so much more graciousness and warmth, comforting on a distant beach with the soft sounds of waves lapping the shoreline.

The treatment continued and as the days progressed Ellie seemed to accept Aye Aye's presence. Not that she reacted, but one presumes what one may even if the deduction is instinctive, as with pet dogs. And now, looking back, I realize that it was I who gained comfort from the Burmese woman. She was… What do we say about those who provide good service? Competent. She had a soft smile as she spoke, a tender touch of my wrist and the top of my hand. Not that there was much conversation. What was there to say? But every night, before we departed, she always said, "You are a good man."

Did the treatment work? It was amazing. Really. Truly. Ellie's memory was restored and, more than that, she remembers her earlier life. After just a week, she wanted to play tennis and learn more languages. Our nights were filled with levity and lust. She wanted to travel more, perhaps to the Himalayas.

Alas! If only it were true. Ellie remained the same, perhaps with softer skin but still mindless and away from this world. But those nights on the beach helped me develop a sense of peace. Now don't go off to an Aha! Hare-Krishna moment. Perhaps it was due to a lack of alcohol and morning hangovers, perhaps being distant from home.

And then there was Ellie, whose side I never left at home. Here, she was off without me while I wandered about, without the daily tensions of caring for the one you love. I knew she was close, safe and cared for and that we would be back together each night.

I had never considered "getting help," the euphemism that suggests one is incapable of dealing with life's complications and with a lover's ailment. How might a stranger, a paid employee, provide the warmth and care of a loved one? I know others are physically or emotionally incapable of "going it alone" and more power to them with a helper. But not me. Not with Ellie. My partner. The thought had never crossed my mind.

But Aye Aye seemed to fit. Ellie responded well to her, or at least did not flinch or react in any way that I could see. The idea came from nowhere, like a reflex. It was the last night of our stay. The three of us sat by the water under a fading light. The air was warm with a soft and sweet sea breeze. All was blue, a fading blue, the water, sky, and dying light on our faces. I looked at Ellie and the small woman and felt so relaxed and at peace.

Without much thought I said, "Aye Aye, I was wondering, would you like to come and help me with Ellie?"

"Yes," she said without pause. She showed no reaction, as if she expected the request.

"Are you sure?"

"I would be happy to come and help you," she said. "If I can. One goes where one must."

I made the arrangements. Dr. Swaraj was more than helpful in allowing Aye Aye to leave. I paid a healthy sum to cover Aye Aye's obligations and the cost of training a replacement. I agreed to make a generous offering to the spa for its continued good works. I turned out to be a good Buddhist, after all.

After almost a year, our world has changed. Aye Aye is a wonder, caring for Ellie so closely and protectively. Is my wife happier? More content? No, that is not in the cards. She still sits and stares out the window or watches television. But each day we stroll to the river, the three of us hand in hand. Aye Aye and I talk quietly, enjoying the breeze, the flowers, and life. She laughs at my jokes, Aye Aye does, although I suspect more out of politeness than anything else.

The apartment is neat and well-ordered. The books on the shelves, dusted as if they were just read yesterday. She cooks Burmese dinners. Asian odors spread down the hall and through the building. In the evenings we watch Burmese television on cable. Aye Aye likes that. I sit by her and read while she laughs at silly shows.

I've always been a solitary man. Ellie would socialize and from time to time I would join her, but I prefer my own company. Aye Aye brought me companionship of a sort, I must confess, and if I feel a little guilty betraying Ellie I know that the young woman's presence is at much for my wife as for me. Rationalization? Perhaps. But Aye Aye is now one of us.

The neighbors descend, upsetting Nirvana. Amy and Liz lead the assault, backed by the co-op board, *nouveaux-arrives* who bought their apartments at the top of the market. Wealthy, self-righteous and secure in their lives, they strut in as if they own the world, money in the bank, country house and private schools for the kiddies: Jim Purcell, the architect with three kids in private school; Dave Huang, the brain surgeon, quiet and withdrawn; and Sam Davis, the lawyer, whose wife is a somewhat famous art critic, their children fully grown. He speaks to me as if he's before a judge.

As they enter, I stare at them, one after the other. Ellie is inside watching television, safe and out of earshot. Not that she understands. She loves game shows with their joyful and cheerful faces, winners jumping for joy, losers smiling and applauding their loss. Everyone as happy as clams. Or she seems to.

I expected something like this, nervous looks in hallways, children staring at the tiny being besides us, conversations cut short as we approached, but not this Star Chamber.

Sam Davis speaks, the lawyer dressed in studied informality, beige cotton slacks we used to call Chinos, a tie and checked shirt, but no jacket. "There is some concern in the building," he says smiling, "and they'd like to understand what's going on." Amy takes a pad out of her bag.

"Is this is an official meeting, to be recorded?" I ask.

"No, that's not necessary." The pad disappears.

"So there is some concern?" I say. "Would you all like some water?" Years of business meetings have taught me to control the agenda.

"Yes," says Davis. "That would be nice. Our concern is about your live-in."

"My live-in?"

"The Asian girl."

"Oh, you mean Aye Aye."

"Is that her name?"

"Yes."

"And she lives here with you?" Davis says, being a lawyer.

"She works for us."

"But she lives here?"

"Yes. What else would you like to know?"

Aye Aye emerges from the kitchen. She places a glass before each guest, nodding and smiling as she pours the water. She withdraws and brings me a glass of Jack with three cubes of ice, the way I like it.

"Anybody wish to join me?" They stare. "Whiskey is God's way of telling us he loves us and wants us to be happy, or so they say." I smile.

She kneels beside me, so petite and calm, so much the opposite of the fierce faces who look at each other in disbelief. She is beautiful, maybe not in a Western sense but a classic beauty for the ages, fingers as slender as reeds, arms like bamboo, and a tight, strong face. She puts a hand on my knee for security.

"Everything OK?" she asks quietly.

"Everything is fine," I respond, squeezing her shoulder.

They look at her. They look at me. They look at my glass. They are unsettled. "This is Aye Aye. She is from Burma. The country they now call Myanmar. But she is not Burmese, she is a Mon."

Purcell, the architect chimes in. He is impatient and direct. "Look, there's nothing personal here. We need to act to protect the community's propriety, ensuring nothing illegal or untoward takes place to bring disrepute upon the building. After all, this is a co-op. We really don't want to call in the authorities and make a big deal about this."

Righteous virtue designed as integrity, I think.

"We are neighbors, Virgil," says Liz the TV woman, smiling as she always does. "We want to settle this amicably. We all share common responsibilities to our neighbors, don't you agree?"

I sip my drink and listen to accusations designed as questions, one after another. How old is she? Where does she sleep? Does she have the proper immigration papers? Is she paid?

They are very confident, these children. Respect for one's elders seems to have gone out the co-op windows a long time past. No, they do not mention the ultimate threat, eviction. But the threat is there like thugs in a dark alley.

I hide my feelings, but maybe not too well. I let them say their peace. I am a native of the city, born and bred, a little angry, paranoid but street-smart. And they? There was a time they lived in suburban and gated splendor with school buses, kids biking on cul-de-sacs, and golden retrievers, all safe with petty judgments shielded in lily-white sub-divisions cocktail parties and behind country club doors. They lived where, as Dr. King said, Sunday morning was the most segregated hour in America, in their Churches.

But all has changed. The split-level avec garden has become the co-op on the river. In stealth they came, bought property, pushed out unfashionable types of darker colors who utter strange and alien languages. They installed their values, these newbies, building meccas in their own vision and staining the urban fabric. "Safe" private schools for the kiddies, enclosed public parks keeping out the riff-raff, choice restaurants and posh art galleries.

"Dr. King," I say to myself. "Churches are no longer segregated. They no longer exist."

"Get over it," Ellie says in my head. "They're good people, perhaps corrupted by power but they have their own families and livelihoods and they don't bother us." Doesn't shut up, does she? Gives me a headache, she does. "They do good works, volunteering and donating to worthwhile charities, they go to benefits and they even have their own foundations. Each of them gives something back. What is wrong with that?"

"Good people," I scoff to her, "high morality amongst their own but somehow the world around them becomes more unequal, filled with poverty and conflict. How to explain that? Good people? $200 a day nannies. $100 dog walkers. Huge crates of groceries delivered by unpedigreed guys named Juan and Xian."

Am I bitter? Bet your ass. Am I crazy, a monster created by these times? Perhaps. And so here we are. Me and Ellie and Aye Aye up against wealthy, self-important moguls who judge, trying to tear my family apart for what they suppose is their moral superiority, holier than the Pope. Whatever happened to respect for elders?

I take a sip and rise. "Well, if this is a meeting we should all be here. I head into the bedroom and bring out Ellie. Aye Aye rises quickly, takes her hand and guides her to the sofa. There we sit, my lost wife and Aye Aye, me in between holding their hands.

"Did I ever thank you, Amy and Liz, for persuading me to go to the spa?" Amy stares at me angrily. "Because Ellie is doing much better these days with Aye Aye here. I am very lucky having two beautiful women in my presence."

"I don't believe this," Amy mumbles. I bet I'm going to get a bumper sticker, I think.

Ellie shrieks in my head, "Why don't you cooperate? They mean well and you are being hostile and confrontational." I plead guilty. I am a bad, bad boy but I am too far into this little match to cede points.

"I wonder if we can ask Aye Aye a few questions," Currey the newscaster says. She smiles at her with perfect white teeth, not a hair out of place and a high-style skirt that reaches just to the tip of her knees and not beyond. She is live, on camera. Always. "Where do you come from, dear? "

"Why you ask?" Aye Aye responds quietly, a discreet rage. Aye Aye's teeth are not white, what remains of them. I sense she understands I have taken the offensive. She joins the fight.

Currey is taken aback. "You wouldn't understand."

Aye Aye nods. "I understand. My people are made slaves and killed. I know bad people." She stares at the TV star. It is the first time I hear anger in her voice but the TV woman doesn't catch on. This interview isn't scripted.

"How old are you with your life of so much experience," the architect Jim Purcell impatiently interrupts. Currey shoots him a look.

"Why you do this?" Aye Aye turns sharply. "He is a good man. You have no right to do this."

"I'm sure he is," says Purcell, "but we have a responsibility to protect you."

"I do not need protection. I protect myself all my life."

"Yes, I'm sure," Currey says quietly, "but if you'd answer the question, perhaps we can proceed."

I lean back, relaxed and content. I sip my Bourbon and nod sagaciously. They have no idea. I had explained to Aye Aye that this group wants to get rid of her or kick us out of our home. She should not worry, I told her, everything will work out but it will not be easy. I also told her not to reveal her age, even if they ask. Aye Aye didn't ask why. She just nodded in agreement.

Ellie continues to pound my cranium, but I must have my sport. What is life without tension? What is old age without some form of amusement?

"I think we should lay our cards on the table," says Amy.

"Yes, the cards on the table," I respond.

"We are worried that this child is being taking advantage of, that she may be underage and maybe even being abused."

"I am not being abused."

"Perhaps a prisoner. There are laws that protect people like this. You can't just buy and sell children, treat them as slaves and hold them in your home." Her voice is rising. She is losing it. "There is morality. You are an old man living with a poor innocent and we can't just let this go on. It is not right."

I put my glass down. "Right, Amy? What is not right? In this building? Your 'help' cleans your toilets, washes your underwear, doing all those chores that not so long ago was called servitude."

"That's not fair. I pay them well."

"You pay them well, just enough for them to feed their families. As long as they smile and dust the foyer."

"This is about you, Virgil," Purcell interrupts. "Not us."

"Really? You like selective morality to mollify your conscience? Does this morality apply to the impoverished in our town, to the wage-slaves who make our clothes in China? To my poor wife Ellie who is handled like a wet-rag in the privacy of my home? Is any of this right?" The Bourbon is taking hold and I'm gaining steam. "I am asking the limits of your righteousness."

Amy shakes her head in desperation. "We are talking about here and now, Virgil, this building. Our morals and our laws, not some god-awful universal truth."

I take Aye Aye's hand and kiss it. "I need to explain something. First of all, don't jump to judgments about taking advantage of a poor innocent. I have no qualms. Aye Aye is a Mon, a member of a group that is abused, oppressed and murdered by its government. Aye Aye saw her friends sold into the Chinese sex trade. She fled and fell under the protection of a man who she paid to smuggle her to America. He sold her as a domestic servant. As an illegal, she had few options. Where else might she go? Then, she was sold to your spa, Amy, the spa that promises peace and tranquility, and obliged to repay her incurred debt over ten years."

There is a collective shuffling and straightening of postures, some of the group look puzzled, some of them grimacing as they see the picture coming together. I notice Dave Huang, the surgeon, is quiet, listening and watching.

"Aye Aye says she is not being held against her will," I say.

"She would," Amy says. "Stockholm syndrome."

"Perhaps," I say. "But let's put our cards on the table as you say. I can let Aye Aye go and my dear wife will suffer. Not because I wish her to but because I am an old man unable to do everything."

"You can get other help," Purcell said.

"Yes, that's an option but frankly, I can't believe anyone would be as wonderful as this woman here. But moving on. I can let Aye Aye go. Worst case, she is deported to a land that doesn't want her and will hurt her. Best case, she returns to the spa where she is forced to work in near-slave conditions, getting minimal salary. Aye Aye, would you like to return to the spa?"

"No," she says emphatically.

"So who is moral here, Amy?"

She shakes her head. Liz Currey speaks. "Perhaps we can clear this up simply. How old is she, Virgil?"

"You see I am in a bit of a quandary here. I have hostile people asking me questions, a lawyer among them."

"We're not hostile, we're only trying to . . ."

I ignore her and turn to Sam Davis, the attorney. "Tell me counselor, if I were your client, would you advise me to answer?"

"That depends upon the answer."

"Precisely, that depends upon the answer. And once I answer one question, there will be another and then another so that I would be opening up a line of inquiry that may not be in my interest, legally speaking. Isn't that right, counselor?"

"Perhaps," he says. "But I don't know the facts of the matter. If you are concerned, you might seek legal representation."

"And if I lawyer up, then what will the board do?"

"No lawyers!" Currey yells, losing her TV cool. "We are trying to settle this amicably."

Amy screams at me. Currey screams at me. Ellie is battering my head, telling me to stop this crazy game. But to me, Aye Aye's age is irrelevant. 15 or 35, it makes no difference. In that other world we do not choose to see the children who marry at puberty, work as prostitutes or in sweatshops sewing our clothes, or are sent to

Arabia as domestics. They work the fields, have babies and struggle to survive before most of my accusers had their first date. Maturity isn't a law but a condition that comes very early. Do our national borders make any difference in morality?

And if I answer these supposedly innocent queries? The next question *cum* accusation will be: Am I taking advantage of a young innocent? Absolutely, I admit. Me, a man in his senior years who uses his American citizenship and wealth to seduce and lure this young person to abandon a life of suffering and servitude for one of wellbeing? If she were 35, I would be taking advantage, too. In my mind, giving her a life without fear and, most important, a future, far outweighs the concerns of this high-minded bunch.

Next question if I allow this process to continue: am I, a man approaching 70, sleeping with her, a much younger woman, perhaps underage?

"This is going nowhere," Purcell says, standing to leave. "I think we have to bring in the authorities."

"What do you think?" I ask Dave Huang, the brain surgeon, sitting subdued. I've been watching him from the corner of my eye.

"Yes, you're from Asia," Purcell says.

"I am not from Asia. I am from Queens," he says, looking down. He clears his throat. "I don't think we should jump to anything. I don't know if any of this is our business."

"It is our business, Dave," says Amy, angrily. "This child is being taken advantage of. I thought we had a common understanding? I bet she doesn't get a salary. Does she have a green card, Virgil? Insurance?"

"On the advice of legal counsel, I must refuse to respond."

"Well then," Amy stands, "I guess we'll have to call child services, the Immigration Department and the Labor Department."

"Call whomever you like."

"I have a suggestion," Davis says. "Why don't you hire legal counsel and our lawyer and your lawyer can sit down and go over everything confidentially. Perhaps we can resolve this quickly."

How sweet, I think. Counselor seeks to resolve the dispute through quiet mediation. I see no profit in that. Negotiations lead to each side giving a little and I am not going to give anything. No, the board can keep probing, invading my space, my life and my existence. Let them give it their best shot.

"Good idea," I say. "I'd like to think it over."

"You are a disgrace," Amy yells. "You should be thrown in jail. Ellie would never have permitted this and now you are taking advantage of us all, including her," she points to Ellie, "and her," she points to Aye Aye. "You are evil."

"No," Aye Aye says gently. "He is good. A very good man." Why am I so lucky?

All these feelings, someone once wrote, from the wardrobe of morality and necessary to cover the defects of our naked shivering nature, to raise our own dignity, exploded in a ridiculous and absurd fashion.

After they depart, Aye Aye brings me another drink. She asks, "Do you miss your wife?"

"No, of course not. She's still here." Aye Aye nods. I wonder if she agrees. "Why do you ask?"

"Because you seem so angry with those people. Are they all so bad?"

"They are trying to hurt me. Us. That is my way."

"You seem so angry," she repeats.

"She's right," I hear Ellie in my head. "You should listen to her."

Just what I need, two sympathetic and caring voices battering my soul.

I have no reason to fight and no one to fight for, now that Ellie is virtually gone. Aye Aye's "are they all so bad?" lingers in my head.

I stare across the river. What do they call it? An involuntary response, a dog marking its turf. I revel in the fight and the tension. This old cur is still alive and barking, defending my territory with all my might, with fury and anger. I need to prove I am alive. To myself.

Not just one more caregiver finding oblivion in my/our damned fate. I will not go quietly into the night. Isn't that what they say?

I take a drink. "I'll try to be nicer," I mumble quietly. "If that's what you want."

Aye Aye smiles. Ellie says nothing.

A SENTIMENTAL EDUCATION

I celebrate myself, and sing myself,
And what I assume you shall assume,
For every atom belonging to me as good belongs to you
—Walt Whitman

THEY SAY THAT WITH AGE COMES WISDOM, although there is considerable evidence to the contrary. But with age comes experience, how to tie shoes, deal with taxes, avoid meaningless arguments and how to survive in a world of constant change and confusing and shifting values.

Experience for me is a life of slipping and sliding from one experience to another, different jobs, different professions and different worlds. How could I put it all together into a single volume? A childhood in the city, roughing it in Central America, hedonism in Paris, doctoral training, college teaching, the corporate world, government work and ultimately a life in development, each having different values. How many countries 30? 50? How many issues? Profit, loss, risk, famine, civil war, corruption. It is all a quagmire that these pages try to put together.

This volume is an attempt to address the sad but inevitable truth, that knowledge and experience are rarely transferred to the next generation or successor. That which we have seen and endured remains with us and us alone. Bureaucracies are famous for failing to preserve "institutional memories" as those who come after fail to gain or appreciate the knowledge gained over years of their predecessors. Reports, analyses, successes and failures are filed away, ignored, destroyed or buried in libraries and archives to remain for future archeologists to explore and brush away, detritus from the mosaic of time.

So too, there is the generational divide, a tendency by the next generation to not only ignore its elders but to consciously employ a *tabula rasa,* most famous in children who reject advice from their parents. I write in these stories of the avoidance of the horrors that were the Second World War by the youth who trampled through Europe just a generation later. This is also true for today, as the trials and travails of the last half of the twentieth century, the famines, diseases and warfare, fade from view as well as the efforts to address these ills.

Many of the efforts of that time failed, results that academics and novelists seize upon in broad, unnuanced judgments. They portray consultants working in the fields of the Lord in a poor light, blaming them for problems not of their making as if a doctor is guilty of the demise of a patient with a fatal illness.

Successes go unnoticed. Consider the huge efforts employed to stabilize newly independent countries and lands freed from the yolk of tyranny, the armies of lawyers that created legal frameworks for democracy, engineers who developed infrastructure, economists who created networks with local officials to further development and tens of thousands of others in health and education who roamed the Earth in those years so that today there is little question that most peoples of Eastern Europe, Africa and Asia live with greater freedom and in better economic conditions than heretofore.

I do not suggest direct causation for the improvement of the lives of millions around the world. To do so would be foolish. But in these times of casting blame, finding fault and denouncing others with all sorts of accusations, nuance is required. There is good. There is bad. There are both positive and negative consequences, many unforeseen, others ignored. But judgments are rarely accurate in international development. What can be noted are the efforts of those who devoted their lives, like my fictional character Walt Whitman Stein, with good hearts and intentions.

The generation of the 1960s was blessed with prosperity and enormous opportunities to choose whatever it wished to do. Cultural revolutions in the arts opened extraordinary vistas for the children who came of age thereafter. Music from an earlier age, the blues, country, musical theater and big band evolved into modern day jazz and finally Rock and Roll. Art moved to abstract expressionism and beyond. The cinema broke the chains held by corporate studios and created a golden age of film, filled with ideas and variety. And the new medium, television, altered the way we could see the world.

The country, once deeply divided, coalesced as media, transportation and the unifying effects of fighting a foreign war against despicable enemies created a sense that America could do anything, at home and abroad. The irony was that an America more unified than ever before became a nation divided on race, politics and social values.

Meanwhile, overseas, the old European hegemony ended. America was seen as leader of democratic and liberal ideals. Newly freed nations experimented with different forms as they struggled to develop their stability, resources and national identities. A broad swath of socialist ideologies emerged in reaction to the old system, post-Stalin Russia, Mao's China, Cuba's Fidel and a host of African ideologies.

"A new generation" came forth in America, announced John F. Kennedy, not without reason, a generation so unlike any ever before, filled with energy and optimism. It was a literate group, thanks to the opening of higher education. Ideas and ideals flowed all about. A million flowers bloomed, in Mao's words, but in America, not China.

This new generation, my generation, *knew* it could change the world. And so we went forth. I was in the Peace Corps in 1968 and 1969 in Costa Rica along with volunteers from throughout the United States. In the years since, most of us devoted our lives to social work, city managers, community developers, teachers and volunteers. We could do it because we were well off, with the resources previous generations created through sweat and suffering. New government institutions enabled and funded us as well as shaping policy. John Kennedy's brother-in-law, Sargent Shriver, was in many ways the Father of this movement, he, still unsung in the popular mind.

The stories in this book describe a time that is rapidly vanishing and may no longer exist. America's efforts to change the world through individual actions and experiments are gone, transformed into a corporatized philanthropy in technology, nutrition, medicine and economic wellbeing. To be trite, the world is so much smaller now, as banks, governments and global charities share common strategies and views, with marketing glossing all efforts.

Once, there were religious missionaries, doing good, spreading the Good Word, some became martyrs but most worked quietly and alone. Then there were us, civic workers who in the last third of the last century spread throughout the world, promoting change, growth and economic well-being in the face of civil wars, ethnic disputes, political interference, corruption, and above all, a lack of experience in government and business. We were young, we workers, also without experience, learning as we went. Some became frustrated and disillusioned while others ploughed on with the optimism of the most zealous missionary.

And we played, oh boy how we played with an open and free morality, judgment free, that has since vanished. We drank, partied, loved and sought all the adventures of lands barely touched by people from our shores. We sought and found authenticity in other peoples. True, we were hedonists but we were devoted to our work.

Then we grew and matured. When communism collapsed, our work expanded, confident that our American experience gave us the right. We knew business. We knew education. We knew health. And we were able to transfer that knowledge into a world that might imitate our success.

And there were those from the '60s who worked in America, rather than abroad, struggling with challenges that ironically grew greater with prosperity, those posed by race, economic oppression and politicized anger and, in recent times, by deindustrialization and technological change. The plight of the poor appeared to be pushed aside while other legitimate concerns, those of gender and ethnicity, were addressed.

We all went forth, back then, because we *knew* we could change the world. And we did, in our own way, with successes and failures. In our work and our lives. We returned home with a worldview so different from that of our friends and neighbors. We were culturally alienated and aware of the great divide between the stable and prosperous land in which we live and those where we worked.

It was an idealistic and heroic effort, those who worked in government and non-profits, consultants and volunteers. We were a great generation, our works spanning half a century and touching every part of the globe.

And now we have been replaced.

MILES WORTMAN
2018

CPSIA information can be obtained
at www.ICGtesting.com
Printed in the USA
BVHW031950180119
537824BV00014B/26/P